The First Amendment,
Democracy, and Romance

The First Amendment, Democracy, and Romance

Steven H. Shiffrin

Harvard University Press
Cambridge, Massachusetts
London, England
1990

For Neesa M. Levine

This book is printed on acid-free paper, and its binding materials
have been chosen for strength and durability.

Library of Congress Cataloging in Publication Data

Shiffrin, Steven H., 1941–
    The First Amendment, democracy, and romance / Steven H. Shiffrin.
        p. cm.
    Includes bibliographical references.
    ISBN 0-674-30275-3 (alk. paper)
    1. Freedom of speech—United States.   I. Title.
KF4772.S45 1990
342.73′0853—dc20   89-28967
[347.302853]   CIP

Acknowledgments

In many ways this book is a collective product. It has been enlivened, shaped, stretched, and pruned in response to the perspectives, arguments, and counterarguments of dozens of friends and colleagues. I would like to thank those who gave me detailed comments on all or a substantial portion of the manuscript: Gregory Alexander, Vincent Blasi, Lee Dembart, John Forester, Kenneth Karst, Gerald Lopez, David Lyons, Jonathan Macey, Frank Michelman, Cass Sunstein, Russell Osgood, Joel Porte, Lawrence Sager, Seana Shiffrin, Aviam Soifer, David Williams, and Susan Williams. Roberto Unger also gave me many useful suggestions, particularly about the relationship between dissent and association.

But many others—too many to thank—contributed valuable suggestions and criticisms during the years I actively worked on or thought about this book. I benefited from exchanges with colleagues and students at conferences or workshops at American University, Columbia University, Cornell University, Duke University, New York University, the University of Texas, and the University of Utah. I also was aided by the responses to my ideas offered at small group presentations I made at the University of Michigan, during my visit there in the fall of 1984 (this was before I realized that my project about democracy and method was really a first amendment project), and at Harvard University, where I visited in 1986–87 (this was after I realized that romance had a lot to do with my project, though I had few clues as to why).

I had once hoped that Chapter 1 and a part of Chapter 2 could be completed in time for the *UCLA Law Review* Symposium honoring the late Melville Nimmer. Mel would have agreed with much and disagreed with much of what I say in this book, but I am sure we would have had a joyous time discussing it—as we did discussing his treatise on the first amendment. I hope this book can stand as a late entry in the outpouring of material honoring and wrestling with his work.

I have been blessed with a merry and capable band of research assistants who have steered me toward material that I "had to read" and set me straight when my readings got "out of hand." In particular, I would like to thank: David Dana, Arthur Edersheim, Sara Harrington, Patricia McCarthy, Elizabeth Miller, Chip Pollard, Michael Robinson, Danaya Wright, and Kathi Wright. In addition, many of my students, particularly those in the seminars I offered at UCLA and Cornell, have probed and criticized positions I have entertained at various stages of this project.

Leah Adams, Bronwin Feeney, Carolyn Lynn, Vera Masur, and Jennifer Smith performed amazing administrative and secretarial feats amidst the jungle that gave new meaning to the word *office*. The librarians at UCLA, Michigan, Harvard, and Cornell kindly looked the other way (most of the time) as my office became an unofficial (catalogued but forbidding) library annex. I am grateful to the Harvard Law Library for giving me permission to take books with me to Cornell for this and other related projects and to the Deans at UCLA, Harvard, and Cornell for helping to subsidize my research with summer research grants.

At Harvard Press I am grateful for the support and suggestions of Lindsay Waters, for the wide-ranging comments of the referees, and for the sharp and careful editing of Kate Schmit.

Finally, I am grateful to Benjamin Shiffrin, Jacob Shiffrin, Seana Shiffrin, and, especially, Neesa Levine. Their very existence is a constant reminder that romance does not depend upon politics.

Contents

The First Amendment,
Democracy, and Romance

Introduction

On July 15, 1838, Ralph Waldo Emerson delivered an address to the Harvard Divinity School. The response was outrage. Emerson was not invited to speak again at Harvard for almost thirty years.

The outrage was provoked. In speaking against "historical Christianity,"[1] Emerson told the "Unitarian clergy to their faces that they were preaching a dead theology."[2] If Christ was important for religion, Emerson said, it should be because of what he said and not because of who he was. To emphasize the authority of Christ, rather than the power of his message, was to "corrupt"[3] all attempts at communication, to engage in "noxious exaggeration"[4] of the personal, and to adopt "petrified ... official titles"[5] and a "vulgar tone of preaching"[6] that "degrade[s] the life and dialogues of Christ,"[7] and "kills all generous sympathy and liking."[8] Such appeals to authority were denigrated as "appropriated and formal,"[9] a "profanation of the soul,"[10] an exhibition of the "sleep of indolence" resting amidst the "din of routine."[11]

Emerson's gesture was not merely a revolt against the use of appeals to authority in Christian preaching. The Divinity School Address expressed and exemplified Emerson's general view that you should respect no authority, no custom, no convention, no habit, no institution unless it makes sense to you. If it does not make sense, Emerson counseled, demanded, insisted that you speak out. Emerson believed that everyone faces the question: "Will you fulfil the demands of the soul or will you yield yourself to the conventions of the world?"[12] The Emersonian message was to trust your own intuitions, to speak out in favor of your own ideals, and to oppose the "strait prison-like limits of the Actual,"[13] to resist the conventions of the "old, halt, numb, bedrid world."[14]

The Harvard divines thought Emerson went too far; perhaps he did. Dissenters often do. But, as luck would have it, Emerson's message carried beyond the corridors of Cambridge. Indeed, his importance as a cultural figure stems in large part from his emphasis on self-reliance and independence and from his lifelong commitment to the "free expression and dissemination of new ideas."[15]

Although Emerson's perspective has helped to shape our literature and our culture, it has yet to be recognized or realized in American law. Emerson's thought has been presented in thousands of classrooms to millions of students, but no Justice has ever even once referred to the free speech views of Ralph Waldo Emerson in any Supreme Court case.[16]

To the contrary, American free speech law has become important but often dreary business. More than half a century ago, Dean Roscoe Pound called upon judges to be "social engineers."[17] Judges, he thought, should reject any characterization of the judicial process as deduction proceeding from unchallengeable premises to conceptually entailed conclusions. Instead, he counseled judges to regard the "social order as an organized human endeavor [designed] to satisfy a maximum of human wants with a minimum of sacrifice of other wants."[18] Judges were to forge "a system of compromises between conflicting and overlapping human claims or wants or desires . . . to satisfy the most they might with the least sacrifice."[19] In forging such compromises, Pound recognized, "social engineering may not expect to meet all of its problems with the same machinery. Its tasks are as varied as life and the complicated problems of a complex social order call for a complicated mechanism and a variety of legal implements."[20] Although the first amendment is nowhere mentioned in Dean Pound's 1923 exhortation,[21] his commentary could easily pass as an apt description of contemporary first amendment law. First amendment law now is, if nothing else, a complex set of compromises. Sometimes speech that presents a clear and present danger is protected; sometimes it is not; sometimes speech is not protected even though it presents no clear and present danger of any ordinarily recognizable evil. The Court periodically formulates exquisitely precise rules; it settles at other times for the most generally phrased standards; often it opts for hazy formulations and relies on the lower courts to fill in the details; sometimes the Court stays its hand and says nothing. The result is a body of law complicated enough to inspire comparisons with the Internal Revenue Code.[22]

It is not difficult to figure out why. To begin with, first amendment doctrine is a committee product. Nine independent social engineers get together to forge agreements on first amendment law, after wrestling with the ghosts of the past. They hedge; they compromise; even then they have trouble agreeing. Committee products are notoriously schizophrenic, and they are certainly short of consistent fidelity to a single organizing vision. The labyrinths of first amendment doctrine thus can well be regarded as a striking example of what we have known all along: if you want a powerful elaboration of principle, find a gifted author; if you want to muddle through, convene a committee.

Gifted authors have tried to put forward organizing visions or powerful elaborations of principle, but the first amendment resists easy capture. Its ally is the complexity and fluidity of social reality. To make decisions about how free speech should be is also to make decisions about the justice of trials; the security of personal privacy and of reputations; the scope of intellectual property; the management of public property ranging from streets and parks to utility poles and prisons; the extent of access to shopping centers, newspapers, and broadcast facilities; the fairness of tax treatment for groups from the Sierra Club to churches to veterans' organizations; the propriety of book selection in schools and libraries, and of personnel decisions and disciplinary efforts in public institutions; the treatment of corporations, unions, and candidates in election law—in short, everything from the content of public morality to the needs of local peace and national security.

Perhaps all of these problems, and a host of related ones, are susceptible to an easy single resolution. Maybe all these problems in fact boil down to one. Attention to this laundry list of issues, however, suggests the difficulty of finding any single premise or set of premises that could dictate acceptable conclusions across the vast range of human conduct implicated by freedom of speech. To formulate an organizing vision for the first amendment is to risk detachment from social reality. If the organizing vision has strong content, it will use a sledgehammer as a substitute for delicate decisionmaking. If the organizing vision has less imperialistic design, it may allow us to see, but not far.

Despite, or perhaps because of, the obvious difficulties, the production of grand and general first amendment theory is a major enterprise in American law schools. The need for such theory is often thought to be apparent. As one scholar puts it, "The outstanding fact about the First Amendment today is that the Supreme Court has never developed any comprehensive theory of what that constitutional guarantee means and how it should be applied in concrete cases."[23] Such words have been a staple for those who build the case for grand and general first amendment theory. For those who build such theories, contemporary first amendment doctrine is the devil. At best it stands in serious need of unifying explanation. At worst, it is ad hoc, unprincipled, and chaotic.

Within the spate of criticism, there is scant recognition of the possibility that social engineering may function best when doctrine is ad hoc. There is little appreciation for "the advantages of thinking small."[24] Instead, if judges are free to decide "small" questions without resort to general theory, it is presumed that the first amendment will be the loser. Genuine commitment to the first amendment is thought to be too fragile, too phlegmatic to withstand the political pressures of the worst of times. What is needed is a theoretical fortress[25] to withstand the pressure which could overcome judges when the roar of the crowd gets too loud. And, in any event, the argument continues, the first amendment is law, not mere preference or policy. "Congress shall make no law . . . abridging the freedom of speech" means just that, not that Congress shall make no such law unless judges can be persuaded that the law is not such a bad idea after all.

In recent years, perhaps in response to these criticisms, the Court has moved in directions, both methodological and substantive, that lend the appearance to its doctrine of being less ad hoc and more lawlike. The methodological innovations appear to provide a structure for first amendment doctrine, and the substantive formulations provide a partial vision. For supporters of these developments, the methodological formulations provide enough "law" to appease lawyers; they also give law students something to "hold on to" for their exams. The substantive developments not only provide ready phrases for Fourth of July speeches; they also offer a plausible explanation of what the first amendment is all about.

In response, I argue this: the methodological development provides a veneer, but not a structure; first amendment doctrine is more rather than less chaotic because of these developments; we have just enough law to be dangerous. The substantive developments rightly attempt to conjoin the first amendment with an understanding of the meaning of democracy. They rightly attempt to make the first amendment central to our understanding of what this nation is all about. But if I am right the Court's understanding of democracy is shriveled.

America has had a romance with the first amendment. It regards the first amendment as an important symbol of what the country means. Thus, the first amendment is more than an exercise in social engineering. Yet, for much of this century, the doctrinal meaning of the first amendment has adjusted and flowed with perceived needs of governance. Platitudes have substituted for substantive vision. We have had social engineering without romance. For the most part, the commentators present organizing visions that lack substantial connections to the demands of social reality. They offer us romance without social engineering. Although the Court recently has recognized the need to connect the first amendment with some basic conception of what the nation stands for, it has, unfortunately, picked the wrong romance.

If an organizing symbol makes sense in first amendment jurisprudence, it is not the image of a content-neutral government; it is not a town hall meeting or even a robust marketplace of ideas; still less is it liberty, equality, self-realization, respect, dignity, autonomy, or even tolerance. If the first amendment is to have an organizing symbol, let it be an Emersonian symbol, let it be the image of the dissenter. A major purpose of the first amendment, I will claim, is to protect the romantics—those who would break out of classical forms: the dissenters, the unorthodox, the outcasts. The first amendment's purpose and function in the American polity is not merely to protect negative liberty,[26] but also affirmatively to sponsor the individualism, the rebelliousness, the antiauthoritarianism, the spirit of nonconformity within us all. That Emersonian ideal of freedom of speech has deep roots in the nation's culture, but it has been subtly denigrated in recent first

amendment theory and seriously abused in practice. I mean ultimately to reflect on the changes we would make if we were to live
up to our first amendment dissenting tradition. In what ways
would we change our society if we protected and supported dissent? How would we organize our national communications
structure if we wanted a nation of vigorous independents? Do we
want a nation of vigorous independents? Is that even possible?
Should we even be asking what kind of citizens "we" want? Does
the inquiry itself invite first amendment difficulties?

Exploration of these issues will force us to choose among first
amendment ideals. One advantage of dissent as an organizing
symbol, however, is that it permits us to remain eclectic about a
host of first amendment values. A major theme of this book is
that the metaphors and symbols we have chosen to stand in for
the first amendment have imposed substantial first amendment
costs. The image of the dissenter would have served us better, but
it is likely that any single organizing symbol is too costly. Nevertheless, I think the first amendment can do double duty. It can
provide a sensible accommodation among a host of conflicting
values in a changing reality, and it can also stand as a shining
symbol of the country. In short, the first amendment can provide
both social engineering and romance.

Chapter 1 indicts the purported structure of first amendment
doctrine. It suggests that our contemporary framework for approaching first amendment questions is an exercise in defective
social engineering. But, equally important, it insists that the
lack of contact between the Court's method and the country's
need for emotional identification with the first amendment is unacceptable. Chapter 2 criticizes the Court's rendition of the central meaning of the first amendment. It argues that politics is the
wrong starting point for first amendment analysis and that a focus on dissent is better. Put another way, romantics like Ralph
Waldo Emerson and Walt Whitman have more to teach us about
freedom of speech and democracy than do Alexander Meiklejohn
or Oliver Wendell Holmes.[27] Chapter 3 explores the value of dissent in greater detail. It argues that the first amendment protects
not only the negative liberty of dissent, but also that the first
amendment reaches beyond its legal applications and functions
as a cultural symbol to encourage dissent. The chapter asks
whether a constitutional commitment to sponsoring dissent runs

the risk of producing an excessively egoistic, individualistic, self-serving society. It argues that such concerns just misunderstand the nature and value of dissent. At the same time, it suggests that the culture has functioned in powerful ways to discourage engagement and dissent. Some of those ways are simply pernicious. But, in other ways, the commitment to protect and sponsor dissent is appropriately qualified and limited. Moreover, helpful as it may be in many cases, a doctrinal focus on dissent is not self-executing. It will not answer a host of important first amendment problems. Nonetheless, a focus on dissent has important implications for how we think about particular first amendment problems, and that leads to the problem of method.

Taken together, Chapters 4 and 5 explore the problem of method, and, in doing so, connect the first amendment with democracy and romance. The central argument of this book is that a commitment to protecting dissent is a vital, but underappreciated, part of the meaning of the first amendment and of American democracy. The philosophical assumptions and the rhetorical dimensions of this argument are deeply rooted in the romantic tradition. Attention to how dissent and the argument of the prior chapters fits within the romantic tradition both deepens the argument and provides a perspective that can forge a strong connection between the substance of the first amendment and its method.

Contemporary scholarship has explored the virtues and vices of methods of decisionmaking variously labeled as pragmatic, contextualized, intuitionistic, feminist, or eclectic, and the journals are filled with discussions of judgment, practical reason, and hermeneutics. Those who favor such approaches (let us call them eclectics) generally deny that moral and political thought can be reduced to single values or to a small set of values, and they resist patterns of justification purportedly based in abstract reason. Like the romantics, then, eclectics resist both Kantianism and utilitarianism in part because society is too diverse and too complicated to justify the expectation that monistic methodologies could be productive. But the resistance of some eclectics is even more strongly tied to the romantic movement. For them, the diversity and complication of social reality is itself positively valued. Moreover, their resistance can be related to that aspect of the romantic tradition that prizes rebellion and dissent. If dissent is important to the first amendment and democracy, it is also a vital part of the romantic tradition. Exploration of the appeal of Kantianism, eclecticism, and romance will lead us to the central claims of the book. The first amendment, democracy, and romance are deeply interconnected. The various uses of the term *romance* do not involve a mere play on words: there is an integrated conceptual structure—a way of looking at the first amendment and the world—that ties them all together.

1

The First Amendment and Social Engineering

Leo Tolstoy was a fox masquerading as a hedgehog. So said Isaiah Berlin.[1] The fox, Berlin explained, knows many things; the hedgehog knows one big thing. Tolstoy "preached not variety but simplicity, not many levels of consciousness but reduction to some single level . . . ."[2] Yet Tolstoy's talent was to depict the multiplicity of nature, and his depictions overwhelmed his metaphysical commitments. He wanted to believe that the massive diversity he described ultimately belonged to one system, but his detailed evocations of the concrete resisted absorption into any well-rounded whole. Nonetheless, Tolstoy persisted in his belief in the one over the many.

The psychological attractions of the one over the many were well understood by Immanuel Kant:

> [I]f we are told that a more searching or enlarged knowledge of nature derived from observation must eventually bring us into contact with a multiplicity of laws that no human understanding could reduce to a principle, we can reconcile ourselves to the thought. But still we listen more gladly to others who hold out to us the hope that the more intimately we come to know the secrets of nature, or the better we are able to compare nature with other aspects as yet unknown to us, the more simple shall we find nature in its principles.[3]

Those trying to understand first amendment law—those who just want to "get a handle on it"—listen gladly to anyone who claims to provide a handle, to any person who would domesticate the fox. Even if the first amendment turns out to be an endless maze, to enter it we must find a starting point. A prominent modern entrance into the maze is a distinction between restrictions directed at communicative content and restrictions directed at communicative conduct.[4] The first scholar to point the way was Melville Nimmer. In an important 1973 article,[5] Nimmer argued that a commonplace distinction should serve as an organizing category for first amendment law. The distinction was that every communicative act has a meaning effect and a nonmeaning effect. If I shout a word—any word—in a crowded theater one non-meaning effect is noise, and the production of that noise could interfere with an audience's enjoyment of the play, whether or not they understood what had been said.

Suppose, however, that the audience accurately translated what I said and that the word I had shouted was "fire." As Nimmer explained the point, the "meaning effect" was not merely the understanding of the word's meaning but also included actions prompted by that understanding. Suppose everyone in the audience takes me to be asserting that there is a fire in the theater. Some believe I am a lying crank and use violence to punish me. Others panic, race out of the theater, and nearly trample one another in the process. In Nimmer's lexicon, both responses are meaning effects.

The state has an interest, to be sure, in preventing both the nonmeaning effects and the meaning effects in the theater example. The state might proceed against me for noise pollution—disturbing the peace—or for attempting to deceive the public in a way that clearly threatened an immediate panic. Nimmer proposed that the crucial starting point for first amendment analysis should turn on whether the state is regulating meaning effects or nonmeaning effects. As Dean Ely put it two years later, "The critical question would therefore seem to be whether the harm that the state is seeking to avert is one that grows out of the fact that the defendant is communicating, and more particularly out of the way people can be expected to react to his message, or rather would arise even if the defendant's conduct had no communicative significance whatever."[6]

By 1978, Nimmer's organizing strategy had become central to the way in which legal commentators thought about first amendment doctrine. The leading treatise on constitutional law, by Laurence Tribe, stated that, "The Supreme Court has evolved two distinct approaches to the resolution of first amendment claims; the two correspond to the two ways in which government may 'abridge' speech."[7] The terminology was somewhat different, but the two ways were Nimmer's ways.

Nimmer's 1984 treatise[8] presented a systematized explanation of the different treatment he thought the two types of regulations should[9] receive. In labeling the two types of regulations, we will think of government action regulating meaning effects as on the *content* track; we will think of government action regulating non-meaning effects as on the *conduct* track.[10]

If the state's action was on the content track,[11] Nimmer argued that the action was "presumptively unconstitutional."[12] This presumption was somewhat mild, however. He was suggesting "an approach, not a formula, whereby doubtful balancing questions are resolved in favor of the speech interest. There is nevertheless a balancing, and the speech interest does not always win."[13] What Nimmer argued for above all was that the balance struck between the free speech interests and government interests should be struck at a level of abstraction that transcended not only the parties before the Court, but also the equities of the individual case.

The issue, argued Nimmer, was whether a particular category of speech should be protected or not protected. In a libel case, the Court would weigh not the importance of the speech in the case before it but the interest in speech generally. It would weigh not the particular damage to reputation in the case before it, but the interest in reputation generally. In so weighing, the Court should formulate a rule or set of rules of general application. Nimmer called this "definitional balancing."[14] In formulating such a rule, the Court would be defining what counted as freedom of speech and what did not. Such a procedure, he argued, was calculated to afford some measure of certainty and to minimize deterrence of speech. "The very existence of the rule makes it more likely that the balance originally struck will continue to be observed despite new and perhaps otherwise irresistible pressures."[15]

As to cases on the conduct track (where the government interests were focused on nonmeaning effects), Nimmer proposed a different approach, but there was an underlying continuity of theme. The task was to formulate rules; again, ad hoc balancing could not be tolerated.[16] Here, however, because there was no intent to suppress speech, government action on the conduct track was presumptively constitutional.[17] Moreover, again, assuming no intent to suppress speech, Nimmer proposed that the test set out in *United States v. O'Brien*[18] should be employed in all cases on the conduct track, namely that such a regulation is "sufficiently justified if it furthers an important or substantial governmental interest . . . and if the incidental restriction on alleged First Amendment freedoms is no greater than is essential to the furtherance of that interest."[19]

There are ambiguities in the test, of course; and Nimmer discussed many of these difficulties with sophistication. Indeed, after the dust clears, what emerges is a picture of a doctrinal structure of first amendment law that many find attractive. It seems to provide a handle on an otherwise mysterious body of law. What I seek to do here is to make the picture less attractive, to argue that at best this picture provides one entry into the maze. Nimmer himself traced the many places where the Court had departed from his proposed structure. Nonetheless, many now see first amendment doctrine through Nimmer's framework; they miss the nuanced "exceptions."

The efforts of Nimmer, Ely, and Tribe are designed to provide an orderly framework for rule making in first amendment law. My purpose is to trace the many ways in which the framework is not helpful. I begin by questioning the axiom that rules are invariably appropriate in first amendment law. I go so far as to suggest that in some contexts first amendment values require ad hoc balancing and not rules, and that, in other contexts, it is hard to tell the difference between the two. I do not prescribe anarchy, but I do insist that the absolute preference for rules—definitional balancing—is overly absolute.

I then aim at the foundation of the distinction between the content track and the conduct track. Underlying that distinction in large part[20] is some variation of the notion that the first amendment stands against government's acting on the basis of its hostility to particular points of view. I make the relatively easy argument that the distinction between the content track and the conduct track is not strongly linked with its ultimate foundation. Moreover, I argue that the "foundation" is itself weak. Government hostility toward particular speech is neither a necessary nor a sufficient condition for a first amendment violation, and, therefore, a structure designed to combat that hostility is ill-suited as a foundation for first amendment doctrine.

This background helps explain why a distinction so prominent in the rhetoric of first amendment law turns out to have so little explanatory force in practice. Regulations on the content track and those on the conduct track are treated by methods that have more in common than is usually appreciated. Paradoxically, these two tracks tend to collapse into one, not because the underlying social reality is so similar, but because of its underlying multiplicity. In order to make good on these claims, I have to follow some doctrinal paths at some length, but the paths are sufficiently interesting in their own right to make the trip worthwhile.

Although both paths turn out to be similar, they are dotted with idiosyncratic signs. That is, the first amendment has developed its own language, and that language may be independently influential and important, even if not in an overarching way. Nonetheless, the language is less important than its place in the doctrinal rhetoric would suggest. Recognition of its *un*importance is a useful corrective to the commentary.

Even in the face of this broadside attack, it might be possible to rescue the centrality of point-of-view discrimination to first amendment law and the distinctive features of the language of first amendment law by relying on distinctions less ambitious than those suggested by Nimmer, Ely, and Tribe. Dean Stone of Chicago has attempted such a defense, but his defense is also thwarted by the multiplicity of first amendment interests and concerns. In fact, it turns out that no general framework rooted in first amendment principle exists. For the most part, the first amendment social engineer just balances the relevant interests and comes to a decision.

Absolutism, Definitional Balancing, and Ad Hoc Balancing

Gifted legal advocates frequently structure their presentations to make it appear as if they are reasonable moderates rejecting the extremes. The extremes that Nimmer set himself against were absolutism and ad hoc balancing. At least in one respect, however, he was an extremist posing as a moderate.

Absolutism is the view that: "Congress shall make no law . . . abridging the freedom of speech" means that Congress shall make NO LAW abridging the freedom of speech.[21] As Nimmer pointed out, laws forbidding speech, however, are commonplace. Laws against perjury, blackmail, and fraud prohibit speech. Much of contract law and securities law abridges speech. Indeed no one has ever contended that citizens are free to say anything, anywhere, at any time. The specter of a man crying fire falsely in a crowded theater crushed absolutism as a serious intellectual position. To be sure, it is possible to say that *freedom* of speech should be absolutely protected or *the* freedom of speech, but the terms are not self-executing. The protective character of any variation of absolutism depends upon the values controlling the definitions. Absolutism need not be absolute; it is either crazy in its full-blown form, or radically incomplete in its more sensible forms.

After destroying absolutism,[22] Nimmer pounced on ad hoc balancing. He described ad hoc balancing as the idea that free speech cases should be decided by consideration of the particular circumstances in concrete cases.[23] This procedure, Nimmer argued, would lead to uncertainty and would fail to insulate judges from strong popular feelings, such as the national hysteria of the McCarthy era.[24] Against absolutism and ad hoc balancing, Nimmer proposed definitional balancing.[25] That is, the courts should define *freedom* of speech not by resort to absolutism, and not by focusing on the circumstances of the individual case, but by assessing the competing interests in the general run of cases and formulating rules. Rules, he argued, were crucial: "[I]n the sensitive and vital area of freedom of expression, constitutional protection must not be predicated on ad hoc balancing."[26] Posed between the extremes of absolutism and ad hoc balancing, definitional balancing was made to appear eminently reasonable.

The difficulty with Nimmer's presentation does not lie in the relationship between absolutism and definitional balancing. Definitional balancing can appropriate many of the advantages of absolutism without accepting its disadvantages. Notice, for example, that a rule fashioned by a balancing of interests can result in absolute protection for speech in any area where that seems appropriate. Nimmer argued against absolute first amendment protection for libelous speech, but that conclusion followed from his assessment of the best social engineering to take account of the conflicting interests.[27] Someone using the same methodology could argue for a different rule absolutely protecting such speech. Many have.

Later I will argue that flexibility of first amendment methodology is a general strength and not a weakness. Now I shall argue that the particular weakness of Nimmer's methodology is its *inflexibility*. Consider the relationship between definitional balancing and ad hoc balancing. There are two things that an advocate of ad hoc balancing might be taken to say. On the one hand, an ad hoc balancer might say that in every first amendment case, there should never be a rule. The qualities of each individual case should be considered, and rules should never be contemplated. So far as I am aware, in the history of the dispute *no one has ever taken this position*. The remaining ground is that in some unspecified areas of first amendment law, courts should consider the equities of individual cases and should try to identify factors that should be weighed and considered, but need not formulate rules. The claim might be that some pockets of first amendment law involve so many competing variables that any rule would lead to intolerable results in too many concrete cases. Indeed, the pattern of common law decisionmaking is case-by-case adjudication, tentative formulation of principles and rules. Rules are sometimes not formulated; when formulated they often change. Rules are not foreign to the common law; indeed, they are common. But the "rule of law" often functions without rules. Principles and policies are often the only guide.

So understood, the extreme character of Nimmer's position ought to be clear. Nimmer's position was that rules had to exist for everything touching on first amendment freedoms; the concrete circumstances of individual cases should never be considered (except, of course, to determine which rule applies); factors are always inferior; ad hoc balancing is *always* wrong.

Extreme positions are often right, and Nimmer's position has some appeal. Rules in first amendment law promise predictability; they afford notice to speakers as to what they can and cannot do; they cabin the arbitrary exercise of discretion; they allow judges to tell the partisan mob that they have no choice but to follow the applicable rule of law.

On the other hand, in some contexts, ad hoc decisionmaking can advance first amendment values more than a regime of rules is able to do. Consider the question of whether reporters can be forced to reveal their confidential sources to grand juries. The Supreme Court's major decision on this issue[28] has been interpreted to authorize ad hoc decisionmaking on the question. Lower courts consider the significance of the investigation, the extent to which the evidence involved bears upon issues important to the investigation, and the extent to which the grand jury could secure the evidence it needs by alternative sources.[29] By contrast, Nimmer proposed a rule that would be less protective of the press. Specifically, his rule would permit grand juries to force reporters to reveal their confidential sources so long as the grand jury was not acting in bad faith.[30] From the perspective of the press, ad hoc balancing in this context is surely better than Nimmer's definitional balance. Of course, ad hoc decisionmaking involves imprecision, but from the press's perspective, there are some things worse than uncertainty. From this perspective, more protection for the press with accompanying uncertainty is better than the certainty of little or no protection.

Admittedly, it is almost always possible to craft a rule that would offer more protection for speech than ad hoc balancing would provide. For example, the rule could be that reporters never have to reveal a confidential source under any circumstances. In any given area, one can resort to absolutism. But absolutism assumes that protection of speech is always more important than other values. The very point of definitional balancing was to reject that brand of dogmatism. If the road to absolutism is blocked, it must be admitted that ad hoc balancing is sometimes more protective of speech than rules.

A related point is that the distinction between rules and ad hoc balancing is not a sharp one in practice. Consider, for example, the rule formulated in *Gertz v. Robert Welch, Inc.*[31] If a private person brings a libel suit against a media defendant, the person may not recover damages without showing fault. The common law had been that people in the media were responsible for the damage caused by defamatory falsehoods even if they had exercised all due care in the publication process. The risk of error ordinarily rested with the publisher, not the victim. *Gertz* changed all that. Concerned that publishers would become too cautious, the risk of error was transferred. The *Gertz* rule substituting fault for strict liability is in actuality the authorization of ad hoc balancing. What does it mean to say that the plaintiff must show fault? Assuming fault is lack of reasonable care, how does one determine what is reasonable? Presumably, by examining the circumstances of the concrete case, by making a judgment, by proceeding to compare cases in the future, by identifying factors to be considered, by forming rules where possible in concrete contexts—in short, by the common law process. The point is not merely a simple replay of the last one (that is, that some protection with attendant uncertainty may be better than no protection). The point is that rules need to be applied in concrete contexts, and how they apply will often necessitate the kind of ad hoc judgments that rules are purportedly crafted to avoid. For example, if a public figure brings a libel suit against a media defendant, the public figure may not recover without showing that the statement was published with knowledge of its falsity or with reckless disregard of the truth. What is a public figure? Figuring that out, one judge has said, is like trying to nail a jellyfish to the wall.[32]

First amendment law is filled with unclear rules. Moreover, in those first amendment areas where ad hoc balancing is the norm, there is sometimes enough shared agreement about the values at stake to afford a strong measure of predictability.[33] The limited point here should not be overdrawn. Rules can confine discretion. They usually provide more predictability than ad hoc balancing. But the line between a "rule" and ad hoc balancing is not sharp. More generally, there is no good reason to suppose that ad hoc balancing is always wrong in first amendment cases. The most one can say is that ad hoc balancing entails costs that are often unacceptable. The distinctions between definitional balancing and ad hoc balancing, between rules and standards, and between nondiscretion and discretion are each useful; they overlap, but are not the same; they can suggest issues; they can not resolve them.

The Distinction between the Content Track and the Conduct Track: The Weakness of Its Foundation

The same ultimately must be said for the distinction between regulations on the content track and those on the conduct track. This distinction is a proxy for something important in first amendment law, but the matter for which the proxy has been created[34] is only one of many important aspects of first amendment law, and the proxy is quite imperfect.

We begin with a truism: the government may never abridge

the freedom of speech. Government may, however, abridge *speech* in many contexts without abridging *the freedom* of speech. Whether one resorts to rules or standards the question to be decided is whether the freedom of speech has been abridged. The "important aspect" is this: government may not abridge speech merely because it is biased against that speech.[35] The focus on meaning effects and nonmeaning effects might be characterized as ultimately proceeding from that concern. The underlying premise or intuition would be that if government seeks to suppress the meaning effects of a communication, it is more likely to be acting from an animus against the speech than if it is acting against the nonmeaning effects of a communication.[36] Thus regulations on the content track could be regarded as presumptively invalid; regulations on the conduct track as presumptively valid.

Note, however, the imprecision of the distinction insofar as it serves as a proxy for government animus against speech. When government regulates the meaning effects of speech, it may be greatly concerned about the harm threatened by the speech. That concern might dwarf, or even be unaccompanied by, any bias toward the point of view expressed.[37] Laws against perjury, blackmail, and fraud regulate speech because of its communicative effects. They are not necessarily accompanied by bias against any point of view.[38] On the other hand, laws that on their face regulate nonmeaning effects may conceal government animus. A law prohibiting the destruction of draft cards may be motivated by a desire to preserve all the purposes for which the cards are issued. On the other hand, such a law might be motivated by an animus toward the message communicated in draft card burning.

Nonetheless, in the general run of cases, one might say, regulations that abridge meaning effects are more likely than regulations abridging nonmeaning effects to reflect government animus or bias against speech. Indeed one way of looking at the structure of first amendment doctrine is that it is *exclusively* designed to combat biased actions by the government. From this perspective, for example, passing the *O'Brien* test (has government advanced substantial or important interests in a manner that is essential to the furtherance of those interests) might be viewed as a reasonable indication that the regulation has been passed without animus.[39]

But analysis of the first amendment can not be reduced to a

concern about government motives. Take the fact situation in *Schneider v. Irvington*.[40] The city had outlawed leafleting not apparently because it objected to the vast array of messages communicated, but because it was concerned about the nonmeaning effect—the harm associated with littering.[41] Nonetheless, even in this simple case, it is likely that the government's motives were somewhat complicated. Admittedly, wholesale animus was not likely present, though the possibility of its presence could not definitively be ruled out. The city council might have hated some messages so much that it was willing to outlaw all leafleting to get rid of some.[42] More likely, its relative enthusiasm for or lack of appreciation for the general run of messages might have played some role in its weighing of the relative advantages or disadvantages of leafleting in the city. Still more likely, the city council might have cared about getting reelected and was responding to the concerns of those citizens who wanted to walk the streets free of strangers trying to hand them things when they want to be left alone. The real objection may well have been more about invasion of privacy than about what is said in the leaflets. Still, it would not be easy to disentangle any asserted privacy interest from attitudes toward the point of view expressed. If the leaflets accurately told people how they could easily acquire large sums of money, or if the leaflets were otherwise thought to enrich their lives, public pressure to ban leaflets would not have been present. Attitudes toward the messages *en masse* influence the outcome; animus, however, may still be absent. Still, animus aside, it could be argued that judicial scrutiny of government regulation of speech is appropriate to the extent that the regulation has been affected by enthusiasm for or against the messages involved.[43]

But *Schneider v. Irvington* stands for something more than a desire to protect against government animus or lack of enthusiasm for particular points of view. It endorses the view that freedom of speech is important wholly apart from government motivation or purpose. It talks about freedom of speech as a fundamental personal right of liberty and concludes that:

> Mere legislative preferences or beliefs respecting matters of public convenience may well support regulation directed at other personal activities, but be insufficient to justify . . . the

exercise of rights so vital to the maintenance of democratic institutions. And so, as cases arise, the delicate and difficult task falls upon the courts to weigh the circumstances and to appraise the substantiality of the reasons advanced in support of the regulation of the free enjoyment of the rights.[44]

The emphasis of the *Schneider* Court is not suspicion about government motives;[45] rather it rings of a denunciation of a bureaucratic mind set—a failure to appreciate the worth of free speech to democratic institutions. More precisely, the *Schneider* Court was indifferent to the motives and attitudes of the government. Rather, it focused on the need to protect the liberty of free speech from unjustified government regulation wholly apart from why the government regulated.[46]

The same can be said for the first amendment protection afforded to some species of libel. The Court speaks of our "profound national commitment to the principle that debate on public issues should be uninhibited, robust, and wide open."[47] It worries about the possibility that defamation law will have a chilling effect upon that debate. It is an "unbeatable proposition"[48] that truth will never emerge in the marketplace if it does not get in, and the Court in its defamation decisions has attempted to preserve the robustness of our national debate without unnecessarily sacrificing reputations. Nowhere in the defamation decisions is there a hint or a suggestion that libel law itself reflects an animus by government to particular points of view. To be sure, the administration of libel law is rife with possibilities for abuse. But the Court's decisions do not depend upon the existence of any such animus. Rather the Court has focused on preserving a particular system of expression in the United States.[49]

Finally, the claim that government, under the first amendment, can bear no animus toward any particular point of view is itself overbroad. Admittedly, there is language supporting that claim, even to the point of insisting on a general posture of benevolent neutrality. *Police Department of Chicago v. Mosley* states that government "may not select which issues are worth discussing or debating in public facilities. There is an 'equality of status in the field of ideas,' and government must afford all points of view an equal opportunity to be heard."[50] That is, government may not censor speeches in public parks or prevent handbill distribution on public streets. But government frequently decides what is worth debating or discussing in public facilities. Government at all levels subsidizes an enormous system of public education. Government decides that astronomy will be taught in the high school, but not astrology. And the decision is one of thousands of content-based decisions in public schools including textbook selection, curriculum development, personnel decisions, even grading exams. Even here we have arrived at only the tip of the iceberg. Public libraries, for example, select books in part on an assessment of what is valuable to the culture. Consider the work of museum curators, or those who administer grants for the universities and the sciences, or the public boards that run concert and lecture halls, or the Superintendent of Public Documents. In short, from the perspective of government there is no "equality of status in the field of ideas." Government plays an enormous role in the intellectual marketplace. By subsidizing some speech and shunning other speech, it rejects the equal status of ideas. Its multibillion-dollar participation in communications belies any vision of a content-neutral government. Government is a participant, not a mere referee.[51]

Government is permitted to subsidize speech and to make content-based decisions in so doing. But, it might be argued, government cannot take its positive or negative attitudes toward speech (or its assessments of the value of speech)[52] into account in deciding whether or not to suppress speech. Putting aside the question of whether this principle has merit as a recommendation for change, it cannot be taken as a plausible statement of existing law. First, some types of speech are deemed to be beneath the protection of the first amendment in large part because of judicial assessments that they lack value. In 1942, the Court stated that:

> There are certain well-defined and narrowly limited classes of speech, the prevention and punishment of which have never been thought to raise any Constitutional problem. These include the lewd and obscene, the profane, the libelous, and the insulting or "fighting" words—those which by their very utterance inflict injury or tend to incite an immediate breach of the peace. . . . [S]uch utterances are no essential part of any exposition of ideas, *and* are of such slight social value as a step to truth that any benefit that may be derived from them is clearly outweighed by the social interest in order and morality.[53]

Much has happened in first amendment law since 1942. Indeed, it has become obvious that many of these classes of speech raise serious constitutional problems, and precious few could muster the temerity to say that any of these classes of speech are well-defined. But the basic technique persists. In declaring some classes of speech not worthy of first amendment protection, the Court continues to assert that these classes of speech are of little value and make at most a slight contribution toward truth.

Obscenity is the most important example. *Paris Adult Theatre I v. Slaton*[54] asserts that the distribution of obscene material is not protected under the first amendment because it debases human personality; it violates the social interest in morality; it interferes with the state's right to maintain a decent society. In short, it is not good speech; it is not valuable. Whatever slight value it may have is said to be outweighed by "the social interest in order and morality."[55] Indeed the very definition of obscenity is filled with decisions about value. To be obscene, material must appeal first to prurient interests; second, must be a patently offensive depiction or description of sexual conduct; and third, must *not* have serious literary, artistic, political, or scientific value.[56]

It is easy to fix on the third prong of the test because it is actually phrased in terms of value. The prurient interest part of the test, however, is an especially clear example of point of view discrimination. Appeals to prurient interests are defined as appeals to a "shameful or morbid interest in sex." The Court has ruled explicitly that appeals to prurient interest can not be taken to include appeals to "normal" interests in sex. That is, appeals to interest in "good, old-fashioned, healthy" sex are constitutionally protected even if they are patently offensive to contemporary standards and lack serious literary, artistic, political, or scientific value. Appeals to "abnormal" interests in sex are treated differently.[57] For them, when the other requirements are satisfied, it is permissible to bring down the full weight of the law.

This is not a prelude to a ringing endorsement of speech appealing to a "shameful or morbid interest in sex." My limited point here is that in determining what speech is or is not protected, right or wrong, the Court regularly makes judgments as to the value of types of speech.[58]

It would be possible to argue that such value assessments should be made (if ever) only at the stage of determining whether or not speech gets any protection at all. On this view, once a type of speech is determined to be within the scope of and protection of the first amendment, judicial judgments about speech value should cease.[59] This position has had impressive support within the Court. Justice Brennan, for example, stated in *FCC v. Pacifica Foundation* that, "For the second time in two years, . . . the Court refuses to embrace the notion, completely antithetical to basic First Amendment values, that the degree of protection the First Amendment affords protected speech varies with the social value ascribed to that speech by five Members of this Court."[60] This, however, is the same Justice Brennan who in ringing rhetoric has extolled the importance of speech on public issues to our national life. Those purple passages have now come back to haunt. The Court has deemed several types of protected speech to be less important than other types of protected speech, such as speech on public issues. Sexually explicit, but not obscene speech,[61] commercial speech,[62] and profane speech[63] each have been deemed to be less important than other types of protected speech. Indeed, Justice Brennan himself has now authored an opinion in which he asserts that profane speech is subject to stringent broadcast regulations, in part because it is not at the "core of First Amendment protections."[64] We shall focus on that core in Chapter 2; the focus now is this: any notion that the first amendment is founded upon the idea of a content-neutral government cannot be squared with existing law; government is permitted to depart from content-neutrality in a wide variety of important circumstances; indeed, first amendment law is rife with judgments about the value of speech. Nonetheless, it is quite accurate to say that the first amendment, *inter alia,* registers a commitment to the view that government ought to act in a neutral fashion toward speech in a wide variety of important contexts. Those contexts, however, do not self-identify, and there is no easy formula for making the identification.

The Distinction between the Content Track and the Conduct Track Applied

That a distinction between the regulation of meaning effects and the regulation of nonmeaning effects would permit us to get a firm grip on first amendment doctrine should now appear unlikely. As a proxy for finding government hostility to points of view, each half of the distinction is underinclusive and overinclusive. Moreover, first amendment law is not exclusively, or even mainly, concerned with government hostility to particular points of view. Finally, government hostility to particular points of view is often acceptable, and evaluations of the value of speech run through the fabric of first amendment law. It should not be surprising to discover, therefore, that the distinction between the content track and the conduct track accounts for much less about first amendment law than is often implied in modern scholarship. The "track" metaphor suggests that doctrine heads off in two different directions. On inspection, the two tracks get to the same stations in much the same way.

The Conduct Track

Professor Nimmer argued that the *O'Brien* test should be employed for all regulations on the conduct track.[65] But any assessment of the effects such a proposal might have if implemented must be preceded by the recognition that the *O'Brien* test is not employed in all cases on the conduct track. Moreover, it may be useful to have a sense of the fragile character of the line separating the content track from the conduct track.[66]

New York v. Ferber[67] presents a useful illustration of the latter point even though the issue in that case is ultimately quite easy. New York prohibited the distribution of films showing children engaged in sexual conduct. The stated concern of the legislature generally had nothing to do with any meaning effects produced by the films. The legislature was concerned about the sexual exploitation of children, and it sought to remove the financial incentives for such exploitation by barring sales of films founded upon such abuse. It believed that it was "difficult, if not impossible, to halt the exploitation of children by pursuing only those who produce the photographs and movies."[68] The production of such films was said to be part of a "low-profile clandestine industry,"[69] but "the need to market the resulting products requires a visible apparatus of distribution."[70] Thus, even though the ordinance at issue in *Ferber* clearly attempted to suppress speech content, the state's principal justification did not depend upon a claim that the content conveyed was itself injurious.

So understood, the case appears nicely to illustrate the distinction between two factors that Professor Nimmer ran together. As he conceived it, a regulation on the content track[71] "attempts to protect a given interest through suppression or limitation of speech content, i.e., particular ideas or subject matter conveyed by speech. *That is*, the content of the message conveyed is thought to be injurious to the [government] interest."[72] As ordinarily conceived, however, *Ferber* is one of those exceptional cases where the state might want to protect a given interest through suppression of speech content without necessarily contending that the message conveyed was itself injurious to the state interest.

But this common rendition of *Ferber* does not take full account of the breadth of the state concerns. The state's concerns were not confined to the initial sexual exploitation. To be sure, the state was not worried about the effects upon the viewers of the film (except for the possibility, however remote, that the child might see the film). But the state was worried about the extent to which the child's fears concerning the film's circulation might exacerbate the psychological harm.[73] In part, the child fears exposure, and, in that respect, a portion of the harm is a straightforward privacy concern. Even in the absence of exposure, children dread the prospect that strangers (friends presumably would be even worse) could be watching the event at any time. At bottom, the child is haunted by the recognition that a permanent and apparently indestructible record of the moment of sexual violation is out there somewhere.

There is a sense in which even these state interests could be characterized as independent of meaning effects. The state could claim, perhaps in good faith, that its concern was not that an audience would see the film and thus invade the child's privacy. Rather the state could insist that its concern was with the child's psychological state and that the child's psychological health was impaired by the existence of the film whether or not an audience ever saw it. In truth, it might be difficult for the legislators themselves honestly to separate out the extent to which their concern was with psychological health and the extent to which they were also concerned with privacy.

When an ordinance is specifically directed at the content of speech, however, it may make sense to place it on the content track whether or not the state interests turn on meaning effects.[74] If distinguishing between meaning effects and nonmeaning effects signals a real possibility of legislative animus toward the regulated speech, the same might be said for regulations that on their face regulate content, even in circumstances where the legislature's stated concern is with nonmeaning effects. In *Ferber* itself, for example, the legislature described the films as "filth."[75] The legislature's hostility to the exploitation of children in the production process thus was matched by hostility toward the content of most of the films.[76]

In a sense *Ferber* has a happy methodological ending. It was treated on the "content" track, and it deserved to be treated on the content track. But focusing on the factors which press one toward one track or another should leave one thinking that the distinctions at work are both subtle and thin.[77] If a great deal turned upon such distinctions, there would be grounds for worrying that too much turned on too little. In fact, less turns on these distinctions than meets the eye, and even less turns on the distinctions than Nimmer had proposed.

Recall that Nimmer would have subjected all cases on the conduct track to the *O'Brien* test, but, as Nimmer well understood, many cases clearly on the conduct track do not follow *O'Brien.* Consider, for example, the line of cases in which persons seek to communicate on government property, but the government seeks to exclude them. The government's desire to exclude often has nothing to do with the content of the communications. It often desires to preserve the property for the uses to which it is "lawfully dedicated."[78] The cases involve communicators seeking access to the streets adjoining legislatures, schools, courthouses, military bases and personal residences, or to the inside of schools and libraries for silent demonstrations or for the right to put unstamped materials in mailboxes at homes and offices, even for the right to put handbills on utility poles. The claims vary in nature, but in most cases the Court has vacillated between two approaches to the problem. One can be labeled the incompatibility test. As the Court put it in *Grayned v. Rockford,* "The crucial question is whether the manner of expression is basically incompatible with the normal activity of a particular place at a particular time."[79] Thus, as the Court explained, a silent demonstration in a public library would not be incompatible with the functioning of the facility, but a speech in the reading room surely would be.[80] The other approach can be labeled the public forum test. Here the "crucial question" becomes whether the property is a "traditional" public forum. Thus some government property "by long tradition or by government fiat [has] been devoted to assembly and debate."[81] Streets and parks are characterized as having been "immemorially . . . held in trust for the use of the public and, time out of mind, have been used for purposes of assembly, communicating thoughts between citizens, and discussing public questions."[82] Other government property is hard to pass off as a traditional public forum. Return to the example of the silent demonstration in the library. The demonstration is constitutionally protected if the question is whether its manner is incompatible with the normal activities of the library. It is not protected if the question is whether the interior of a library is a traditional forum for demonstrations.

Much controversy has surrounded these two tests, but neither of them is the *O'Brien* test. It would be possible to argue that if either or both of them would be satisfied, it could be conclusively presumed that the *O'Brien* test had been satisfied. But if that maneuver were accepted, the *O'Brien* test could be said to apply in every area of the law virtually all of the time. Neither the incompatibility test nor the traditional public forum test can be equated with a requirement that a substantial state interest be furthered by means essential to the furtherance of the interest. The traditional public forum test seems to require less; the incompatibility test seems to require more.

City Council of Los Angeles v. Taxpayers for Vincent [83] provides an excellent illustration of the point. Los Angeles had outlawed placing signs on public property including sidewalks, crosswalks, street lamp posts, hydrants, and the like. The specific issue before the Court was whether the ordinance constitutionally could be applied against those who wished to place signs on utility poles. Vincent argued that the ordinance was unconstitutional under either of the two tests applied. Placing signs on utility poles could hardly be described as incompatible with the functions of the utility pole. Moreover, it is easy to make the argument that people have been placing signs on utility poles "time out of mind," that they have functioned as a traditional public forum for messages ranging from "Vincent for City Council" to "Dog Lost—Reward."

If the Court had followed its most recent precedent, it would have asked whether the utility pole was a traditional public forum.[84] If the answer were yes, the ordinance could not constitutionally be applied to utility poles.[85] If the answer were no, the question would be whether the exclusion was "reasonable and not an effort to suppress expression merely because public officials oppose the speaker's view."[86] But the Court pulled a rabbit out of the hat. And the rabbit turned out to be the *O'Brien* test. Noting that there was no "hint of bias or censorship in . . . this ordinance,"[87] the Court stated, "In [*O'Brien*], the Court set forth the appropriate framework for reviewing a viewpoint-neutral regulation of this kind."[88] The offhand ease with which the relevant test is identified connotes that the Court is not embarked on anything new, that it is just invoking long-settled practice. One would not have a clue from the sentence that in literally a score of prior cases no Justice ever expressed the hope or the fear, no Justice even dropped a hint that the *O'Brien* test might apply to cases involving access to public property. In a footnote the Court stated that asking whether the utility pole should be deemed a public forum was a question of "limited utility[89] in the context of this case."[90] Its description of "the context of this case" turned out to be one which would apply to any close case.[91]

Having selected the *O'Brien* test as the appropriate test, the Court proceeded to argue that the ordinance furthered a substantial state interest (the interest in avoiding visual clutter) by means essential to the furtherance of that interest. The dissent argued that the *O'Brien* test had been misapplied, but it too "solemnly [went] along with the gag."[92] It too acted as if the *O'Brien* test had always been applied in public forum cases.[93]

This branch of the discussion should shed light on what a small part of the first amendment story would have been told if it turned out that the *O'Brien* test applied to all cases on the conduct track.[94] The *O'Brien* test has all the virtues and vices of flexibility. Indeed the application of the test is even more flexible than its wording suggests. On its face, the wording of the *O'Brien* test implies that *if* a state regulation does in fact serve (to some unspecified extent) an important or substantial state interest by means essential to the furtherance of that interest, the regulation is constitutional. The implication is that the furtherance of a substantial state interest by the appropriate means *always* outweighs the free speech interest, at least on the conduct track.[95]

In *Vincent,* however, the Court purported to follow the *O'Brien* test but rephrased it to say something quite different. It asked whether the state interest was *"sufficiently* substantial to justify the effect of the ordinance on appellees' expression."[96] So understood, the *O'Brien* test is simply a mangled attempt to state that on the conduct track, the Court will consider the competing interests and arrive at a decision.[97] It is mangled because it is not precise about the general factors it will take into account. Worse, it conveys a distorted picture of what it really does and of what it wants lower courts to do.[98] That will become clearer when we compare and contrast the conduct track and the content track. The Court's methodology on the conduct track can best be described as eclectic. It assesses the competing interests and will fashion a variety of tests and techniques to cope with the perceived exigencies of social engineering. To know that is not to know very much about first amendment law, but knowing that the first amendment is a fox is better than thinking it is a hedgehog.

The Content Track

Those who would rescue some pattern from "chaos" would insist that the content track is different from the conduct track. Indeed, the point could be put sharply. Finding that open-ended balancing occurs on the conduct track is nothing new. "Everyone knows that," but the structure of first amendment doctrine is fashioned to bring order to those instances of regulation that fall on the content track. Moreover, the doctrine, it could be argued, is designed to provide a firmer ground for protecting such speech than would be afforded by a comprehensive balancing methodology. Thus John Hart Ely argued that the Court was "beginning to understand"[99] that on the content track all speech is protected *"save that which falls within a few clearly and narrowly defined categories."*[100] If the Court achieved a proper level of understanding in Ely's view, it would eschew balancing on the content track altogether.[101]

The difficulties with Ely's approach become clear if one tries to imagine how he would decide upon the "few clearly and narrowly defined categories" that would constitute exceptions from the principle that speech is protected from regulations on the content track. Certainly the existing exceptions could not be relied upon. There is nothing clear or narrowly defined about *them*. From the terms of the obscenity definition (prurient appeal, patent offensiveness, serious value) to the terms of defamation law (opinion, public figure, fault, defamatory remarks) vagueness, not clarity, pervades. Even if the definitions were clear, any declaration that the categories of nonprotection were to be frozen now and forever would require more justification than a pithy passage about the glory of free speech. For example, there is no recognized category in which to fit the "fire in the theater" example. Ely would have to create a category to cover it, which he surely would want to do. That leads to a difficult inquiry. How does one decide a case in which a new category is formed? Alternatively, how does one decide a case if it is proposed that an old category be liquidated? Ely does not propose an answer, yet he must if he is to argue that balancing can be banished from the content track.

Nimmer, of course, argued that balancing (albeit, definitional) was necessary on both the conduct track and the content track. He had proposed the *O'Brien* balancing test for the conduct track, but he did not propose a test for the content track. He settled for a prescription that such regulations were presumptively unconstitutional. Would it not be remarkable if *the* test for determining whether speech were protected on the content track turned out to be the *O'Brien* test!

In fact, the Court sometimes uses tests quite close to the *O'Brien* test on the content track, sometimes speaks as if a stronger test were required, but often does not speak in terms of tests at all. In *Gertz v. Robert Welch, Inc.*,[102] for example, the Court fashioned a set of rules to resolve the conflict between reputation and the freedom of speech and press. It spoke of the need for rules and of a need to find a "proper accommodation"[103] of the competing interests, but it did not invoke any particular standard of review.[104] It just balanced the interests.

In the obscenity area, the Court has fashioned a standard it has described as "an accommodation between the State's interests in protecting the 'sensibilities of unwilling recipients' from exposure to pornographic material and the dangers of censorship inherent in unabashedly content-based laws."[105] In forging that accommodation, the Court did not require the state to demonstrate that a substantial state interest had been furthered by means essential to the furtherance of that interest. Instead, in important passages, it invoked a posture of deferring to legislative wisdom. "The fact that a congressional directive reflects unprovable assumptions about what is good for the people, including imponderable aesthetic assumptions, is not a sufficient reason to find that statute unconstitutional."[106] In the absence of an obvious violation, the Court declared that it was not the Court's task to resolve empirical uncertainties so long as the opinion of the legislature was reasonable.[107]

If the treatment of the obscenity issue seems less stringent than that connoted by *O'Brien,* the treatment of speech in other contexts seems somewhat more stringent. For example, the Court sometimes requires that speech be regulated only if the state shows a compelling rather than a substantial or important state interest.[108] Sometimes, even while recognizing that the regulation is on the content track, the Court purports to follow tests that are much like that in *O'Brien,* for example, when it deals with content regulation of commercial advertising[109] or of editorials in broadcasting.[110] To be sure, commercial advertising regulations and broadcasting regulations are said to be special contexts, but just what is special about them has been somewhat hard to pin down. Moreover, the stringency of the review can be quite unrelated to the phrasing of the test. When the Court has applied the *O'Brien* test to the regulation of commercial advertising it has acted like an inconsistent parent—strict on one day,[111] looking the other way on the other.[112]

Perhaps the best illustration of the *in*significance of the phrasing of the standard of review is contained in *Buckley v. Valeo.*[113] The Court there examined the constitutionality of the Federal Election Campaign Act of 1971 (as amended in 1974) and considered at some length whether the *O'Brien* test should apply. For pages, it argued in detail why the *O'Brien* test was inappropriate and why the regulation of contributions and expenditures was on the content track, not the conduct track.[114] All this argumentation was designed to help the Court establish the appropriate standard of review, and the Court said that the state regulations must be subject to the "closest scrutiny."[115] Having arrived at this point, the Court fell asleep. The test of "closest scrutiny" was put in these words: "Even a '"significant interference" with protected rights of political association' may be sustained if the State demonstrates a sufficiently important interest and employs means closely drawn to avoid unnecessary abridgement of associational freedoms."[116] Recall that the *O'Brien* test would have required that the state *further* an important or substantial interest by means *essential* to the furtherance of the state interest. As phrased, the *Buckley* test omits a furtherance requirement and substitutes a "closely drawn" requirement for an "essential to the furtherance of the state interest" requirement. If one looked only at the wording of the tests, one could easily conclude that the *O'Brien* test was more protective than the *Buckley* test. It is clear, however, that the Court did not quite mean what it said. It did not reject *O'Brien* either to adopt a less protective test or to adopt the same test. What it actually purported to mean was that it is adopting a form of the "closest scrutiny."

In fact, as many commentators have demonstrated, the degree of scrutiny employed in *Buckley* varies from paragraph to paragraph.[117] Naive passivity about legislative wisdom is followed by naked cynicism about legislative sagacity. The Court turns from sycophant to antagonist from section to section. The discussion of the appropriate standard of review is a fitting prelude to the constitutional schizophrenia that is to follow. Extreme as it may be, *Buckley* is one of many cases illustrating that standards of review do not bind those who do not wish to be bound and do little to guide those who wish to be led.

In fact, *Buckley* is almost a cartoon example of a larger point. Having explained for pages why an approach used on the conduct track is inappropriate, the Court adopts the ways of the conduct track *in haec verba*. The larger point is that the content track functions almost exactly like the conduct track. Balancing *is* the order of the day. Rules are framed in order to accommodate clashing interests of importance. This is not to say that there is *no* difference between the content track and the conduct track. The factors that cause a regulation to be placed on one track or the other are of *some* importance in first amendment law. They are, however, but few of the many factors important in first amendment law. That a regulation is on the content track tells one little about the outcome of a case. Of itself, it is no guarantee that any form of strict scrutiny will be applied. Perjury, fraud, and blackmail all ride the content track. Examination of the constitutionality of such restrictions would be unlikely to trigger any form of strict scrutiny. If a five-year ban on the use of paper were imposed—to protect the trees—the regulation would ride the conduct track,[118] but the regulation would surely invite searching and hostile scrutiny. The distinction between the content and conduct track is not meaningless, but the distinction does not separate the dangerous regulations from the benign, and it fails as an organizing framework for first amendment law.

The First Amendment and Standards of Review

If one seeks to understand the Court's methodology, far more important than any distinction between the content and conduct tracks is a recognition of the nature of balancing that guides the Court on either track. Whether stated implicitly or explicitly, the Court evaluates the importance of the state interest, the extent to which the state regulation advances the interest, and the extent to which the interest might have been furthered by means less restrictive of free speech values; compares the importance of the free speech values at stake; and judges the extent to which such values have been infringed.[119] Guided by general factors such as these,[120] the Court decides to formulate a rule, to identify a number of more specific factors to be applied, or opts for ad hoc case-by-case adjudication. One, but only one, of the factors in the calculus[121] is whether the state regulates meaning effects or non-meaning effects. Meaningful standards of review, therefore, can not be based on the distinction between the content track and the conduct track because those categories themselves embrace regulations that affect free speech values in radically disparate ways. If a standard of review were said to be triggered by such overinclusive and underinclusive categories, one would hope and expect that the standard of review would provide the pretense but not the reality of restraint. Only this can explain the pervasive sloppiness with which the Court states standards of review in the first amendment area. The ordinary language of a test is often stronger or weaker than the Court intends; the Court often leaves out relevant factors it could not mean to exclude; it offers rephrasings of tests that change a test's meaning without any apparent recognition that a change has been implemented; in short, its phrasing of tests in the first amendment area belies any notion that careful attention has been paid to the enterprise.[122] This carelessness suggests that the "standard of review" in first amendment law functions primarily as a ritual, as an incantation, as a prelude to the statement of result, but not as a guide.

Often, however, the ritual contains a substantive point. In *Buckley,* for example, the Court meant to say that the impact on first amendment values was more significant than that involved in *United States v. O'Brien* and that more justification would have to be provided in *Buckley* than was provided there. In the obscenity context, the Court was saying that the impact of first amendment values was less than in other contexts. Accordingly, less demanding requirements of justification were required than normal. In *Gertz,* the Court was faced with a strong impact on first amendment values and a strong state interest. It tried to forge the best set of rules it could under the circumstances. Standards of review are a way of trying to generalize the requirements of justification in particular classes of cases. One difficulty with the technique is that the strength of state interests and the impact on speech values interact in too many complicated ways to make the prospects for standards of review realistic. After all, the only occasion for their use is in circumstances where the categories of regulation at issue are too unmanageable to have given rise to rules. Thus, it is understandable that standards of review in the first amendment area quickly deteriorate (or ripen—depending on your perspective) into general balancing tests.

At worst, however, standards of review might be taken seriously. The danger is that busy judges and lawyers will take the English language seriously. The case against standards of review is that judges and lawyers might think that the absence of a factor from a standard of review really means they should not take account of it or that a similar standard of review, as phrased, *means* the same thing in commercial advertising regulation, as it does in broadcast regulation, as it does in draft card burning cases, as it does in adult theater zoning cases, as it does in cases involving election campaign reform. In reality, the same standard of review sometimes means different things in the *same* general context[123] and often means different things in different contexts. The standard of review is a bankrupt form of social engineering. If it is designed to make first amendment law more methodical, it is a failure. If it is designed to guide the lower courts, it leads with sloppy and inaccurate signs. Ultimately, the standards of review are overconfident or cynical. If they are designed with the view that they state the factors to be weighed with appreciation for the needs of diverse situations, they reveal a stunning naivete about the complexities of social reality. If they are designed to mask the subjective aspects of first amendment decisionmaking, by providing a "test" that makes an ad hoc process *appear* determinative, they mask cynicism.

Objections, Clarifications, and Caveats: Attempts to Kill the Fox and Rescue the Hedgehog

A predictable response to the foregoing discussion is that it portrays first amendment law as murkier than it is and that more meaning can be salvaged from the content track/conduct track distinction than has yet been considered. By way of clarification, my argument is not that first amendment law is murky (although much of it is). The argument is that first amendment law is extraordinarily complicated, and that its general features reveal no clearly outlined structure. Whether or not they concede these points, some would argue that there is more to the two-track distinction than has yet been admitted. The least serious of these objections would point to the incomplete character of the critique of Ely's approach to the content track. Even conceding that general balancing were needed to form the categories of unprotected speech, the objector might argue, once that balancing has taken place, first amendment law absolutism prevails on the content track. This response would mischaracterize first amendment law in several ways. First, as previously discussed, some first amendment "protected" speech gets less protection than other protected speech. Commercial advertising,[124] sexually oriented speech,[125] and so-called private speech[126] get some measure of first amendment protection but are subject to forms of regulation that would not be permitted for political speech. Second, political speech on the content track can be regulated in certain special contexts. For example, public employees can be prohibited from electioneering,[127] despite the fact that electioneering is undoubtedly protected speech. Finally, political speech can be prohibited when a sufficient justification is forthcoming. The Supreme Court has stated that the presumption against ad hoc restraints on such speech is "heavy."[128] That is a far cry from stating that such restraints are impermissible. As witness, for some period of time the *Progressive* was restrained from publishing an article describing how to make an H-bomb.[129] Thus, even after the categories are in place, ad hoc balancing is permitted on the content track. The Court is prepared to admit the possibility of special contexts and prior restraints. Absolutism is absent from both tracks.

These lines of cases also thwart one of the most sophisticated approaches to rescuing the hedgehog currently alive in the literature. Dean Geoffrey Stone argues that the distinction between content-based and content-neutral restrictions on expression is "the Burger Court's foremost contribution to first amendment analysis, and it is, today, the most pervasively employed doctrine in the jurisprudence of free expression."[130]

In support of this contention, Stone states that "[E]xcept when low value speech is at issue, the Court has invalidated almost every content-based restriction that it has considered in the past quarter-century. Thus, whether the Court evaluates such restrictions by an 'absolute protection' approach, a 'clear-and-present danger' test, a 'compelling government interest' standard, or some other formulation, it clearly applies a different and more stringent standard to content-based than to content-neutral restrictions."[131]

These pronouncements sound sweeping, but they ultimately address only a corner of first amendment doctrine. In order to establish that "almost every content-based restriction" has been invalidated, Stone has to provide a narrow construction of the term *content-based.* Moreover, he relies on a "low-value" exception that looms larger than the rule.[132]

The Narrow Construction of "Content-Based" Restrictions

In order to establish that the Court has invalidated almost all content-based regulations it has recently considered, Stone relies on a much narrower conception of "content-based" restrictions than was employed by Ely, Nimmer, or Tribe.

What Stone ultimately wants for first amendment law is solid recognition for the idea that regulations discriminating against types of speech *on the basis of their point of view* can be justified only when an especially stringent standard of review is satisfied.

Point-of-view regulations are suspect, according to Stone, principally because they are often accompanied by justifications or motivations rooted in intolerance or unjustifiable paternalism and because they threaten to distort public debate significantly.[133] Stone's taxonomy of first amendment categories is driven by his concern for these particular first amendment values. That is, his understanding of the application of those values to a particular context controls his decision to classify a particular regulation as content-based or content-neutral.

Take, for example, government restrictions designed to limit the use of profanity in broadcasting. At first glance, it is hard to see why anyone would label such regulations "content-neutral." If, for example, George Carlin says "2 + 2 is 4" on the radio, the government restriction does not apply. If he says "Fuck," the restriction applies.[134] It is the charged content of the script that changes the result. Stone, of course, recognizes this: "[R]estrictions on the use of profanity are content-based in the most literal sense . . . ."[135] But, he continues, "such restrictions do not pose the dangers that underlie the Court's use of stringent standards of review to test the constitutionality of content-based restrictions."[136] He suggests that "Analytically, offense at language is more like offense at noise than offense at ideas. And restrictions on the use of profanity are no more likely to involve improper governmental motivation, in the form of official disapproval of ideas, than most content-neutral restrictions. Thus, although restrictions on offensive language may seem at first glance to be content-based, they are more appropriately analyzed as content-neutral."[137]

There is much that could detain us here—the privileging of "ideas" as the important part of discourse; the narrow construction of ideas; the benign interpretation of government motivation. The point, for now, is that Stone is prepared to relegate regulations of speech to the content-neutral department whenever he concludes that the perils of point-of-view discrimination are not present. To take another example, suppose the state forbids public employees from engaging in partisan political activity. This too seems clearly content-based. Public employees can give public speeches about chess or bridge without fear, but partisan public speeches about political candidates are regulated. From Stone's perspective, regulations directed at classes of subject-matter rather than at point of view present intriguing complexities.[138] At one level, they are literally content-based. In some circumstances, however, they do not involve the same evils as point-of-view discrimination. Stone would argue that bans on public employees' participation in political campaigns are, for the most part, viewpoint-neutral. He concludes that "this type of subject-matter restriction poses problems virtually indistinguishable from those posed by content-neutral restrictions."[139]

By so concluding, Stone has not argued that limits on profanity or public employees' speech are beneath constitutional scrutiny. Stone would apply a "relatively demanding standard of justification"[140] even for "content-neutral" regulations.[141] The importance of the first amendment doctrinal structure as he sees it, however, is that it helps isolate those point-of-view discriminations that deserve the strictest scrutiny. So understood, however, the size of the content-neutral category enlarges and that of the content-based category shrinks.

Moreover, as a descriptive matter, the Court has made the content-neutral category even larger than Stone would allow. *Renton v. Playtime Theatres, Inc.,*[142] for example, considered a municipal ordinance that prohibited movie theaters that presented sexually explicit material from locating within a thousand feet of any residential zone, church, park, or school. A theater specializing in films like *Bambi,* however, could locate in any business district. It takes special training to come to the view that such a distinction is not content-based. After all, the single variable affecting the zoning classification is the *content* of the films shown. Nonetheless, the Court ruled that the ordinance was "content-neutral."[143] Why? Because, the Court explained, the ordinance was not designed to suppress unpopular views. The ordinance reflected concern about the impact of adult theaters on the quality of urban life. It was focused on the *effects* of the theater's location, not on its *content*. Yet, as Dean Stone has observed, the films suppressed by such zoning restrictions "carry an implicit, if not explicit, message in favor of more relaxed sexual mores. Such restrictions, in other words, have a potent viewpoint-differential impact. . . . To treat such restrictions as viewpoint-neutral seems simply to ignore reality."[144]

Given that understanding, however, it becomes necessary to discount any suggestion that a content-neutral/content-based distinction explains much of first amendment law. If one uses

Stone's terminology, the phrase *content-neutral* already becomes far broader than one would initially expect, and its usage in the case law is, in important areas, even broader than Stone would want to allow. The broader the category, the less the distinction explains because the distinction is set up to assist results when regulations are characterized as content-based, not the other way around.

The Low-Value Exception

Dean Stone is also quite willing to concede that dozens of important cases are not explained by the content-neutral/content-based distinction. He clusters these cases together under the umbrella of "low value theory."[145] "Whatever the merits of the low value theory," he says, the "theory is not the focus of the content-based/content-neutral distinction."[146] Nonetheless, Stone explicitly recognizes that low-value theory justifiably plays a major role in the jurisprudence of the first amendment.[147] It is necessary, he argues, because we otherwise would have to apply the same standards to private blackmail that we would apply to public political debate, because if we do not treat harmful but relatively unimportant speech differently, we will dilute the expression "at the very heart of the guarantee."[148] As Stone characterizes the law, "The Court, applying [the low-value] approach, has held that several classes of speech have only low first amendment value, including express incitement, false statements of fact, obscenity, commercial speech, fighting words, and child pornography."[149] Once the Court has decided that speech has low value, it then, according to Stone, engages in "categorical balancing, through which it defines the precise circumstances in which the speech may be restricted. In attempting to strike an appropriate 'balance' for each class of low value speech, the Court considers a number of factors, including the relative value of the speech and the risk of inadvertently chilling 'high' value expression."[150] This is all said by way of contrast with high-value speech, where "the Court employs, not a balancing approach akin to its content-neutral balancing, but a far more speech protective analysis."[151] That "far more speech protective analysis" also turns out to be a form of balancing, but one with a stricter standard of review.

The role that assessments of the value of particular speech or categories of speech should play in first amendment theory is much contested. Some argue that judges should never make assessments about the value of speech in resolving first amendment questions; others argue that they must. Everyone agrees, however, that at *some point* judges should be barred from making assessments about the value of particular speech in deciding whether it may be regulated or prohibited. Moreover, the image of a content-neutral government, at least as a regulative ideal, haunts first amendment law and its commentators. That the Court makes judgments about the value of speech embarrasses the notion that the first amendment stands for openness, tolerance, diversity, or what-have-you. Since most commentators tend to be cheerleaders for the first amendment, descriptions of first amendment law place judicial judgments about the value of speech offstage. Such judgments are described as "exceptions." The "norm" is said to be that speech is protected and that judgments about the value of speech are foreign to the judiciary. As a recitation of everyday life, these descriptions are correct. The vast majority of people spend day after day speaking without fear that government officials will arrest, fine, or otherwise punish them for what they say. For some, the fear of legal consequences is a daily part of the job; consider, for example, editors of newspapers. Even for them, however, the occasions when the law strikes are rare. The socializing effects of law have something to do with this, of course; but the law has a recognizable interest in only a tiny fraction of the speech uttered in any American day.

The picture of first amendment doctrine looks quite different from the picture of everyday life. The doctrine is obsessed and preoccupied with the "exceptions." It may even be that the doctrine is best captured by turning the picture of everyday life upside down. That is, the doctrine recognizes that numerous types of speech are not valuable or that they have "low value." From one angle at least, that speech is the focus of first amendment doctrine. It must be given "special treatment." It may be that the best place to start learning about the first amendment is by examining its treatment of "disease." By finding out what is not valued, we may learn more about what really is valued. By looking in the dark, we may find some light.

Stone's characterization of the doctrine is unorthodox in its frank recognition that low-value theory is a necessary and important feature of first amendment law. The orthodoxy of his analysis lies in its placement of the treatment of "protected" or high-value speech in the foreground. If low-value theory is brought to the foreground, however, many important features of the doctrine become obvious. Most important, for purposes of this chapter, is the recognition that there is no sharp dividing line between low-value and high-value speech. Consider two examples. Advocacy of illegal action is protected unless it is directed to inciting imminent lawless action and is likely to incite or produce imminent lawless action.[152] Is unprotected advocacy a form of low-value speech?

One approach might be to say that any speech that can be prohibited is of low value by definition. This, however, would substitute tautology for analysis. Moreover, it would mistake Stone's description of the methodology. As Stone describes the methodology, the Court first asks whether low-value speech is present, then balances to see how much protection the speech should get, if any. Any conclusion of nonprotection arises after the determination of low value has been made. It, therefore, would not work to slide from the conclusion of nonprotection to the conclusion that the speech involved was low-value speech. Moreover, even Stone recognizes the possibility that high-value speech might be prohibited in certain circumstances.

In the absence of fiat, however, it becomes hard to accept the characterization of "incitement" as low-value speech. It would not be fruitful, for example, to argue that advocacy of illegal action is itself low-value speech, even though the Court has apparently so held at the bleaker moments of our history.[153] But non-inciting advocacy of illegal action, without more, is protected speech under the first amendment. Moreover, this conclusion has been arrived at in light of powerful opinions by Holmes and Brandeis about the enormous value of such speech.[154] Under Stone's taxonomy, advocacy of illegal action appears to be "high-value" speech.[155] The reason why some types of advocacy of illegal action can be prohibited seems to have less to do with their value as speech than with their potential for harm. Alternatively, even if the Court had silently repudiated Holmes and Brandeis, the label "low-value speech" would obscure the decisionmaking process. The Court did not start and need not have started its advocacy of illegal action analysis by asking whether the category of speech was valuable or not. Indeed, the Court in dealing with the issue has ordinarily begun with an assessment of the state interests. What ultimately is at stake in this context is an accommodation of the values of order and free speech. If the rules in the advocacy of illegal action context are good ones, it is because they have protected order without *unnecessary* sacrifice of first amendment values. But first amendment values have surely been sacrificed. If the advocacy of illegal action rules has the effect of muffling the voices of those who are most agitated against the system, we have suffered a substantial first amendment loss. It demeans the speech and shortchanges that loss to think about this as a part of low-value theory.

The same can be said for the rules regulating defamation. Certainly, from one perspective, the speech at issue is high-value speech. Criticism of public officials and public figures, many think, is "at the very heart of the guarantee." To fashion a set of rules in which plaintiffs get to ask juries to scrutinize that criticism risks a major chilling effect. Moreover, the "factfinding" process may simply mask the unleashing of juror prejudices about what speech should be free. As the second Justice Harlan once said:

> [I]n many areas which are at the center of public debate "truth" is not a readily identifiable concept, and putting to the pre-existing prejudices of a jury the determination of what is 'true' may effectively institute a system of censorship. Any nation which counts the *Scopes* trial as part of its heritage cannot so readily expose ideas to sanctions on a jury finding of falsity.[156]

Perhaps the protection of reputation requires findings of truth and falsity by juries, but that "protection" must be accompanied by a sense of first amendment loss. To characterize any such process as a part of low-value theory would deemphasize the major risk to "high-value" speech however the latter might be defined. The conflict between reputation and free speech necessitates a difficult choice. Something important must be abandoned, and that fact deserves emphasis.

Yet, in a shameless paragraph in *Gertz v. Robert Welch, Inc.,* the Court attempts to disguise the bitter pill: "Under the First Amendment there is no such thing as a false idea. However pernicious an opinion may seem, we depend for its correction not on the conscience of judges and juries but on the competition of other ideas. But there is no constitutional value in false statements of fact."[157]

Never mind John Stuart Mill's observation that even a false statement can bring about "the clearer perception and livelier impression of truth, produced by its collision with error."[158] Forget how much we each have learned by experiencing the correction of our own false perceptions. Discard any notions of the role of individual self-expression as part of why we cherish speech. Two other things, however, cannot be ignored, forgotten, or discarded.

First, to say that there is no constitutional value in false statements of fact begs the first amendment question. It assumes that there is a bevy of infallible Platonic guardians ready, willing, and able to separate the true from the false. Even if such a group existed, there would be a basis for arguing that we should not rely on them. The first amendment may value participation and freedom more than truth. But, if the first amendment means anything, it means that a careless epigram about false statements of fact cannot be the right starting point for first amendment doctrine.

Second, the distinction between facts and ideas is too fast. Let us pass over the difficulties involved in distinguishing between the two. Any suggestion that the government can generally control false facts without major conflict with first amendment values is worse than idle. We surely would not tolerate a regime in which the Federal False Facts Commission rooted out false facts from the nation. And we would laugh (or cry) if the Commission said, "Not to worry, under our Constitution, there is no such thing as a false idea." Fortunately, when the Court emerges from its foolish paragraph, it steers a more defensible course. It recognizes that false statements of fact can cause serious damage to reputation that the marketplace will never fully cure,[159] but it also recognizes that the process of safeguarding reputation is imperfect and that such a process can threaten first amendment values in a serious way. Right or wrong, the Court made a set of difficult choices with full recognition that much was to be lost by whatever choices it made. It would have been the first to recognize that its rules safeguarding reputation placed high-value speech at risk.

Dean Stone also would be near the front of the line in recognizing the difficulty of the choices made in the defamation area. Nonetheless, he classifies defamation law as part of "'low' value theory."[160] He argues that false statements of fact are low-value speech and that "In attempting to strike an appropriate 'balance' for each class of low value speech, the Court considered a number of factors, including the relative value of the speech and the risk of inadvertently chilling 'high' value expression."[161]

Although Stone characterizes defamation law as part of low-value theory, a fuller characterization might understand defamation to be a doctrinal area in which low-value theory and high-value theory run together. For Stone, regarding advocacy of illegal action and defamation as low-value exceptions serves to preserve the autonomy of "high-value" speech from government regulation. At best, these characterizations are an ingenious way of cutting first amendment losses. At worst, they amount to apology that shrinks from the truth. So-called high-value speech is subject to government regulation if a strong enough showing can be made. Stone takes the sting out of some of these regulations by calling them content-neutral. The sting is removed from others by the label "low-value" speech. But the very concept of low-value speech is an embarrassment to first amendment orthodoxy.[162] To say that government cannot suppress speech unless the speech is of low value sounds like a parody of free speech theory. The censor will always be inclined to say that the speech suppressed is of low value. Thus, the low-value exception mocks the rule. It seems almost like saying that South Africa has a humane racial policy except for its treatment of the blacks. Stone's enterprise is noble, but the orthodoxy cannot be salvaged. There are better ways to save the first amendment.

When the Dust Clears

The reality of first amendment doctrine overwhelms the orthodoxy. In truth, it turns out that nothing is sacred. The first amendment owes more to Roscoe Pound than to Holmes or Brandeis, Milton, or Mill. Decisionmaking in the first amendment arena is not much different from decisionmaking in other policymaking contexts. Freedom of speech is an important value, but when it comes into conflict with other important values, like order and reputation, accommodations are made. Attention is paid to the seriousness of the state interest, the extent to which it is advanced by the regulation, and the possibility of less restrictive alternatives, together with the impact on first amendment values. Because a multiplicity of factors[163] are employed in first amendment analysis, it is possible to come into the maze from any number of points. One can cut through the material by looking at the doctrine from the perspective of what it does with point-of-view discrimination, content discrimination, liberty, the marketplace of ideas, and numerous other first amendment values. It is also productive to come at the material by focusing on the state interest or the doctrine of the less restrictive alternative. Even if we ultimately could perceive the maze in its entirety, however, our starting point would influence what we were able to see. But descriptions of first amendment law (my own included) are also influenced by what we want to see, and most first amendment commentators do not want to see mere social engineering. They want to see principle, and when they do not find it, they seek to shape it.

Their impulse is in us all. The first amendment is supposed to stand for something in our culture and in our Constitution. It surely ought to stand for something more than the notion that a state regulation has to advance a substantial, important, or even compelling interest in the least restrictive way. We may not demand absolutism; but we do demand some meaning, some integrity, some substance from interpretations of the first amendment. We want more than social engineering.

2

The First Amendment and Democracy

Everyone thinks the first amendment stands for something, even balancers. To say that speech values are not all-important or to say that they must give way in concrete circumstances may be thought of as realistic or, alternatively, as dangerous. But to balance is not to deny first amendment meaning or value. Indeed, any notion that one could balance first amendment values without some notion of what they were would be incoherent.

What first amendment values are and should be, however, has recently been much contested. For decades the Supreme Court had been rather unselfconscious about the nature of first amendment values. It has published purple paragraphs about the glory of the first amendment and repeated them on those occasions when it thought some eloquence was required. Meanwhile the commentators have understood that numerous values can conceivably be linked to the first amendment, that some of those values conflict, and that it is important to get straight about why the first amendment is a good thing.

After a series of fits and starts, the Supreme Court has finally begun to settle on a "central meaning"[1] of the first amendment. This "central meaning" links the first amendment to a particular conception of democracy. It is a conception shared by a number of prominent scholars and has wide acceptance on the Court. What is often not noticed is that this "central meaning" changes from case to case and even drifts around within the same case. It is an unstable center. I want to argue not only that the central meaning is fuzzy, but also that it proceeds from a fundamentally wrongheaded understanding of the first amendment, the Constitution, and American democracy. My project here, however, is not destructive but, instead, transformative. My object is not to sever the link between the first amendment and democracy but to re-characterize both. The recharacterization I offer, however, is not an academic lawyer's shuffle. Paradoxically, I hope to show that this recharacterization has deep roots, not only in the American experience, but also in how we perceive that experience and want to perceive it. Before transforming the existing conception of the relation between free speech and democracy, though, we need to get a "handle" on what the current conception is. Finally, we will find some order amidst the chaos.

The First Amendment and Alexander Meiklejohn: The Seeds Planted

Current interpretations of the first amendment owe much to Al-exander Meiklejohn and to Harry Kalven, Jr., his more moderate supporter. Meiklejohn argued for a somewhat extreme view of the first amendment, but his animating ideal resonated strongly with important aspects of American tradition. Meiklejohn's understanding of the first amendment proceeded from the hy-pothesis that "[t]he principle of the freedom of speech . . . is a de-duction from the basic American agreement that public issues shall be decided by universal suffrage."[2] The notion is that the Constitution's commitment to freedom of speech is nothing more than a reflection of our commitment to self-government.[3] Under this approach, speech relevant to self-government is absolutely protected under the first amendment;[4] speech not relevant to self-government is beyond its scope and fair game for government regulation so long as due process requirements are respected.[5]

The attraction of this politically based interpretation is easily understood, and its pull has drawn favorable commentary from a diverse group of respected commentators.[6] As a strategy for pro-tection of communications, it offers the pragmatic prospect of pre-venting the government from intruding into areas where its potential for bias is particularly acute. As a theory of communi-cation, it offers the legalistic neatness of permitting the conclu-sion that the absolute terms of the first amendment protect abso-lutely that speech within its scope. It confines the area within which the judiciary may impose subjectively derived values. And, finally, it offers a grand and romantic appeal by conjoining first amendment theory with the basic theory of American government.

Even if one accepts Meiklejohn's understanding of American democracy, however, the Meiklejohn view of free speech is overdrawn and fuzzily conceived. If the first amendment protects only political speech, it seems especially important to get clear about what political speech is. Initially, Meiklejohn declared that the first amendment applied only to speech which bears, "directly or indirectly, upon issues with which voters have to deal—only, therefore, to the consideration of matters of public interest."[7] So considered, the theory was capable of being interpreted to preclude first amendment protection for most literary, philosophical, and scientific writing.[8] If a first amendment theory designed to provide absolute protection for political speech can do so only by excluding protection for Shakespeare, Aristotle, and Einstein, something is seriously amiss.

In later writings, Meiklejohn sought to plug this hole by asserting that philosophy, science, art, and literature were areas from which the voter derived "knowledge, intelligence, sensitivity to human values: the capacity for sane and objective judgment which, so far as possible, a ballot should express."[9] But the idea that literature's claim to first amendment protection depends upon its relevance to political life simply does not ring true. The notion that the classics of literature cannot be suppressed solely because of their relevance to voter decisionmaking bears all the earmarks of pure fiction. Indeed, if the classics of literature are to be characterized as political speech, it is hard to see how any speech could be called nonpolitical. Specifically, in making decisions voters are called upon to make evaluations of the character of candidates for political office.[10] As a practical matter, assessments of human personality by most voters are rarely based on sensitivity to human values derived from literature,[11] but are surely based in large part upon experiences with others in private life and on values formed through communications about other individuals in private life.[12] The impact of private speech on assessments of human personality and politicians surely dwarfs the impact made by art, literature, or science. If art and literature are protected on the theory that they have political impact, private speech is protected *a fortiori*. In short, once the door is opened, it becomes difficult to close. Either a politically based theory excludes speech such as literature which virtually everyone (including the Founders)[13] agrees is deserving of protection, or, by making adjustments to include such speech, it is unable to justify a stopping point. In the absence of a stopping point, the Meiklejohn position unravels. Beginning with the proposition that political speech must be absolutely protected and moving to the proposition that all speech has political relevance yields the necessary conclusion that all speech must be absolutely protected. The distinction between public and private speech, so carefully developed, thus evaporates.

Claiming absolute protection for whatever political speech turned out to be was another, perhaps less stunning weakness of the Meiklejohn theory, but it also insured a lack of pragmatic success. If I successfully urge a howling mob to throw bottles at soldiers entering the Pentagon or if I embark on a malicious defamatory campaign against a public official, my speech would surely be regarded as political, but the likelihood of judicial protection for such speech is low. Despite its many attractions, one might guess that Meiklejohn's influence would be confined to the halls of academe; one would not expect it to be influential among those who actually decide first amendment cases.

If Meiklejohn's theory was to have any practical effect in the courts, it needed a talented public relations expert. In fact, Meiklejohn had something much better on his side—an enormously gifted scholar and advocate, Harry Kalven, Jr. Kalven was shrewd enough to recognize the limits of the Meiklejohn theory, the nature of its appeal, and the occasion to put it forward.

The occasion was *New York Times Co. v. Sullivan,* a case which even when read broadly stood only for the narrow proposition that a public official could not recover in a defamation suit without proving that the statement complained about was made as a knowing falsehood or in reckless disregard of the truth.[14] But the holding was accompanied by strong language. In ringing terms, *New York Times* announced that the first amendment represented our "profound national commitment to the principle that debate on *public* issues should be uninhibited, robust, and wide-open"[15] and that the "central meaning of the First Amendment"[16] is that "prosecutions for libel on government have [no] place in the American system of jurisprudence."[17] In an

important article in the *Supreme Court Review,* Professor Kalven
enthused that the Court had written "an opinion that may prove
to be the best and most important it has ever produced in the
realm of freedom of speech."[18] The occasion for praise was that
the Court "almost literally incorporated Alexander Meiklejohn's
thesis that in a democracy the citizen as ruler is our most important public official."[19] The hope for the future was said to be that
the Court "will slowly work out for itself the theory of free speech
that Alexander Meiklejohn has been offering us for some fifteen
years now."[20] Kalven reported that he had "occasion this summer
to discuss the *Times* case with Mr. Meiklejohn. Before I had dis-
closed my own views, I asked him for his judgment of the *Times*
case. 'It is,' he said, 'an occasion for dancing in the streets.' As
always, I am inclined to think he is right."[21]

Without calling attention to the fact, however, Kalven rejected
both of Meiklejohn's major principles. Kalven did not believe that
the scope of the first amendment was confined to political
expression[22] nor did he think that political expression need be
absolutely immune from government abridgment.[23] For example, the *New York Times* proviso that knowing or reckless
falsehoods about public officials could trigger liability was en-
dorsed by Kalven, at least insofar as it applied to calculated falsehoods.[24] But that endorsement was a square rejection of absolute
protection for political speech. From the Meiklejohn perspective,
that was no occasion for dancing in the streets. That was heresy.
Closet[25] heretic though he may have been, Kalven recognized the
appeal of the Meiklejohn position. First amendment theory no
longer needed to start from the picture of a man yelling fire
falsely in a crowded theater.[26] Instead it could start with the image of the citizen-critic—"our most important public official."[27]
Without flirting with absolutes, the Court could make the first
amendment stand for something fundamental in the American
polity. To be sure, Kalven himself had unrealistic hopes for what
would follow in a regime where the amendment was thought to
be centrally concerned with self-government. He predicted the
demise of the clear and present danger test[28] and the destruction
of other parts of the Court's methodology that had served to un-
derprotect speech.[29] Kalven thought the dialectic progression
from protection for speech about public officials to protection for
all speech in the public domain would prove overwhelming.[30]

As luck would have it, within a year, Justice Brennan, the author of *New York Times v. Sullivan,* was asked to deliver the Alexander Meiklejohn lecture at Brown University. There, Brennan quoted Kalven's article several times. He too referred to the central meaning of the first amendment. Quoting Kalven, he said, "This is not the whole meaning of the Amendment. There are other freedoms protected by it. But at the center there is no doubt what speech is being protected and no doubt why it is being protected. The theory of the freedom of speech clause was put right side up for the first time."[31]

In embracing Kalven's praise, Brennan was careful to mention the limits of his endorsement. Brennan rejected any thought that political speech would be absolutely protected. He referred, for example, to calculated falsehoods as beneath constitutional protection: "That speech is used as a tool for political ends does not bring it automatically under the protective mantle of the Constitution."[32] Moreover, like Kalven, Brennan rejected any notion that political speech was the only speech protected under the first amendment: "'There are other freedoms protected by it.'"[33]

The metaphor of centrality, however, was bought by Brennan—hook, line, and sinker. And, on this point, Brennan spoke for a full Court. In *Garrison v. Louisiana,* for example, the Court, per Brennan, stated that "speech concerning public affairs is more than self-expression; it is the essence of self-government,"[34] and mentioned again our "profound national commitment to the principle that debate on *public* issues should be uninhibited, robust, and wide-open."[35]

Perched as he then was, a liberal centrist—outflanked on what was then perceived to be the left on speech issues by Justices Black and Douglas—Justice Brennan may well have thought that the rhetoric about self-government and its centrality to freedom of speech had largely progressive possibilities. He certainly must have recognized that if there were a center of the first amendment, there might also be a fringe. We do not know whether he initially saw any danger to that fringe in embracing the Meiklejohn-Kalven rhetoric. One of his strategies, however, was to define the core as broadly as possible. The various Brennan majority opinions talk of central protection not merely for speech on *political* issues, but for speech on *public* issues or public affairs,[36] or for speech of *general* interest.[37] The core of the first amendment or its center seems to move around even within a single Brennan opinion.

In *FCC v. League of Women Voters*,[38] for example, the Brennan majority opinion states that "editorial opinion on matters of public importance . . . is entitled to the most exacting degree of First Amendment protection";[39] later that the expression of editorial opinion [without further qualification] "lies at the heart of First Amendment protection";[40] later that expression on public issues "'has always rested on the highest rung of the hierarchy of First Amendment values'";[41] later that the "Framers of the Bill of Rights were most anxious to protect . . . speech that is 'indispensable to the discovery and spread of political truth'. . . ."[42] Finally, we are told by Brennan that this editorial commentary (that you will remember "lies at the heart of First Amendment protection") *"includes within its grip a potentially infinite variety of speech, most of which would not be related in any way to governmental affairs, political candidacies, or elections. Indeed, the breadth of editorial commentary is as wide as human imagination permits."*[43]

The *League of Women Voters* opinion simply makes no distinctions between political speech, speech on public issues, or editorial opinion on any thing at all; and it is surely not making distinctions between the core, center, or heart of the first amendment. The Brennan hierarchy does not exhibit any stratification. For Brennan, political speech may be the first among equals, but it is more equal than first. He appears to imagine a first amendment center without a fringe, a hierarchy in which the top is all there is.

If this perspective reflected a strategy to protect as much speech as possible, there were important victories. The Court's treatment of whether to extend first amendment protection for commercial advertising is one example. In attempting to justify protection for commercial advertising, the Court in *Virginia State Board of Pharmacy v. Virginia Citizens Consumer Council, Inc.*,[44] focused on the connection between commercial speech and political speech. One might think that commercial advertising could experience difficulty in a regime where the center of the first amendment was thought to radiate from a concern for political speech. Through such a lens, advertisements for beer, marshmallows, and jello might easily be thought of as speech on the first amendment fringe. But the Court was not troubled. Indeed, with an air of insouciant moxie, the Court in *Virginia Pharmacy* suggested that commercial speech might be more important than political speech. "[T]he particular consumer's interest in the free flow of commercial information . . . may be as keen, if not keener by far, than his interest in the day's most urgent political debate."[45] Without breaking stride, the Court opined that commercial speech is political speech, for while it furthers "the proper allocation of resources in a free enterprise system, it is also indispensable to the formation of intelligent opinions as to how that system ought to be regulated or altered."[46] Yet, in the midst of this, the Court threw up its collective hands to say that it knew some commercial speech lacked public interest or importance and some did not, but it could not tell which was which:

> Obviously, not all commercial messages contain the same or even a very great public interest element. There are few to which such an element, however, could not be added. Our pharmacist, for example, could cast himself as a commentator on store-to-store disparities in drug prices, giving his own and those of a competitor as proof. We see little point in requiring him to do so, and little difference if he does not. . . . [N]o line between publicly "interesting" or "important" commercial advertising and the opposite kind could ever be drawn.[47]

Thus the politically based center got larger, and the fringe became increasingly difficult to imagine. It began to seem that no line between the center of the first amendment and its fringe might ever be drawn. So Brennan had apparently hoped, but it was not to be.

The Political Center and the Nonprotected Fringe

The Meiklejohn rhetoric was in tension with another first amendment rhetoric, that which called up the image of a fair, tolerant, content-neutral government. From the standpoint of speech protection, the image of a content-neutral government has the advantage of protecting the fringe by its refusal to establish a center.[48] As we have seen, Justice Brennan avoided conflict between the two rhetorics by expanding the center and by refusing to see a fringe.[49] In *Young v. American Mini-Theatres, Inc.*,[50] however, the two rhetorics collided, and Brennan blinked.

The issue was whether Detroit could zone adult motion picture theaters in ways different from other motion picture theaters. The Detroit ordinance prohibited adult theaters from locating within one thousand feet of establishments like liquor stores, pool halls, adult bookstores, or other adult theaters. The ordinance was designed to combat urban blight and was billed as an Anti–Skid Row ordinance. Sensible as Detroit may have considered its actions, the ordinance presented a knotty first amendment question. Obscenity is deemed to be beneath the protection of the first amendment, but no one contended that the adult theaters were exhibiting obscene movies. Nonobscene movies were fully protected under the first amendment. From the perspective of the doctrine then current, for Detroit to engage in selective zoning of protected speech was to discriminate against protected speech. The ordinance runs right into the jaws of a first amendment premised on a content-neutral government.

Justifying the ordinance seemed to require a different rhetoric, and Justice Stevens, speaking for a plurality of the Court, employed a rhetoric that rang of Alexander Meiklejohn. "[E]ven though we recognize that the First Amendment will not tolerate the total suppression of erotic materials that have some arguably artistic value, it is manifest that society's interest in protecting this type of expression is of a wholly different, and lesser, magnitude than the interest in untrammelled political debate . . . ."[51] Stevens thus argued that adult films get some first amendment protection but not as much protection as political speech or philosophical discussion: "[F]ew of us would march our sons and daughters off to war to preserve the citizen's right to see 'Specified Sexual Activities' exhibited in the theaters of our choice."[52]

Justice Stevens does not elaborate on his "marching to war" standard for speech protection. A later decision involving draft registration reveals that Justice Stevens is apparently unwilling to send *our daughters* marching off to war for any purpose.[53] If he kept strictly to the standard implied in *Young,* apparently no speech would ever be protected. But the Stevens epithet was just that—a passing stylistic flourish—a cheap shot.

Stevens's reliance on the Meiklejohn rhetoric in *Young,* however, was a significant move designed to apply the Meiklejohn insight to establish a real first amendment center and a real first amendment fringe. If political speech was at the center, thought

Stevens, sexually explicit movies must be out at the fringe. If the Meiklejohn perspective had initially been adopted with speech protection in mind, Stevens's approach must finally have aroused doubts about the sagacity of the strategy.

Perhaps the most significant aspect of the *Young* opinions is the character of the response to Stevens. One familiar with feminist theory might have expected Brennan to take on Stevens directly: to affirm that sexual speech is indeed political. None of the five justices rejecting Stevens's proposed hierarchy of protected speech tried to argue that sexual speech was political speech. Neither Brennan nor any other justice met Stevens on Meiklejohn's ground. Instead the Brennan focus abandoned the Meiklejohn vocabulary almost entirely. Justice Stewart spoke for the Brennan forces, and the response was shrill. Stevens, he said, had adopted an approach that "rides roughshod over cardinal principles of First Amendment law."[54] The trampled-upon cardinal principle apparently was the idea that even "'[w]holly neutral futilities'"—those utterances that do not address issues of social and political importance—"'come under the protection of free speech as fully as do Keats' poems or Donne's sermons.'"[55] Except for a somewhat half-hearted aside, the Brennan forces handed over the Meiklejohn rhetoric to a coalition including Justices Stevens, Rehnquist, White, and Chief Justice Burger. The Brennan group retreated to the model of a content-neutral government. In a sense, however, the Brennan group won. Although the Detroit ordinance was upheld, there were only four votes for the proposed Stevens hierarchy of protected speech. But the progressive resonance of the Meiklejohn perspective had been stolen. Despite the doctrinal victory, there was no dancing in the streets.

Even the doctrinal victory was short-lived. A series of subsequent decisions have established that there is a fringe of protected first amendment speech that stands well outside the core. Sexually explicit speech is at the periphery;[56] so is indecent or vulgar speech, at least on the radio at certain times;[57] so is commercial speech[58] despite *Virginia Pharmacy's* rhetorical flourishes; so, finally is speech about issues not of public concern, at least in certain contexts.[59] It may be that some of these decisions are justified. Nonetheless, there is something quite odd about suppressing speech in the name of democracy. If robust debate about public issues is implied by the concept of democracy, does it follow that we should be committed to pallid debate on private issues? Is a public issue/private issue distinction part and parcel of a democratic vision? Before we can assess whether it is a good idea to forge a strong link between democracy and freedom of speech, perhaps we need to know more about what democracy is taken to mean in constitutional law.

Democracy and Constitutional Law

Two of the leading constitutional works in modern times quickly fuse the concept of democracy with majority rule. In *Democracy and Distrust,* Dean John Hart Ely states that "We have as a society from the beginning, and now almost instinctively, accepted the notion that a representative democracy must be our form of government. . . . Our constitutional development over the past century has therefore substantially strengthened the original commitment to control by a majority of the governed . . . [*M*]*ajoritarian* democracy is . . . the core of our entire [system]."[60] Similarly, in *Judicial Review and the National Political Process,* Dean Jesse H. Choper begins by recognizing that the term democracy is vague, but he asserts: "[C]ertain critical elements are beyond reasonable doubt. Whether one looks to such classical theorists as Aristotle, Locke, and Rousseau, to such mainstays of American political thinking as Madison, Jefferson, and Lincoln, or to this nation's constitutional development from its origin to the present time, majority rule has been considered the keystone of a democratic political system in both theory and practice."[61]

If majority rule is seen as the core of democracy, it is easy to see how the right of the people to know and the concern with self-government could come to be regarded as the center of the Constitution and, accordingly, the center of the first amendment. But the starting assumption is exactly what I now mean to place in question. I mean to question the strength of our commitment to majority rule, and specifically to deny that "majoritarian democracy is . . . the core of our entire system." It is not "beyond reasonable doubt" that majority rule is the "keystone of a democratic political system in both theory and practice." Indeed, I would contend that majority rule is *not* the keystone of our theory or our practice. I do not question the importance of self-government or democracy, but rather contend that neither self-government nor democracy make much sense in the American system if *majoritarian* democracy is thought to be the "core" of the system or the "keystone of the system." Once it is understood that majority rule, self-government, and democracy are not tightly connected, any Meiklejohn-like claim that political speech (or speech on public issues or speech of general interest) deserves a privileged place in the first amendment becomes correspondingly less attractive. It would no longer be possible on that understanding to connect the first amendment with any realistic conception of democracy.

Political scientists have long understood that the centrality of majority rule to the American system is very much in doubt, yet the writings of Ely and Choper reflect a powerful and for many years the dominant theme[62] in the legal literature.[63] In fairness, it should be stressed that scholars as good as Ely and Choper are by no means unaware of the aspects of our system that fail to fit a majoritarian picture. Part of their task is to reconcile the anomalies. Nonetheless, for them the starting point is a commitment to majoritarian democracy, and that starting point is problematic.

From that starting point, important features of the American system look strikingly out of place. If the country is committed to majority rule, why do nine unelected people wearing black robes get to veto decisions that have been approved by the political branches of government? From this perspective, judicial review is simply undemocratic. Thus, Deans Choper and Ely, along with dozens of other American legal scholars, have set out to address the "counter-majoritarian difficulty"[64] of judicial review.[65]

If majority rule were in fact the American perspective, there looms an even more striking feature of the American system that seems out of place: the Bill of Rights,[66] including the first amendment. Congress shall make no law abridging the freedom of speech, presumably even if a deliberate and broadly based majority of the country wishes to do so.[67] When members of Congress take an oath to support the Constitution, they, in important respects, take an oath against majority rule.

Scholars like Choper and Ely, of course, are not prepared to dispense with the first amendment or the rest of the Bill of Rights. They recognize that majority rule must be tempered with respect for minority rights.[68] The Bill of Rights and the institution of judicial review in part express that principle; they promise to make American democracy workable; they promise to protect those who are frozen out of the political process. Some provisions of the Bill of Rights are hard to characterize, however, as rights of discrete and insular minorities.[69] In fact, some provisions have been used to protect groups with substantial political power. The press, for example, is a powerful institution. Politicians confront it at their peril. Nonetheless, the Constitution specifically protects the press, even against legislation respecting and implementing the will of an overwhelming majority. Dean Ely suggests that protection of the press is a justifiable feature of the American Constitution not because it protects minorities (though, of course, it sometimes has that effect), but rather because freedom of press helps to assure an open and effective democratic process.[70] Thus, majority rule is compromised, but only to assure a good process. Democracy ends up being a commitment to majority rule on matters of substance, but not on matters of democratic process.[71] The pull to narrow the first amendment to public or political issues becomes increasingly attractive.[72]

Majority Rule and the Structure of Power

The equation of American democracy with majority rule, however, cannot be squared with either the original understanding of the Constitution or with modern constitutional practice. It can not and should not serve as an organizing principle for American democracy. Of course, there are majoritarian features to the American Constitution, and their presence is not accidental. Article I, Section 2 provides that the House of Representatives is to be elected by the people;[73] moreover, there is abundant evidence that Congress was given the power under Article 1, Section 4 ultimately to control the time, place, and manner of elections to the House of Representatives in order to assure that the will of the majority, rather than a faction under the control of a state legislature, might be expressed. The debate surrounding Article I, Sections 2 and 4 was prominent in the Constitutional Convention and in the ratifying conventions. Some objected to introducing any majoritarian features into a republican form of government,[74] but the voices for majoritarian democracy prevailed. It was decided that the voice of popular opinion should be directly[75] felt in at least one part of the government.[76] But no fair reading of the overall design of the Constitution can plausibly yield a notion that majority rule is a central feature of the document.[77] Tiny Delaware was given as many seats as populous New York in the United States Senate. This was not an accident. The Senate is an institutional rejection of majority rule. So is the Bill of Rights. So is judicial review. The Constitution is simply not a populist document; it is calculatedly antimajoritarian.[78] Madison made this clear in *Federalist* 10. The Constitution was designed to combat the types of evils perceived to exist under the state constitutions, namely, that "the public good is disregarded in the conflicts of rival parties, and that measures are too often decided, not according to the rules of justice and the rights of the minor party, but by the superior force of an interested and overbearing majority."[79]

The antimajoritarian character of the American polity is revealed not only in the makeup of its formal governmental structure,[80] but also in the strength, power, and influence of the institutions that are placed at one remove or another from the governmental process. The antimajoritarian character of these institutions is usually taken for granted. I have in mind first the relationship of powerful "private" corporations to governmental institutions. That relationship is by no means unique to the United States; but many Americans see the relationship as a fundamental part of what the country is all about. In communist countries, the leaders of automobile companies, steel factories, and oil producers are public officials. By contrast, General Motors, United States Steel, and Mobil Oil Corporation are led by private citizens, not public officials. The major means of production are owned and, for the most part, controlled by nongovernmental actors. They are outside the day-to-day control of the democratic process.

It is easy to see how one could make a democratic case against this set of arrangements. The move from the premise that people have a right at the voting booth to control those who exercise substantial control over their lives to the notion that powerful conglomerates should not be free to wield power outside the democratic process is easy to make. Charles Lindblom, for example, after asking how the American corporation fits with democratic

theory and vision, answers simply, "[I]t does not fit."[81] Even conservatives like Irving Kristol admit that the apparent lack of
"fit" between the substantial power of American corporations
and the "accepted ideology of the American democracy" requires
justification.[82]

The puzzle cannot be avoided by invoking any notion of private
property. Of course, if federal law provided for a national election
of the head of General Motors (or for Presidential appointment),
the property rights of General Motors shareholders would be di-
luted. But no constitutional barrier would prevent such legislation.[83] Some may think that socialism (of this sort) is "un-
American"; it is not unconstitutional.

These property arrangements did not emerge from thin air
here any more than did their quite different counterparts in Eastern Europe. The property arrangements which placed enormous
power in nongovernmental hands were created by governmental
actors and could be changed if there were a will to do so. The lack
of will to do so suggests something important about the American
conception of democracy, namely, that American democracy permits the exercise of enormous power without substantial electoral control. If the lack of democratic control of American business corporations were to be defended, references to Madisonian
concepts of dispersed power might be useful, and those who have
an interest in defending the current arrangements seize on just
these defenses. Thus Irving Kristol ultimately is moved to say
that, "In our pluralistic society we frequently find ourselves defending specific concentrations of power, about which we might
otherwise have the most mixed feelings, on the grounds that they
contribute to a general diffusion of power, a diffusion which creates the 'space' in which individual liberty can survive and pros-
per. . . . The general principle of checks and balances, and of de-
centralized authority too, is as crucial to the social and economic
structures of a liberal democracy as to its political structure."[84]

To be sure, the modern business corporation is subject to governmental checks. Even there, it is not neurotic to worry that the
existing system allows the regulated to control the regulators.[85]
At the very least, the process of "checking" the power of business
corporations is tricky. From any reasonable perspective, the modern business corporation is a significant example of the extent to

which the American polity is *not* committed to majoritarian control.[86]

The institutional press is in some respects an even better example. It too illustrates the extent to which the polity resists majoritarian control of powerful institutions. Consider a fictional
example that has nonfictional counterparts in hundreds of American cities. Imagine a large metropolitan city with one major
newspaper, the *Times*. The paper is owned by a single family, the
Pattersons. The paper makes recommendations on election day
for dozens of local offices. Tens of thousands of voters (who pay
only dim attention to local politics) read the *Times*'s recommendations and act upon them. The *Times*'s recommendations are
made by three editors who interview the candidates. From time
to time owner Patterson will reverse the board and dictate a particular selection. He *is* the owner.

The *Times* has broken mayors, helped to elect mayors, and
been a substantial factor in determining whether a mayor will be
re-elected. Owner Patterson is surely a powerful figure in this
fictional city. To be sure, he is not all-powerful. Local politicians
have sometimes bucked the editorial demands of the *Times* and
succeeded. But the position of the *Times* is a substantial factor to
be taken into account in the political reckoning of a person who
seeks or strives to keep local office in the city.

Let us suppose that Patterson's father ran the paper before him
and that Patterson hopes his son or daughter will run the paper
after him. Once again, it is easy to sketch the democratic case
against such arrangements. One could argue that disproportion-
ate power to influence the electorate has been fixed in the hands
of a single unelected family. To think these arrangements are
sound, it could be argued, would be to favor the power of a single
family over the power of the majority. Moreover, it is easy to
think of arrangements that would place the press inside the democratic process. In order to further majoritarian democracy, the
city could institute eminent domain proceedings against the paper and bring about a forced sale to the city. The publisher could
become a public official elected by the people or appointed by the
mayor. One could contemplate a variety of other possibilities: the
Federal Communications Commission could appoint the publisher (or the editorial board);[87] the losing candidate for mayor

could have appointive power or a blue-ribbon commission of journalists. One could imagine a host of further possibilities regarding the selection of the "blue-ribbon" commission.

I have discussed possibilities such as these with many different people in many different places. The most typical reaction is nervousness. This nervousness is sometimes manifested in extreme forms of denial. Many people deny the power or influence of the press. These denials usually slide from the demonstration that the local press is not all-powerful or invariably influential to the conclusion that it is not powerful or influential. Denials sometimes take the form of shrill and extreme propositions about the capacity of the marketplace to sort out the truth. People suggest that if the editorial policy of the paper is "out of line," the paper will go out of business. They argue that the "people" somehow find out the "truth" about local candidates despite the paper. Or they argue that the press tells the people what they want to hear.

These responses are not even half-truths; they are just kernels. The Pattersons of the nation have a lot of influence and power; it makes a difference whom they appoint to write for the paper. And the difference runs not merely to the election and re-election of public officials, but to the fate of commercial enterprises from land development to restaurants. The local newspaper can ruin the reputation of a day care center or a local teacher. The same people who deny the power of the press in one context are the first to recognize that the truth rarely catches up with a lie; they know that reputations can be savaged by a single article.

What motors the denials of press power is skepticism and fear about the alternative possibilities. People do not want electoral majorities controlling newspapers. Nor are they inclined to trust alternative political arrangements designed to assure that dissenters have a voice in the paper. People tend to think that America is committed to an independent press. They want it independent of money, power, and the passions of the majority. This is in part what they think the first amendment means. So if democracy means majority rule, the first amendment is at war with democracy.

That the first amendment is at war with democracy, however, is, of course, quite unacceptable. And it seems clear what has to give way if peaceful relations are to be assured. What must go is not the first amendment (or judicial review, or the Bill of Rights);

what has to give is any notion that the organizing principle of American democracy is majority rule.

Majority Rule in Practice

If majority rule is not the central principle of the Constitution, it might be said that it is at least an important feature of the American Constitution. Even if majority rule does not apply to the press, even if it does not directly apply to business corporations, and even if the Constitution (principally through the Bill of Rights) places some side constraints on what elected representatives can do in response to popular majorities, the fact remains that the members of the House and Senate and the President of the United States do stand for election and their chances of reelection do depend in fact upon their responsiveness to the will of the electorate. It can be argued that in practice the majority, subject to limited side constraints, does and should rule.

Even this line of argument overstates the importance of majority rule in theory and in practice. Before exploring its limits, however, we should examine its core of truth. The "truth" is this: Elections are a vital feature of the American Constitution. Politicians are to some extent influenced by public opinion, and they should be. No plausible conception of American democracy would exclude elections. A commitment to elections and a commitment to representative democracy, however, is not a commitment to majority rule. For the most part, as political scientists have pointed out for decades, the majority can not rule on specific issues.[88] Consider the presidency, and take, for example, the elections of Ronald Reagan. Ronald Reagan was elected because of voter perception about his leadership qualities. Voters admired his strength, his warmth, his determination, his general personality. At the same time, voters disliked many of his policies (indeed, some have argued, most of his policies). Thus the majority of the voters elected Ronald Reagan, yet he may well have implemented many policies they opposed, for example, concerning farm policy, the environment, civil rights, women's rights, and education. The Reagan presidency may be an extreme case of division between voters' conception of *who* they want and of *what* they want in terms of policies.[89] But that division is always present. Voters frequently complain that they are faced with the lesser of two evils. If they vote, they always vote for people whose views they reject on one issue or another. So long as issues are complicated, so long as interests are multiple, so long as people have diverse values, most voters will vote for a candidate whose policy preferences are something other than a carbon copy of their own views and perspectives. This phenomenon applies not merely to Ronald Reagan, not merely to the presidency, but to every Senate election, every House election, indeed every election in every city and hamlet.[90]

Politicians, then, need not be responsive to the electorate on every issue that comes before them, and they are not. Most members of the House of Representatives have "safe" seats.[91] On some well-publicized issues they must be responsive to the electorate,[92] but for much of their work they need not be.[93] By the same token, there are many issues upon which politicians must be responsive to campaign contributors. Responsiveness to campaign contributors is not well correlated with majority will or the public interest, however much "pluralists" might contend to the contrary.[94] For a wide range of issues, then, neither the President nor the members of Congress need be responsive to the majority. For many issues, they respond to the demands, perceived or otherwise, of campaign contributors. For many other issues they act on their own independent judgment. For still others, they act in response to a patchwork of these and other factors. One need not even refer to the seniority system, to the committee structure, to the filibuster, or to a myriad of other institutional oddities to discern the existence of substantial limits on majority rule. Public opinion and the prospect of elections is an important factor in the legislative process; still, majority rule is a fiction.

Should legislators be responsive to the will of the majority on every issue? The question presupposes, of course, what will never be the case, namely, that there is a majority will on every issue. Suppose, however, that through polling we were able to get the views of the constituents on every issue. Or imagine that voters in their homes could press a button and quickly signal their views to their representatives on every issue. Worse, or better, depending upon your perspective, forget the representatives. Suppose we could turn the nation into a technological town hall every night. Would it be a good idea to have people across the nation voting from their homes on the day's national legislative agenda? One person's democratic dream is another person's democratic nightmare.

For this thought experiment, we should assume what we do not have, a nation of people who know the identity of both their Senators and the content of the Bill of Rights, a populace that reads the newspaper, a people vitally interested in national politics.[95] Before making this assumption, however, permit a brief confession. As I write this, I have been living in Massachusetts for six months. I know the name of only one Senator from Massachusetts (guess which one). I can identify only a few votes he has cast in the last six months. I could not name every member of the President's cabinet if my life depended upon it. I sneak glances at two papers every morning while getting a five-year-old ready for kindergarten, humoring a two-year-old, and negotiating with my wife about day-to-day life. I am more interested in national politics than most people, but I do not have time to read the *New York Times* with a microscope. Suppose I and everyone else did and would. Should we rule?

Even if we read the newspaper every day (and many periodicals cover to cover), we would be ill-informed about many of the issues facing the Congress. I have views on the environment, arms control, and United States–Soviet relations, but I have no doubt that knowing more about the questions before the Congress would affect my views on numerous issues. If I am asked for my opinion on current issues before Congress, I can respond to a poll-taker. I can give *an* answer. So can most people. Our answers will be different, and they can be quantified. Even if we assume a well-read people, is it at all clear that a legislator should take those poll answers as gospel?

More realistically, of course, we are not a nation of well-informed people. We do not have a paid staff exploring issues for us. To ask representatives to follow majority opinion on all issues would ask them to be bound by the relatively blind.

There is an alternative to a notion of lock-step, rubber-stamp representatives. One might postulate that representatives should enact what a majority would enact if they were more fully informed. This postulate is perhaps less meaningful than it sounds. How fully informed do we imagine the citizens to be? For example, in approaching legal or medical questions, do we imagine that they know enough about law to think like lawyers, enough about medicine to think like doctors? Even recognizing that expertise among lawyers and doctors varies and that neither lawyers nor doctors can claim a privileged position with respect to dozens of "legal" or "medical" questions, what we know to some extent determines who we are. If the people constituting the majority knew more than they do, they would not be the same people. Imagining what they would think if they knew what we know is not meaningless, but it is usually fruitless.

Beyond this relatively simple problem are issues about what the majority would think if they fully appreciated the intensity of the preferences of those in the minority and how a representative should act if he or she thought the fully informed majority was callous about or even had antipathy for the plight of the minority.

I am left with the view that representatives should take constituents' views into account in a serious way, but that they should be fully prepared to make, and should be encouraged to make, independent judgments about what is best for the polity.[96] The argument is not that representatives are smarter or even wiser than the people they represent. It is rather that decision-makers with more time for deliberation about difficult issues are likely to make better decisions than those with less time for deliberation. To that extent, majority rule is undesirable in theory and in practice.

Several considerations mitigate against the force of this conclusion, however. Legislators may make many more decisions on the basis of their own judgment about what is wise for the polity than is often supposed. Many vital decisions are made, however, not on the basis of their best independent judgment about what is good for the country, but on their best judgment about what campaign contributors want.[97] Money and power, not wisdom, often guide the legislative process. Moreover, power corrupts in other ways. The arrogance of politicians, their loss of touch with the people, their provincial outlook, their easy ability to equate the narrow interests of their friends with the general interests— all these considerations make it hard to settle on any a priori sunny view regarding the independent judgment of a member of Congress from Bakersfield, California, or Orlando, Florida,[98] or the collective judgment of their ilk.

The case for judicial review rests on that part of the picture

which sees a legislative failing to make independent judgments.[99] That picture imagines legislators giving up independence in several ways: rubber-stamping the wishes of an aroused
but insensitive majority (while ignoring the rights and needs of a
minority) because the majority casts more votes in elections than
the minority; responding to the demands of a lobby against what
would otherwise be the legislator's conception of the public interest because the lobby has substantial dollars to contribute;[100] responding to the deal struck between powerful interest groups and
enforced by legislative leaders (a deal that insufficiently responds to the needs of groups with less legislative power) because
of a desire to maintain the good graces of the legislative leadership.

Judicial review is seen by many as an important check on these
potential failures in the legislative process. Federal judges with
life tenure should be less responsive to insensitive majorities
(federal judges do not seek votes) and less responsive to campaign
contributors (federal judges do not seek contributions). Their in-
sulation from the election process should allow them to make
genuinely independent judgments. They thus should be able to
protect minorities and to safeguard fundamental values.[101] In
short, they should be able to make judgments independent of
money, power, and the roar of the crowd.

At the same time, judges may be *too* independent. Power corrupts, even without campaign contributions. Judges too can be
arrogant, out of touch with the people, provincial in their outlook.[102] They may too easily substitute the narrow vision of their
own class and background[103] for the more eclectic outlook needed
to formulate wise policy.[104] And they may do this all in good faith;
they may not be arrogant or simpleminded. Everyone's perspective is partial.[105] Judges are no exception.

Independent decisionmaking by legislators and judges may be
informed, prudent, and wise; it may also be self-serving, myopic,
and corrupt. If majority *rule* is undesirable, undesirable also
would be the absence of populist power in the governmental process.

Some argue that populist power is important because participation is valuable for self-realization or, even more strongly, because it is constitutive of what we are, that is, social and political
animals. Leaving these important considerations aside,[106] it is

important to recognize that providing for some populist power is likely to produce better decisions overall.

Martin Redish, however, has argued for the opposite position. He suggests that popular participation and power cannot be justified on any notion that it produces better decisions. He suggests that in any contest between a presumably informed political leadership and a relatively uninformed populace there is no reason to believe that the populace is right and the leadership is wrong.[107] On that point, Redish may well be correct, but the focus on any particular contest is not well calculated to judge the efficacy of popular participation. The real question is whether a process relatively devoid of popular power will produce better decisions over the long term than a process in which the population has power from time to time to change political leaders. In the absence of mechanisms for electoral power, leaders are far more likely to be uninformed about popular concerns, more likely to be arrogant, corrupt, and self-serving. Although majority rule may be a deficient ideal in theory and a myth in practice, there would be a substantial case for popular power even if the only matter of concern were the quality of the decisions made over the long term.

But recognizing that popular power is of some importance in the American system is a far cry from supposing that majority rule is central to the American system or that the "citizen-ruler" is truly its heartbeat. Even if one should characterize the system as a representative democracy, it becomes important to ask what the leaders are supposed to be representative of. Not the majority. Perhaps the best interests of the citizenry. So conceived, however, representative democracy is elitist democracy. If the first amendment is centrally tied to that conception, it loses much of its luster.

Ultimately, there can be no evasion: the citizen-ruler is a myth; a town hall meeting is not a realistic metaphor for the American system. Substantial power is exercised in the American system with no direct popular control over the leaders. Consider again the varying degrees of independence ceded to business leaders, to the press, and to federal judges. Finally, we can engage the central point of this section: if democracy rests on majority rule, if majority rule is truly the cornerstone of a democratic system, democracy is not desirable, and, in any event, on that understanding, America is not a democracy.

Democracy as a Contested But Bounded Concept

In World War II, American soldiers fought and many died in defense of American "democracy." I find it extremely doubtful that any soldier's opposition to Hitler or Mussolini would have faltered if he or she had focused on the unreality of a town hall conception of democracy or realized that the composition of the Senate or the protections of the Bill of Rights were resolutely antimajoritarian. In the postwar period, American Presidents have lauded American democracy while castigating Soviet tyranny. Even recognizing the cynical capacities of politicians, we can assume that their praise of "democracy" carried a measure of sincerity and that it was not based on any simpleminded conception about the workings of the American political process.

As we probe the concept of democracy, it is useful to recognize that the Soviet Union also regards itself as a democracy.[108] To be sure, this is difficult for most Americans to credit. Much of Communist doctrine is diametrically opposed to American understandings of democracy. For example, from the Communists' perspective, "The Communist Party is the lever of political organization, with the help of which the more progressive part of the working class directs on the right path the whole mass of the proletariat and the semi-proletariat."[109] Proceeding from this premise, Lenin argues that when the party has reached a decision, there can be no dissent. The danger, he thinks, is that, "[T]o belittle the socialist ideology *in any way,* to *turn aside from it in the slightest degree* means to strengthen bourgeois ideology."[110] From Lenin's perspective, the risk of dissent from the Communist Party is the reestablishment of a state used as an organ by capitalists to exploit the proletariat. And *that,* from the Soviet perspective, would be undemocratic. Thus, as Benn and Peters explain:

> Marxist critics of "bourgeois democracy" complain that, despite formal equality of political rights, anti-capitalist [programs] reach the electorate only in the distorted versions served up by the bourgeois press. The poorly educated masses are all too sus-

ceptible, they say, to capitalist propaganda. So far from being sensitive to a wide range of interests, liberal democracy is a formal facade obscuring domination by an economic class. Should it ever threaten to be other than that, the mask would be dropped and the brutal features of power exposed.[111]

Whatever the merit of the Marxist criticism of American democracy, the gulf between the Soviet Union's conception of democracy and the typical American conception is apparent. From an American perspective, any system of government that tells its citizens that they may not dissent "in any way" from the ideology of the ruling party is by that fact alone an undemocratic government.

By that standard, it may well be that many governments are undemocratic. Yet, a 1949 UNESCO inquiry that had sent questionnaires to scholars in many countries concluded that "'democracy' is claimed as the proper ideal description of all systems of political and social organization advocated by influential proponents."[112] It might be possible to divine a definition of democracy—at a high level of abstraction, to be sure—that would accommodate the various uses of the term throughout the world.[113] Any such definition, however, would either exclude factors regarded as necessary conditions of democracy in America or would need to include terminology vague enough to accomplish the transcendent task.

If the term *democracy* is to play a role in the interpretation of the American Constitution, the reference point must not be a worldwide abstraction but a conception firmly fixed in the American culture and experience. That understanding, of course, does not take us far. First, there is a somewhat circular quality about the relationship between the idea of democracy and the American culture and experience. To a large extent, the term *democracy* has functioned in America less as a concept independent of the American ideals and experience than as a surrogate for those ideals and experience.[114] Many American political scientists have attempted to describe the meaning of democracy by describing the nature of American institutions.[115] These "descriptions," however, could not possibly be decisive even if we forget that the complexity of American institutions often renders them reductive, value-laden, and subject to change. Such descriptions could not be decisive because the term *democracy* stands in for American *ideals,* and the extent to which those ideals have been unfulfilled in practice is always open to argument.[116] Moreover, those ideals themselves conflict. As William Connolly explains, the term *democracy* has long functioned as a contested concept in American politics. Indeed, "Central to politics," Connolly argues, is the

> ambiguous and relatively open-ended interaction of persons and groups who share a range of concepts, but share them imperfectly and incompletely. Politics involves a form of interaction in which agents adjust, extend, resolve, accommodate, and transcend initial differences within a context of partly shared assumptions, concepts, and commitments. On this reading, conceptual contests are central to politics; they provide the space for political interaction.[117]

In fact, the "desire to expunge contestability from the terms of political inquiry," he writes, is itself the manifestation of a desire "to escape politics."[118]

Nonetheless, as Connolly himself would emphasize, that democracy is a *contested* concept in American politics does not prevent it from being a *bounded* concept. American understanding of democracy may embrace a combination of ideals about freedom, participation, equality, community, and welfare, ideals that themselves can conflict in concrete contexts. But there are some shared ideals, and some other ideals are in fact—to use a dangerous phrase—"un-American." Consider, for example, the ideals of Mussolini:

> For the fascist, all is comprised in the State, and nothing spiritual or human exists—much less has any value—outside the State. In this respect fascism is a totalizing concept, and the Fascist State—the unification and synthesis of every value—interprets, develops, and actualizes the whole life of the people.[119]

Thus fascism's motto: "Everything for the State; nothing against the State; nothing outside the State."[120] Or consider the Nazi ideal as expressed by Goering:

> In the old parliament, Authority and Responsibility were in reverse order. Responsibility went from top to bottom, and Authority went from bottom to top. That was a sin against natural law ... Here however the old principle holds good: Authority goes from top to bottom, but Responsibility always from bottom

to top. Each is responsible to him who is called to stand next above him. The Leader carries final Responsibility. What the Leader wants will be done. His will is law for us.[121]

However diverse American conceptions of democracy may be, they are not so capacious as to reach the authoritarianism idealized by Nazism or Fascism. More specifically, American conceptions of democracy simply rebel against the notion that dissent can be repressed in the name of any ideology. The rejection of authoritarianism so strongly implicated in the valuing of dissent does not exhaust the shared understandings of American democracy, but it is surely a major part of the meaning of American democracy. Whether American democracy depends upon genuine majority rule is open to debate, but American democracy would not exist in the absence of a commitment[122] to safeguarding dissent. Understanding American democracy requires an understanding of the first amendment, and understanding the first amendment requires an understanding of American democracy. They are symbiotically related.

Democracy and Dissent: Emerson, Whitman, and Free Speech

After a brief introduction, most American law students begin their study of the first amendment with the 1919 case of *Schenck v. United States*.[123] Justice Holmes there attempts to justify the imposition of criminal penalties for a conspiracy to circulate an antidraft leaflet to persons accepted for military service.[124] The leaflet recited the thirteenth amendment's ban on involuntary servitude, claimed that the conscription act violated constitutional principles, that conscription was "despotism in its worst form and a monstrous wrong against humanity in the interest of Wall Street's chosen few."[125] In the course of its antiwar and antidraft commentary, it insisted that recipients should "not submit to intimidation."[126] Instead they were told to "Assert Your Rights."[127]

As wars go, World War I was relatively popular. It would be surprising if many American conscripts read this leaflet inveighing against "cunning politicians"[128] and the "mercenary capitalist press"[129] and raced off to "assert their rights." In fact, there was no evidence that anyone, anywhere, at any time was influenced in any way by the leaflet in question.

Nonetheless, Justice Holmes purported not to see "what effect [the leaflet] could be expected to have upon persons subject to the draft except to influence them to obstruct the carrying of it out."[130] His opinion refers to a "clear and present danger."[131] Indeed, he asks us to think of this leaflet in the same way we would think of "a man . . . falsely shouting fire in a theatre and causing a panic."[132]

Schenck v. United States is a sobering introduction to American ideals about freedom of speech. Packing dissenters off to jail is an activity we associate with tyranny, not with democracy. Moreover, the *Schenck* opinion is bereft of any indications about why Americans might value freedom of speech. To be sure, Holmes admits that in other places and at other times the defendants "in saying all that was said in the circular would have been within their constitutional rights."[133] But this compounds the insult. The defendants in essence were told they had a constitutional right to dissent—some of the time.

Schenck introduces a long line of cases dealing with the advocacy of illegal action. If *Schenck* is a sobering introduction, the whole line is simply depressing. No one can read these cases without becoming increasingly cynical about the binding force of legal doctrine and about the willingness or capacity of the judiciary to protect dissent. The cases reveal a judiciary that mirrored the moods of the people. Judges, too, were caught up in the hysteria of World War I;[134] they too responded to the anticommunist scare of the McCarthy era. In cooler times, they protected dissent. In the best of times and the worst of times, doctrine was manipulated, shaped, and changed to serve the perceived needs of the moment. Only rarely did judges transcend the censoring passions of the day.

There is a large lesson in the line of cases from *Schenck* to *Brandenburg*,[135] and the lesson has to do with the limitations of legal doctrine. Law can play a role in shaping culture, but legal doctrine is a part of the culture and is frequently hostage to it. Censorship becomes unthinkable only insofar as the collective conscience of a culture has placed it beyond the bounds. Moreover, judicial capacity to draw upon traditions of freedom is enhanced if the vitality of those traditions resonates in the precedential materials. What is disturbing about *Schenck* is not only the lack of courage reflected in its result, but its overall blindness to the rich American cultural understanding of freedom of speech. Even in later cases when Holmes gets around to speaking up on behalf of freedom of speech, he draws on only a small part of the available tradition. Moreover, it is that partial rendition of the American tradition that is internalized in the vocabulary of lawyers, commentators, and judges. The legal community is afflicted with a serious case of Supreme-Court-itis. At the very least, it is fair to say that the legal profession relies heavily upon the existing judicial tales about freedom of speech. When a Meiklejohn narrative was added to the then-existing set of tales about freedom of speech, it was easy for Kalven to create an air of excitement. The Meiklejohn perspective was new and old at the same time. It was new to judicial opinions, but it connected to long-standing traditions. What in retrospect might be surprising is that judicial discussion of freedom of speech could have continued for so long without entertaining the Meiklejohn perspective. Seriously flawed as it may be, it is a part of this nation's first amendment story.

What I want to emphasize here is that another part, indeed a more important part, of that story has been largely missing from the pages of the *United States Reports*. The side of the story I have in mind has been most eloquently presented by the American romantics, but it has been a persistent theme throughout American history. In short, I want to argue that Ralph Waldo Emerson and Walt Whitman understood more about the relationship of freedom of speech to American democracy than did Oliver Wendell Holmes or Alexander Meiklejohn, that their insights are closer to prevailing conceptions of American democracy than those currently prevailing in the legal commentary, and that if their insights were taken seriously, the impetus to repress speech on public or private issues would be substantially diminished.

In establishing these claims, I will use the little-noticed case of *Connick v. Myers*.[136] It exhibits the impoverished character of legal discourse about freedom of speech as well as any case I know. Sheila Myers was an Assistant District Attorney in New Orleans for five-and-a-half years. As the Court put it, "She served at the pleasure of . . . Harry Connick, the District Attorney for Orleans Parish."[137] Sometime in 1980 Connick decided to transfer Myers to a different section of the criminal court. Myers objected to the transfer and to a number of other aspects about the managerial policies of the office. She expressed her concerns to Dennis Waldron, one of the First Assistant District Attorneys, who apparently countered that her views were not shared by others in the office. Apparently in response to that comment, Myers prepared a questionnaire soliciting the views of her co-workers, fifteen district attorneys, "concerning office transfer policy, office morale, the need for a grievance committee, the level of confidence in supervisors, and whether employees felt pressured to work in political campaigns."[138]

Upon learning of the questionnaire, Waldron phoned Connick at home and told him Myers was creating a "'mini-insurrection'"[139] within the office. Connick returned to the office and informed Myers soon thereafter that her distribution of the questionnaire was "an act of insubordination."[140] Connick fired Myers, and after litigation over the issue, the District Court found that he fired her because she had distributed the questionnaire. Myers argued that her discharge was unconstitutional. She argued that her distribution of the questionnaire was a protected exercise of free speech.

The federal district court in the Eastern District of Louisiana agreed with Myers; so did the United States Court of Appeals for the Fifth Circuit. But the Supreme Court agreed with Connick. By a 5–4 vote, it upheld the firing of Myers. In approaching the question for the majority, Justice White concentrated on whether Myers's speech was political in character. After parading a series of quotations about the importance of political speech and self-government, Justice White concentrated on whether Myers's speech addressed a "matter of public concern."[141] The general inquiry was said to be grounded on the issue of whether the subject matter was one upon which "'free and open debate is vital to informed decisionmaking by the electorate.'"[142] The Court stated that if the speech was not of public concern, there was no first amendment protection against dismissal.[143]

The Court found that most of the questions on Myers's questionnaire did not relate to a matter of public concern. Questions involving office morale, the possibility of a grievance committee, the transfer policies of the office, and the processes by which they were implemented were all deemed to be outside the scope of public concern. The Court did find that one of Myers's questions touched upon a question of public concern. The question (number 11 of 14) asked whether Myers's co-workers felt pressured to work in political campaigns on behalf of candidates supported by the District Attorney's Office. Nonetheless, the Court concluded that the government interests outweighed the first amendment interests. Connick, it was said, did not need to "tolerate action which he reasonably believed would disrupt the office, undermine his authority, and destroy close working relationships."[144] At the same time, the Court observed that different fact situations involving public employees might support a constitutional claim: "Although today the balance is struck for the government, this is no defeat for the First Amendment."[145]

In dissent, Justice Brennan complained that "the public will be deprived of valuable information with which to evaluate the performance of elected officials."[146] He thought that Myers's entire questionnaire addressed issues of public concern "because it discussed subjects that could reasonably be expected to be of interest to persons seeking to develop informed opinions about the manner in which the Orleans Parish District Attorney, an elected official charged with managing a vital governmental agency, discharges his responsibilities."[147] As to whether Myers's critical comments had so far interfered with the operation of a government office as to warrant dismissal, Brennan concluded that the Court's deference to Connick's fears about the impact of Myers's statements was excessive. He saw no reason to overturn the lower court's finding that "'[I]t cannot be said that the defendant's interest in promoting the efficiency of the public services performed through his employees was either adversely affected or substantially impeded by plaintiff's distribution of the questionnaire.'"[148]

In assessing these opinions, we might recognize at the outset that the government has a substantial interest in the character of working relationships in a district attorney's office, that these relationships could be disrupted by a single obstreperous "bad actor," and that federal judges might have a difficult time discerning, after the fact, what the true interpersonal state of affairs might have been at the time of a dismissal. One can at least understand why some members of the Court might want to stay out of disputes of this kind. Nonetheless, I insist that *Connick v.*

Myers is indeed a defeat for the first amendment. And the most substantial aspect of the loss is that no one on the Court, not even Justice Brennan, seemed to appreciate the character of the values at stake.

There is nothing very complex about the values involved. I suspect they would be the first resort of anyone who had not been exposed to the reigning judicial precedents. We might imagine how Sheila Myers might have thought about the case before she saw a lawyer. Myers, of course, *is* a lawyer; so that background might have infected her capacity to see the situation clearly. Her vision, too, might have been clouded by the existing community of legal discourse with its paeans to democracy and self-government. If not, I suspect her first reaction would have nothing to do with public issues or private issues. Her assumption might well be that the first amendment guaranteed the right to speak about any subject and that it most especially guaranteed the right to dissent against existing customs, habits, conventions, processes, and institutions. It is possible that Myers was gathering evidence so that she could go to the voters with her information. But she may have had more "modest" goals in mind. She might simply have wanted to speak out against the management of the office. She presumably wanted to stimulate others in the office to begin discussing office policies and management. For all we know, Myers's questionnaire might have spelled the beginning of a union organizing campaign.

In any event, we do know that Sheila Myers had a view of employer-employee relationships different from Dennis Waldron's or Harry Connick's. Waldron thought the distribution of the questionnaire constituted a "mini-insurrection"; Connick called it "insubordination." Myers, on the other hand, thought that employer-employee relationships included the possibility of vigorous dissent.

So understood, Myers's claim stands in a great first amendment tradition. It was a tradition well understood by Ralph Waldo Emerson and Walt Whitman. For them, and I would argue for most Americans, the point of Myers's claim has little to do with whether there were voters out there combing the pages of the local *Times-Picayune* to learn about office morale in the District Attorney's office. For them, American democracy meant that Americans could speak out against any of the existing institutions, habits, customs, and traditions.[149] Emerson and Whitman may have celebrated a mythical American, but they celebrated an American who was not wedded to the comforts of the present nor tied by the bonds of the past. They celebrated the courage of the nonconformist, the iconoclast, the dissenter.[150] In urging self-reliance and independence of thought, in praising the heroism of those willing to speak out against the tide, they sided with the romantics—those willing to break out of classical forms. Their conception of democracy had little to do with voting and everything to do with the American spirit. They sided with John Stuart Mill, in recognizing the ease of conformity. And, with Mill, they sponsored nonconformity.

In so doing, they struck a responsive chord. Emerson spoke at a special time in American history. It was a period when there was substantial discussion of the failure of Americans to produce a genuinely independent literature,[151] a period when Tocqueville and others were observing that the abstract American commitment to freedom and civil liberties was not matched by the spirit of its people.[152] Indeed Tocqueville, reacting to his concern about the tyranny of the majority and of public opinion, had insisted that "I know no country in which, speaking generally, there is less independence of mind and true freedom of discussion than in America."[153] For whatever complicated reasons, as Barbara Packer observes, Emerson's recurrent pleas against the fear of speaking out "came to seem, to a whole generation, [as] an agent of liberation."[154] Arthur Schlesinger has come to call Emerson the "quintessential American"[155] and Walt Whitman is called America's greatest poet.[156] For my purposes, however, no one need think that Emerson is the quintessential American. One might grant such a title to Washington, Lincoln, Jefferson, or, even better, one could rail against the very concept of a quintessential American.[157] Indeed, for present purposes, it is perfectly satisfactory if one rejects (or accepts) Emerson's idealism,[158] his stance toward evil,[159] his glorification of intuition,[160] the character of his individualism, his views about the relationship between the one and the many, or his rendition of the relationship of humanity to nature. It is enough to recognize that Emerson and Whitman eloquently express an important part of the American tradition—the part that encourages an independent spirit.[161]

It is that tradition to which I appeal. Anyone who takes that tradition seriously must flinch at the Court's mindless observation in *Myers* that, "This is no defeat for the First Amendment." The *Myers* case tells public employees everywhere to shut up or get fired. The loss is not merely that voters will lose information. The loss is the failure to appreciate that the protection of dissent and its nurturance is a major American value.

One can only speculate what the outcome of *Connick v. Myers* might have been if a different rhetoric had animated first amendment decisionmaking from *Schenck* onward. The usual range of first amendment metaphors did not serve Myers's needs. The self-government-town-hall perspective, of course, led down a path to fantasyland. Even the often-used metaphor of the marketplace of ideas was not difficult for the Court to sidestep. The Court was able to portray the Connick-Myers dispute not as a contest for Truth emerging in the Marketplace of Ideas, but as an everyday squabble in the workplace, something best left outside the federal courts. If the first amendment were regularly conceived as specially prizing dissent, however, Myers's claim could have been articulated in terms that placed her in the center of first amendment traditions, not at its periphery.

The *Myers* case is not uniformly regarded as a first amendment outrage. Some believe that the government interest is substantial in public employment contexts and that the litigation process is likely to exacerbate difficulties in the workplace. Even if that view were accepted, it would be a mistake to indulge the comforting delusion that free speech values are not at stake. If workers are not free to speak out in the workplace, if they are habituated to knuckle silently under authority, their speech is not free. Perhaps most Americans or the Court believes that workplaces can not be run effectively if workers are free to criticize their bosses, but anyone who believes that should be forced to recognize that free speech values have been compromised; one ought not be able to pretend that those values are not involved.

It might be argued that the Court's treatment of first amendment values in *Myers* is merely an aberrational and undeliberative reflection of its desire to avoid involvement in particular employment disputes. But the Court's failure to recognize the first amendment value of dissent is not confined to employment disputes. There are many other important cases, and these cases are the inevitable reflections of the Court's general approach to first amendment questions. Some of these cases have been sharply criticized by the commentators. What gives these criticisms particular energy and sting, I would argue, has been the Court's failure to protect dissent.

A striking example is the case of *FCC v. Pacifica Foundation*.[162] There the Court upheld the imposition of sanctions against a radio station for broadcasting a George Carlin monologue called "Filthy Words." Carlin's humorous monologue was a satire against societal verbal taboos. In a "variety of colloquialisms,"[163] he repeated over and over the words that "will curve your spine, grow hair on your hands and [laughter] maybe, even bring us, God help us, peace without honor [laughter], um, and a bourbon,"[164] namely, "shit, piss, fuck, cunt, cocksucker, motherfucker, and tits."[165] The monologue evoked frequent laughter from a live studio audience, but the FCC was not amused. It moved against the radio station for broadcasting "indecent" language, and the Supreme Court upheld the FCC's action. The words were considered too vulgar and too offensive for the radio, at least in the early afternoon and in the manner presented by Carlin. The Court observed that "[a]dults who *feel the need* may purchase tapes and records or go to theaters and nightclubs *to hear these words*."[166]

Most people with any first amendment bones in their bodies are troubled by the *Pacifica* case. But the nub of the first amendment insult has little to do with self-government or with the marketplace of ideas. The concern does not flow from a worry that voters will be deprived of valuable information. Concern that the truth about vulgar language might not emerge in the marketplace of ideas may be well placed, but it is not a sufficient concern to explain the widespread outrage against the decision. Again, the decision is an affront to a notion of content-neutrality, but there are many of those. The *Pacifica* case produces heat precisely because Carlin's speech is considered by many to be precisely what the first amendment is *supposed* to protect. Carlin is attacking conventions; assaulting the prescribed orthodoxy; mocking the stuffed shirts; Carlin *is* the prototypical dissenter.

It matters not at all whether the target of his invective is society at large or a public official.[167] The outrage is that the stuffed shirts are in a position to silence Carlin, or at least in a position to keep him from "offending" the mass audience.[168] Justice Brennan put it well in his dissenting opinion when he found in the majority opinions "a depressing inability to appreciate that in our land of cultural pluralism, there are many who think, act, and talk differently from the Members of this Court, and who do not share their fragile sensibilities."[169]

Looking at the first amendment through the lens of dissent puts speakers like Myers and Carlin near the center of the first amendment (if there is a center),[170] but, in any event, not in their current location—at the fringe. It also should afford an important place to those whose methods of communication are unconventional. A leading case is *United States v. O'Brien*,[171] another instance where, from the perspective of dissent, the Court was dead wrong. David Paul O'Brien was convicted and sentenced to the custody of the Attorney General for "supervision and treatment" for burning his draft card. He argued that the burning of his draft card was protected speech. The government argued that burning a draft card was burning a draft card. It was not speech. Yet, the law used to prosecute O'Brien was passed precisely because members of Congress did not like the message communicated by the burning of draft cards.[172] And there can be no doubt: O'Brien intended to communicate an antiwar message by burning his draft card, and he successfully communicated that message. Nonetheless, the Court put its head in the sand: "We cannot accept the view that an apparently limitless variety of conduct can be labelled 'speech' whenever the person engaging in the conduct intends thereby to express an idea."[173] O'Brien, by this analysis, was not at the fringe of first amendment protection. He did not even get inside the circle.

Once again, neither the town hall metaphor nor the marketplace of ideas metaphor is quite apt as a symbol for why *O'Brien* is a first amendment horror story. Town hall meetings can function without the burning of draft cards. And it is hard to claim that truth was kept from the marketplace of ideas. *O'Brien* is one of those not infrequent cases where government prosecutions assist the dissemination of the dissenter's message. Yet, *O'Brien* is perhaps the ultimate first amendment insult. O'Brien is jailed because the authorities find his manner of expression unpatriotic, threatening, and offensive. When he complains that his freedom of speech has been abridged, the authorities deny that he has spoken.

Cases like *Myers, Pacifica,* and *O'Brien* suffice to show that, judged by the value of dissent, the Court's approach to the first amendment is in disrepair. The dissent value affords a basis for criticizing these decisions, not for explaining them. Nonetheless, the dissent value can assist in explaining some important aspects of first amendment doctrine. The dissent value affords at least a partial explanation for the Court's second-class treatment of commercial advertising. Commercial advertising arguably makes a contribution to the efficient allocation of economic resources, and some regard that contribution as political. But no one would contend that the typical commercial advertisement is an exercise in dissent.[174] When David O'Brien burns a draft card, we witness an act of dissent. When General Motors gives us a pitch about the glory of Chevrolet, we run for the refrigerator. To sing "We shall overcome," is to join a protest movement; to sing "Things go better with Coke," is to protest nothing.[175] Moreover, the distinction makes a difference. If protestors are banned from city streets, the first amendment affords protection. If commercial advertising is prohibited on city streets, the first amendment affords no refuge.[176]

The first amendment treatment of literature presents an even better example. One would be hard pressed to say that the value of literature is political. Indeed, Judge Robert Bork once went so far as to argue that the first amendment should be interpreted to protect only explicitly political speech.[177] On this view, he wrote, freedom for literature would depend not on constitutional protection, but "upon the enlightenment of society and its elected representatives. That is hardly a terrible fate. At least a society like ours ought not to think it so."[178]

At one level, Judge Bork might be correct. Even if the first amendment afforded virtually no protection for literature, literary freedom might still be quite expansive in most communities. For most authors, the abolition of the first amendment would have no practical effect on the dissemination of their work. Judge Bork's claim, however, carries plausibility at this point in our history[179] in part because his theory of the first amendment has not ever been accepted in this country.

Suppose a book by D. H. Lawrence, for example, were publicly burned by county officials in some rural area of the United States. There would be a public outcry, of course, and those resisting might well quote from Milton and Holmes in drawing upon a marketplace of ideas rhetoric. Yet, it is at least doubtful that the marketplace of ideas is threatened by the burning. D. H. Lawrence's publications would still be available in the vast majority of American communities. Indeed the actions of zealous prosecutors in provincial towns might, in fact, enhance the demand for his work. The depth of passion against bookburnings, however, runs deeper than fears that truth will ultimately lose out in its battle with falsehood in the proverbial marketplace.

Literature is commonly prized for its capacity to broaden our perspective, to challenge our limited ways of looking at the world.[180] Literature challenges and shatters conventions. A provincial community that attacks a book of D. H. Lawrence attacks more than a book. It attacks an American value. People have come to understand that American democracy protects literature even if it is threatening to existing conventions and traditions. The fight to protect a work of D. H. Lawrence is less a fight for truth than it is a struggle to maintain a symbolic understanding of America as a country where people have the right to experiment, to be independent, to dissent from the everyday understandings. If I am right, then Judge Bork is wrong, wrong not only about literature and the first amendment, but also about the principles of American democracy.

As Bork conceives American democracy, the preeminent responsibility of the people acting through their elected representatives is to establish, maintain, and refine the public morality.[181] Accordingly, Judge Bork sees the legislature as the repository of democratic wisdom, and regards it as a part of society's responsibility to decide whether books by D. H. Lawrence appropriately belong within the evolving tradition of civilized discourse. Within this framework the courts pose a threat of interfering with the *democratic* task of defining the public morality and that is why Judge Bork would have them stay their hand when elected representatives seek to purge uncivilized discourse from the public forum.[182]

Judge Bork is importantly wrong and not merely because he misconceives the relationship between courts and legislatures or even because he endorses a breed of censorship that is alien to the American tradition. Those failings are but symptoms of an even more fundamental misunderstanding.

Judge Bork, of course, recognizes that his conception of the relationship of courts to legislatures is counter to longstanding tradition. He knows that courts have long been unwilling to concede to legislatures the unbridled authority to define our public morality. From his perspective, the courts have thus usurped American democracy. If courts are the ultimate definers of our public morality, thinks Judge Bork, we have substituted aristocracy (or tyranny) for democracy, and we have lost the idea of self-government. Against Judge Bork, some would say that the Bill of Rights and the establishment of judicial review settled this question, and they did. But that response does not speak to Judge Bork's puzzle about democracy.

A better response is that the legislature can not be taken to be *the* representative of the people in the American system. Rather, the Constitution embodies an elaborate scheme designed to assure that the will of the people will be collectively expressed through the *combination* (checked and balanced) of decisions and expressions by the legislative, the executive, and the judicial branches. The constitutional hope is that this elaborate scheme is the safest means of assuring that governmental decisions are ultimately responsive to the needs and interests of all the people.

On this understanding any *authoritative* rendition of public morality would need more than the endorsement of a duly elected legislature and the support of the executive. It would also have to pass muster under reigning judicial understandings of our constitutional traditions. On this view, no legislature could fairly claim to hold a constitutional monopoly on the will of the People. Moreover, there would be no need under such a view to entertain anything like Judge Bork's narrow notions of civilized discourse or his crabbed conception of the first amendment's scope.

Even still, the whole notion of government's providing an authoritative rendition of public morality is democratically problematic, no matter how enlightened that rendition might be. Let us concede that government has a role to play in nurturing, and even in creating, public values.[183] Any notion of authoritative governmental pronouncements is nonetheless questionable. Indeed, I question the very idea that the people act through their representatives or the related view that when government speaks, the people speak. For most constitutional scholars the question is disturbing. They think it crucial for Americans to believe that government actions are the actions of the people, and they have worked hard to justify such belief. If they fail, they fear that the legitimacy of American democracy will be imperiled.

But they cannot possibly succeed. The best they could ever do would be to show us that the constitutional scheme is well calculated to produce decisions *for* the people. But we live in a diverse country of more than two hundred million people. Only someone with a mature capacity for strained metaphor or for serious self-delusion could endorse the idea that governmental decisions are *of* the people or *by* the people.

The notion of American democracy depends upon no such demonstration or metaphorical flight, and both Emerson and Whitman had a more realistic and more vibrant conception of American democracy than that which has customarily prevailed among American academic lawyers. By the lights of Emerson and Whitman, government could *never* provide an authoritative expression of public morality.[184] Indeed, it is a dangerous idea to suppose that government ever *authoritatively* expresses the popular will on any subject.[185] Government may *purport* to speak *for* the people and in the name of the people, but whether it has successfully done so is always for *us* to decide. Emerson and Whitman understood in the nineteenth century what Frank Michelman has so well observed in the twentieth: We are not the military; we are not the judges; we are not the legislature; we are not the government.[186] Self-government does not reside in the government;[187] self-government resides in us.[188]

Emerson and Whitman understood that democracy was much more than a set of governmental arrangements.[189] For them, democracy stood against the whole idea of authoritative pronouncements whether they were to emanate from government[190] or were more subtly couched in customs, habits, or traditions. A century before *West Virginia State Board of Education v. Barnette,*[191] they understood that if "there is any fixed star in our constitutional constellation, it is that no official, high or petty, can prescribe what shall be orthodox in politics, nationalism, religion, or other matters of opinion."[192] They understood that democracy and orthodoxy are always potentially at war. They knew that democracy and dissent run together.[193]

3

The First Amendment and Dissent

Richard Parker has written that conventional modes of constitutional argument "figuratively communicate ideological assumptions—general assumptions of political life—through their characteristic rhetoric and their characteristic metaphor."[1] Development of first amendment doctrine has unquestionably been influenced by striking pictures and powerful rhetoric. As I wrote some years ago, "[T]he specter of a man shouting [fire falsely] in a theater [still preoccupies] first amendment scholarship. And so the commentators (not to mention the courts) try to decide whether Nazis marching in Skokie, communists advocating revolution, pornographers selling their wares, publishers defaming all manner of plaintiffs, or ambulance chasers soliciting customers are somehow like that man in the theater."[2]

If the "fire!" metaphor reminds us that speech can be dangerous, other pictures have been more positive. Justice Holmes imagined an open and competitive marketplace of ideas;[3] Judge Learned Hand spoke of the supposition that right conclusions are more likely "to be gathered out of a *multitude of tongues,* than through any kind of authoritative selection."[4] Alexander Meiklejohn pictured citizens deliberating about public policy in a town hall assembly.[5]

My object, of course, is to highlight another portrait in the first amendment gallery. Without obliterating the other pictures, I seek not only to associate images of the dissenters, the eccentrics, the rebels, and the iconoclasts with the first amendment, but also to forge a strong connection between the first amendment and those who would speak out against prevailing conventions, norms, authorities, and institutions. But what would be the implications of emphasizing the dissent value in first amendment discourse? Is dissent merely to be tolerated or is it actively to be encouraged? And what dissent is to be tolerated or encouraged? Is the claim that all dissent is valuable? Perhaps, some might argue, America has come to the point that we have too much dissent—too much self-seeking egoistic individualism. Perhaps a value emphasis on dissenting rebels and iconoclasts risks further destruction of the increasingly frail bonds of American community. Symbols unfurled build a life of their own. No one can fully predict the evolution of a concept or metaphor in practice, but it is reasonable to inquire about what the implications might be and to wonder whether those implications might be for better or for worse.

American Culture and the Affirmative Side of the First Amendment

In his book, *The Tolerant Society,* Lee Bollinger argues that the first amendment does more than protect freedom of speech and that "the free speech idea" is "one of our foremost *cultural* symbols."[6] As Bollinger sees it, protecting "free speech involves a special act of carving out one area of social interaction for extraordinary self-restraint, the purpose of which is to develop and demonstrate a social capacity to control feelings evoked by a host of social encounters."[7] And Bollinger is indisputably correct. The idea of free speech does not merely protect the negative liberty of freedom of speech: it has indeed functioned as a cultural symbol[8] to promote tolerant attitudes in American society.[9] But, as a cultural symbol, free speech has done more than promote tolerance: as a cultural symbol, the first amendment has enlivened, encouraged, and sponsored the rebellious instincts within us all. It affords a positive boost to the dissenters and the rebels. It has helped to shape the kind of people we are, and it influences hopes about the kind of people we would like to be.

Thus, the first amendment plays a role in American culture that ranges beyond its legal bounds. The common understanding of lawyers and judges is that the first amendment applies only to *governmental* abridgments of speech.[10] It ordinarily provides, for example, no legal protection for students wearing black arm bands (or otherwise dissenting) in private schools, for workers criticizing the practices of corporate conglomerate employers,[11] or for demonstrators seeking access to the grounds of privately owned shopping centers.[12] The students can be expelled; the workers can be fired; the demonstrators can be thrown off the property; the first amendment provides no protection.

That the first amendment has such narrow legal scope comes as a surprise to law students; some are quite baffled. Prior to legal study, many of them had come to regard the first amendment as a shining symbol of a country that values and protects dissent. Indeed, that untutored understanding reflects a cultural significance that may be more important than the first amendment's legal significance. Students, workers, and demonstrators in private contexts will often invoke their "right to free speech," and such invocations will have persuasive power despite the legalities. Thus, the social and political force of the first amendment goes beyond its legal force. Indeed, its social and political force has sometimes resulted in legislation limiting the discretion of private schools, employers, or businesses to discriminate against persons because of their speech.[13] In any event, the symbolic force of the first amendment is there. It affects the consciousness of the entire society.

A major share of the credit or blame for this phenomenon belongs to American educators. They have long believed that a goal of American education was to prepare citizens for participation in the American democracy. *At least in the abstract,* a major part of what this has come to mean is that students should be prepared to become skeptical, independent, open-minded, and inclined to challenge outmoded customs, traditions, and habits. Indeed, Allan Bloom complains in *The Closing of the American Mind* that openness is "the only virtue, which all primary education for more than fifty years has dedicated itself to inculcating."[14] Part of his criticism is that promotion of the distrust of absolutes leads to a relativistic ideology, that is itself close-minded. But the inevitable result of education will in any event produce a close-mindedness of one sort or another.

However much the educational system promotes skepticism and open-mindedness, and however much it encourages dissent *in the abstract,* it will oppose dissent *to some extent* in the concrete. That is, society in general, and compulsory education in particular, promote a particular conception of the good life.[15] Suppose, for example, that an illiterate farming couple do not want to send their child to school. The couple contend that to send the child to school will irretrievably prevent the child from pursuing the good life, namely that of an illiterate farmer. To teach a child how to read will undermine her life, say the couple. In response, the state tells the couple that whether the child shall be educated is not their choice to make and that the child will not be raised as an illiterate farmer. Indeed, the state hopes to close off the option of illiteracy for all children. To be sure, literacy opens many different windows of opportunity, but it closes off possibilities as well. In short, the state is not neutral about the good life. It regards literacy as an important part of that life.

If literacy is a dramatic example, the entire educational process is rife with questions about what is good for people. From curriculum development to selection of textbooks, library books, and personnel, the state is inescapably involved in decisions about the good life. To be sure, the emphasis is often on promoting diversity and broadening opportunity. But when the state makes editorial decisions in any of the areas I have mentioned, it makes these decisions in a social context in which some perspectives are regarded as worth exploring in depth and others are not.

It may be that a life promoting astrology, cat-beating, sadomasochism, racism, or witchcraft is the good life, but a grammar school pursuing any of the above in any substantial way would not be accredited. If the state were truly neutral about the good life, education would not be compulsory; and the accreditation process would exhibit no interest in textbooks or curriculum.

Decisions concerning children are not the only examples of state decisionmaking about the good life.[16] Consider the involvement of government in museums, public libraries, public television, public universities (particularly the humanities), and subsidies for the arts in general. Such governmental involvement uses compulsory taxation to support activities which many people regard as a waste of time—not part of the good life. Such programs encourage people to become involved in the arts and various humane pursuits. By so doing, government takes a stand on a part of the good life. Moreover, it aims to cultivate a particular kind of people.[17] Indeed, quite extravagant claims have been made about what a rich education in literature, the arts, and the humanities will do for a person.[18] Be that as it may, what is striking about such governmental activity is how far removed it is from any general commitment to neutrality about the good life. Such neutrality is not possible, and even if it were, there would be no neutral way to defend a commitment to neutrality.[19]

Even if we admit, then, that education inevitably produces some close-mindedness, that it may irretrievably foreclose certain ways of looking at the world, that it identifies certain values as malevolent, and that it channels, structures, and encourages other values, it remains the case that American culture promotes, albeit in a culturally relative and constrained way, an open-mindedness, a willingness to challenge habits and traditions.[20] Moreover, this promotion is nurtured by general conceptions of American democracy and by the force of the first amendment as a cultural symbol.

Individualism, Association, and Truth

It might be argued that the encouragement of dissent has been counterproductive. The American people might be seen as too individualistic, too selfish, too prepared to go their own way, too unprepared to accept the bonds of community and of commitment with their fellow citizens.[21] The ready encouragement of dissenting postures might be seen as contributing to a destructive form of individualism.

The notion that promoting dissent leads to excessive individualism is a legitimate concern. Promoting dissent can promote egoism, self-indulgence, narcissism, and self-absorption. Undoubtedly such an emphasis would have significant negative effects for some individuals and in that respect negative consequences for the society. The question, however, is what the likely results would be for individuals generally and for the American society overall. From that perspective the concern about excessive individualism is not only exaggerated, but also involves a fundamental but widespread misunderstanding of dissent in particular and of freedom of speech in general. To press the point, American legal commentary exhibits an almost bizarre failure to recognize the connection between associational values and freedom of speech. It is quite common for courts and commentators to say that one of the values of freedom of speech is *self*-expression, *self*-realization, or *individual* autonomy. And freedom of association has traditionally been conceived as "an independent right, possessing an equal status with the other rights specifically enumerated in the first amendment."[22] Nonetheless, it seems obvious that associational values are inextricably a part of freedom of speech. No doubt, freedom of speech contributes to individual self-realization, but speech is at the same time a *social* phenomenon. Speech is predominantly interpersonal[23] and associational, no less in the case of dissent.

In challenging existing habits, traditions, and customs, dissenters seek to persuade others that they are right; they frequently seek to form groups of like-minded individuals that will transform the society. Dissent is predominately a form of social engagement whether groups or individuals are leading the charge. Dissenters seek converts and colleagues. To promote dissent is ordinarily not to promote anomic individualism; to promote dissent is to promote engaged association.

To build on the point, each new association is a transformation of the existing society. A focus on dissent emphasizes forms of collective action that are obscured by the individualism celebrated by the marketplace analogy. The marketplace calls up an image of buyers and sellers each maximizing their own private individualistic desires in countless individual transactions. When David O'Brien burned his draft card as an act of dissent, however, he was engaged with others in group activity in an effort to plead with others to join with them in collective action to transform the society. This was not anomic or selfish individualism. When Sheila Myers sent a communication to her fellow employees soliciting their views in an attempt to criticize the management of the District Attorney's office in New Orleans, Louisiana, she was seeking to associate with them in bringing about change in the office. When George Carlin used vulgar language on the radio in an effort to mock existing customs and conventions, he may not have sought to form an ongoing group, but his action was indisputably social.

Dissenters do not "sell" ideas in the manner depicted by the marketplace metaphor. Yes, dissenters are sometimes paid for expressing their ideas, that is, newspapers, magazines, and books are sold, and sometimes a dissenter is an author. Important parts of the intellectual marketplace function without sales, however.

People talk at breakfast, lunch, and dinner and between meals. They "exchange" ideas in universities, over back fences, on airplanes, at baseball games, even in bathrooms. They talk on radio, on television; they are quoted in newspapers, books, and magazines. One could *impose* a market model on this process. But dissenters are not like auto dealers. By and large they do not sell their ideas. They seek something other than the monetary profit of a commercial transaction; and their appeal generally is not tailored to whatever will sell. They seek agreement, support, and, often, group mobilization and collective action. Even when their subject matter is not political, their collective aspirations are more like politics than the market. Any conception that an emphasis on dissent flirts with the stereotypical evils of market individualism misunderstands dissent.

Those who fear the promotion of dissent may put their worries another way. A society of 240 million O'Briens, Myers, and Carlins would be ungovernable, a prescription for anarchy. That may be true, but we will never know. What John Stuart Mill said in 1859 remains true today: society "practises a social tyranny more formidable than many kinds of political oppression, since, though not usually upheld by such extreme penalties, it leaves fewer means of escape, penetrating much more deeply into the details of life, and enslaving the soul itself."[24] The pressures to conform in every society are enormous.[25] However much dissent is encouraged, the process of socialization will continue to produce and reenforce customs, habits, and traditions that are broadly shared and to a large extent not even the subject of conscious recognition. However much our educators emphasize independence and participation, the millions in the vast majority will not be like O'Brien, Myers, or Carlin. Anarchy is not around the corner.

Indeed, America's primary socializing source for destructive individualism is outside the schools. Children spend a fair amount of time in school; they also spend some three to four hours[26] a day exposed to another medium that has the effect, if not the design, of educating children. Simply put, American television is a powerful educator, and the kind of person encouraged by American television is substantially at odds with the kind of person encouraged in American schools.

American television is organized as an advertising medium.[27] An American child is exposed literally to hundreds of thousands

of powerful commercials during the course of his or her education.[28] What commercials say to American adults and children
many times an hour is that the acquisition of products is vitally
important for human happiness and for a sense of identity. It
would be surprising if there were *no* impact from daily exposure
to this commercial deluge. Rather, one could reasonably expect
that daily exposure to televised commercialism would promote
a hedonistic, acquisitive, materialistic,[29] self-seeking, money-
hungry culture. It is a program of communications likely to promote individualistic alienation and to discourage civic virtue.[30]
More to the point, it is likely to promote a privatized, non-
engaged citizenry. So while American educators encourage persons to participate in the body politic as "citizen-critics," American television teaches people to be hedonistic consumers. Those
two options are by no means mutually exclusive. One can be both
a "citizen-critic" and a "hedonistic consumer," but if Americans
disproportionately devote their lives to self-seeking consumerism, American television is a more likely culprit than American
educators.

Fostering dissent is part of the solution to destructive individualism; it does not pose any realistic danger of creating an excessively individualistic society. None of this is to deny that an
inclination toward dissent can lead to narcissism, cynicism, or
self-indulgence. Promotion of dissent *can* have bad consequences
in individual cases just as promoting industrious and disciplined
work habits can lead to pathological compulsion. The key question in building a Constitution, however, is the overall consequences for most individuals and for the society at large. Promoting dissent can promote its own pathologies, but the sponsoring
of dissent is necessary for any healthy individuality to flourish.
Societal pressures for conformity, as Mill put it, "fetter the development, and, if possible, prevent the formation, of any individuality not in harmony with its ways, and compels all characters to
fashion themselves upon the model of its own."[31] Individuals
flourish and are largely constituted through their association
with others. But if there is no room in association for individuality, association is unduly repressive.[32]

Sponsoring dissent is also allied with one of the major underlying values of the marketplace analogy, namely truth. As Emerson writes in his essay on "Self-Reliance": "[M]ost men have

bound their eyes with one or another handkerchief . . . [to a community] of opinion. This conformity makes them not false in a few particulars, authors of a few lies, but false in all particulars. Their every truth is not quite true."[33] He elaborates in his essay on "Intellect":

> God offers to every mind its choice between truth and repose. . . . Between these, as a pendulum, man oscillates. He in whom the love of repose predominates will accept the first creed, the first philosophy, the first political party he meets,— most likely his father's. He gets rest, commodity, and reputation; but he shuts the door of truth. He in whom the love of truth predominates will keep himself aloof from all moorings, and afloat. He will abstain from dogmatism, and recognize all the opposite negations, between which, as walls, his being is swung. He submits to the inconvenience of suspense and imperfect opinion, but he is a candidate for truth, as the other is not, and respects the highest law of his being.[34]

Emerson's passage speaks to more than the issue of truth. It underscores how some might fear that the sponsoring of nonconformity would undermine the bonds of association and lead to excessive individualism. There is no question that a commitment to truth about anything and everything can lead to a lonely life. Some writers and some academics perhaps come closest to the Emersonian model. The vast majority, however (I include most academics and most writers), need the shared values of association and unconsciously temper, adjust, and shape their views to maintain, nurture, and build their associations. At the same time, a proud moment for many is the point in their life when they refused to "go along," when they stood up for what they believed. Sponsoring that kind of behavior, Emerson argues, not only causes individuals to flourish but also leads toward truth in society. When someone has the nerve to say that the Emperor has no clothes, others begin to see and to talk about what they have previously concealed from themselves and others. Truth, too, can nurture associations. Indeed, Emerson recognizes that a sovereign aspect of friendship "is Truth. A friend is a person with whom I may be sincere. Before him I may think aloud."[35] Our public aspect of civility is of vital importance for the functioning of day-to-day life, but intimate associations thrive on our ability to be our "real" selves.[36]

It might be objected that the connection forged here between dissent and truth is too close. Dissenters are often wrong. To sponsor dissent, however, is not to suppose that all dissenters are right. Still less is it to assume that any truth spoken by dissenters will emerge in the marketplace of ideas.[37] Indeed, an Emersonian commitment to sponsoring dissent does not require a belief that what emerges in the "market" is usually right or that the "market" is the best test of truth.[38] Quite the contrary, the commitment to sponsor dissent assumes that societal pressures to conform are strong and that incentives to keep quiet are often great. If the marketplace metaphor encourages the view that an invisible hand or voluntaristic arrangements have guided us patiently, but slowly, to Burkean harmony, the commitment to sponsoring dissent encourages us to believe that the cozy arrangements of the status quo have settled on something less than the true or the just. If the marketplace metaphor encourages the view that conventions, habits, and traditions have emerged as our best sense of the truth from the rigorous testing ground of the marketplace of ideas, the commitment to sponsoring dissent encourages the view that conventions, habits, and traditions are compromises open to challenge. If the marketplace metaphor counsels us that the market's version of truth is more worthy of trust than any that the government might dictate, a commitment to sponsoring dissent counsels us to be suspicious of both.[39] If the marketplace metaphor encourages a sloppy form of relativism[40] (whatever has emerged in the marketplace is right for now), the commitment to sponsoring dissent emphasizes that truth is not decided in public opinion polls. So understood, sponsoring dissent encourages a robust, burgeoning marketplace.[41] To sponsor dissent is to encourage talk that the marketplace metaphor unwittingly discourages (if truth has emerged, what is left to say?). And, in that way, sponsoring dissent forges a stronger connection with truth than the marketplace metaphor, for, as Harry Kalven once said, "It is an unbeatable proposition that the truth will not emerge in the marketplace if it does not get in."[42] But more fundamentally, the Emersonian conception of dissent forges a closer connection to truth just because it denies that the status quo represents the truth. As John Stuart Mill argued, with respect to many of the great political questions of the day:

> If either of . . . two opinions has a better claim than the other, not merely to be tolerated, but to be encouraged and counte-

nanced, it is the one which happens at the particular time and place to be in a minority. That is the opinion which for the time being, represents the neglected interests, the side of human well-being which is in danger of obtaining less than its share.[43]

Dissent, therefore, should be valued not only for its contribution to individual self-realization and to association, but also for its contribution to the realization of truth. It should also be valued as an instrument of necessary change and as a means of combating illegitimate abuses of power.

Dissent and Change

In addressing the subject of change, we need not indulge in any pollyannaish views about dissent. Dissent does not invariably seek change, let alone desirable change, nor does it invariably combat power, let alone illegitimate power. My claim, however, is that the sponsoring and protection of dissent generally have progressive implications.

Begin with the proposition that millions of hierarchies are unavoidable in a nation of 240 million people. Any notion that the promise of the future lies in returning us to face-to-face "communities" is pure fantasy.[44] Encouraging more equality of participation in schools, factories, and institutions is an important and laudable goal, but hierarchies and bureaucracies are unavoidable.[45] Decisionmakers in millions of small and large institutions will, therefore, exercise power, and will often abuse that power. Their self-interest is to defend what they do, and it is in society's interest to check the abuse of power. To accept dissent as a value in this connection is to assume that wielders of power have advantages in defending their position and that their use of power is more often self-serving than they admit—even to themselves. Again dissent may often be unfair. Hierarchies engender envy, and dissent may be fueled and distorted by that envy. The threat of dissent too can chill useful exercises of power. On balance, however, dissent and the threat of dissent make hierarchy less oppressive. Dissent communicates the fears, hopes, and aspirations of the less powerful to those in power. It sometimes chills the abuse of power; it sometimes paves the way for change *by* those in power or *of* those in power. The democratic value of dissent in this connection transcends the voting booth; it is a part of the daily dialectic of power relations in the society.

In important ways, however, the American Constitution is structured to prevent change. To the extent that change is not possible, dissent is discouraged. Moreover, if one really believes in the value of dissent, it might be argued, the structure of institutions should allow dissenters to prevail when they achieve majority support. Instead, the structure of the federal government was calculatedly designed to prevent transient majorities or "factions" from instigating rapid change. Those who would change the system by legislative action must persuade not one but two legislative houses, avoid a Presidential veto, survive judicial review, and, if enforcement is needed, secure cooperation from law enforcement authorities and the courts. The Founders feared that factions might secure rapid, problematic change; the structure of the federal government is designed to limit that possibility. Moreover, as federal power has grown, the importance of that structure has grown as well.

There are a variety of political perspectives from which one might question the current federal structure. Roberto Unger, arguing from a radical political perspective, maintains that the federal political structure is an unjustifiable barrier against radical democratic change.[46] From a reformist perspective, many have argued that the British parliamentary system is more receptive to change and promotes more effective governance. They suggest that the American system allows interest groups to tie up the legislative process and thwart needed change.

The focus on the structure of the federal government is under-inclusive if one is concerned with dissent or change. That is, many important customs, habits, and traditions can be criticized and changed without governmental action of any kind, let alone from the federal government. Indeed, some who argue from a radical perspective charge that liberals and conservatives unduly focus on government as the center of politics. If politics is the struggle for power, many of the most important American political struggles (consider the overlapping questions of gender, race, and the workplace) have been as important outside legislative halls as inside.

Nonetheless, the federal government has undoubted power. One bomb can make "private" political struggles irrelevant. Federal health and environmental action can affect the quality and duration of countless lives. I raise the example of the federal constitutional structure not necessarily to side with those who would change it, but to make a number of related points about the relationship between dissent and the American system.

The structure of the federal government was initially designed with an eye to the ends it would produce. This was not cheating. Stacking the deck is not per se wrong in setting up governmental arrangements; the question to be pursued is how the deck should be stacked. The Founders, for example, wanted to prevent debtors from passing measures that would impair the rights of creditors. They wanted a mix of interests to have power in the legislature. They thought, for example, that the economic and social background of an individual, the time spent in office, and the size of the representative's constituency would have an impact on the policies that would be promoted. They took those views into account in arranging the governmental structure. The structure was result-oriented.

Similar thinking has substantially influenced the debate over judicial review. In the pre-1937 era, liberals assailed the undemocratic character of judicial review; conservatives defended the Court's power. In the Warren era liberals celebrated the Court; conservatives assailed the undemocratic character of judicial review. I will not develop the argument here, but it seems entirely appropriate that one's stance about judicial review might depend upon the likely consequences of judicial review in the long run. If conservatives and liberals have been disingenuous about the issue of judicial review, their guile has touched only their reasons, not their conclusions. Particularly if one believes that a commitment to democracy involves a commitment to particular notions of freedom and equality, it is reasonable for one's support of judicial review to hinge upon assessments of whether that review will advance or retard democratic commitments.

If this perspective is reasonable in assessing the institution of judicial review, it is all the more reasonable in assessing the federal structure. Certainly if one thought that the structure disserved the public interest regarding national defense, the environment, the economy, and the like, the case against the structure would be strong. My first observation is that any assessment of the federal structure should lean heavily on the consequences the structure is likely to produce.

The larger point to notice is that a part of the current instrumental perspective includes hostility to certain forms of dissent. The Bill of Rights, for example, is another constitutional commitment to the notion that it should be extremely difficult for certain dissenters to have their way. Indeed, to affirm the value of dissent is itself to take a stand against certain forms of dissent. Thus, the first amendment involves a constitutional commitment to the principle that those dissenters who wish to abridge speech or press will have formidable barriers placed in their path.[47] Any argument that it should be easy for dissenters to bring about rapid change has to contemplate what the forms of dissent are likely to be, whether important values would be threatened, and whether newly contemplated institutional structures would provide appropriate safeguards.[48] In short, the constitutional commitment to protect and encourage dissent is part of a larger framework[49] that channels, cabins, and otherwise limits[50] the effectiveness of dissent.

The right to dissent, therefore, does not imply any right to succeed in transforming institutions. Nonetheless, any strong and general commitment to the value of dissent must be accompanied by a commitment to structuring institutions so that dissent has substantial opportunities to be effective in bringing about change. If dissenters are to have an opportunity to build associations and coalitions in a meaningful way, and have a meaningful chance to effect change, courts must be sympathetic to claims of access for communicative opportunities involving large audiences. A serious commitment to the value of dissent would treat cases involving claims of access to property where large groups are gathering as a test of that commitment[51] rather than as an occasion for sermons about deference to government administrators or for homilies about the "private character" of the streets and sidewalks of shopping centers.[52] Unless one thinks that the gatekeepers of the print and broadcast media afford meaningful access to dissenters, a strong commitment to the value of dissent should tilt one toward upholding schemes of regulation designed to afford meaningful access. Instead, the government appoints a corporation to manage a station reaching millions of people and grants the corporation virtually unfettered discretion to decide what issues will be discussed and who will discuss them. One need not be a follower of Alexander Meiklejohn to think it strange that broadcasters will allow anyone to buy time to sell

products, such as automobiles, but will allow no one to buy time
to attack those commercials and advocate mass transportation.[53]
By allowing broadcasters to engage in blanket denials of paid access for controversial noncommercial messages, government has
set its own appointees with nearly total control of access to a
quite powerful communications medium. To be sure, broadcasters have been required under the fairness doctrine to be "fair"[54]
but such vague and general injunctions have been notoriously
unproductive. As Justice Brennan has stated, "[I]n light of the
strong interest of broadcasters in maximizing their audience,
and therefore their profits, it seems almost naive to expect the
majority of broadcasters to produce the variety and controversiality of material necessary to reflect a full spectrum of view-
points."[55]

As current law stands, dissenters have no constitutional right
of access to public or private workplaces, no constitutional right
of access to shopping centers, and no constitutional right of access
to the broadcast or print media. Moreover, legislation to assure
access to the print media has itself been summarily dismissed as
unconstitutional.[56]

To be sure, some of the issues concerning access involve difficult issues. Honest and intelligent people who care about dissent
can disagree from question to question. These issues deserve (but
will not here get) quite detailed consideration.[57] Nonetheless,
when the dust clears, it has to be said that the Supreme Court
has treated access claims without substantial regard for the
value of dissent.

The Scope of Dissent and Its Limits

But what precisely is dissent? Is dissent really itself a value or is
it just a proxy for other values? Is the value of dissent exclusive
to the first amendment? Does the value of dissent exhaust the
first amendment? Should dissent invariably be protected? If
there are to be exceptions, what is the appropriate methodology
for separating the protected from the unprotected?

These are lawyers' questions, and some of them are easy. Ultimately, I want to argue that the difficult questions are difficult
because they are placed at too high a level of abstraction. But
first, it ought to be clear that by insisting that the value of dissent

should be given greater prominence in free speech and press law, I am not arguing for a constitutional revolution. I am not suggesting that the speech and press clauses should become the exclusive constitutional vehicle for protecting dissent, nor that the speech and press clauses should be exclusively concerned with dissent, nor that dissent always deserves constitutional protection.

The religion clauses protect religious dissent, and the equal protection clause is an important repository of protection for those who somehow offend the powers that be. Without question, in protecting dissent, constitutional guarantees overlap. This is not unusual. The same can be said for the protection of privacy and of property. Although overlap may offend the sensibilities of those who yearn for clean lines and watertight categories, it may be salutary in a document designed for government, rather than aesthetic contemplation. Moreover, the existence of overlap perhaps suggests that values protected in so many ways are of particular constitutional importance.

The overlap is sometimes quite conspicuous. Some government repression of dissent may at once offend many constitutional clauses. If government tried to permit Catholic speakers in the park, but not Anglican speakers, its attempt would quite obviously affront the free speech clause, the free exercise clause, and the equal protection clause. What is less obvious perhaps is the extent to which the Constitution might afford some protection for dissent even in the absence of protection by the speech or press clause.[58] The establishment clause, for example, is sometimes understood to provide prophylactic protection for religious dissenters.[59] So, for example, when the Court strikes down some forms of aid to religious education on establishment clause grounds, it may provide preemptive support for religious dissent, but in circumstances that would trigger no accompanying support from the speech or press clauses.

The speech and press clauses are thus by no means the exclusive repositories for the protection of dissent. It is obvious, however, that they are important guarantors of dissent. But the existence of dissent is neither a necessary nor a sufficient condition for speech or press clause protection. Some dissent is not even within the scope of the first amendment. Suppose, for example, that a person thoroughly alienated from the culture and life within it commits an act of mass murder, such as spraying machine gun fire into a random crowd of people. The act of mass murder might be the product of and a manifestation of the person's dissent against the culture, and any good psychiatrist might find it to be highly revealing and expressive. But no one, so far as I am aware, would argue that this act is "expression" or "speech" for first amendment purposes. I suppose that conventional usage might countenance the use of the term *expression* to describe such conduct, but would not similarly license the use of the term *speech*. My preliminary point, albeit obvious, is worth stating explicitly: terms like *expression* and *speech* have the meaning we give them and the meaning we give them is at least largely dependent on what will make them useful in the contexts in which we expect to use them. In a legal context, there is no reason to expect that usage will slavishly follow conventional usage.[60] And one need not be a legal beagle to recognize that the legal community would be unlikely to find any utility in employing terms like *expression* or *speech* to describe murder.

To make the point even a bit sharper, suppose that the person committing the act of mass murder actually intends to communicate a message by the act, that the act is a terrorist "political demonstration" against the culture, and suppose it is so interpreted by the audience. There are two ways to handle this example. One is to say that the action in this context is speech, but the values of expression are so substantially outweighed by the government interests in order and security that any free speech claim is frivolous. Another option is to say that murder is not speech whatever the communicative intent and that the first amendment is not involved in any way.

There is little doubt that the courts would incline toward the second option. The courts would not be willing under any foreseeable circumstances to characterize "speech" as embracing murder even as a form of "demonstration," yet they are quite prepared to use the term to embrace many other kinds of nonverbal demonstrations. Thus, to wear a black arm band or to place tape on a flag or to engage in a sit-in or to march is considered speech for first amendment purposes, at least when it is intended to communicate a message and when it is perceived to communicate a message. It makes no difference to the courts that, like the other examples, a march is not a speech in conventional usage. Indeed the ready willingness of courts to stretch conventional usage in the context of demonstrations might be considered substantial evidence of the court's perception that dissent is an important first amendment concern.

Why then would courts be reluctant to consider expressive terrorist acts to be within the scope of the first amendment? Certainly that reluctance can not be ascribed to any fear that murder might ultimately get protected under the first amendment. Nor would it work to distinguish the other demonstrations on the ground that murder is illegal. Many constitutionally protected demonstrations have proceeded in the face of government prohibitions. The very question to be decided in such cases was whether such prohibitions passed first amendment muster under the circumstances presented. Perhaps what distinguishes the murder example (together with violent examples as a class) is that the nonexpressive aspects of murder so overwhelmingly outweigh the expressive aspects that countenancing that form of expression as a part of the first amendment would not only trivialize the first amendment, but also would be symbolically offensive. In any event, even if murder as a form of demonstration were somehow included within the scope of the first amendment, any argument that such dissent merited first amendment protection would be universally regarded as perverse.

Dissent is also appropriately limited in cases where there is no doubt about the speechlike character of the act in question. I may have a right to dissent against the President's policies, but I have, for example, no right to make a speech in the Oval Office of the White House in so doing. Nor, for example, does anyone have a right to engage in speech that is directed to inciting or producing imminent lawless action and is likely to incite or produce imminent lawless action.[61] Examples could be multiplied, but the point is narrow: arguing that dissent deserves greater appreciation in first amendment law is not a demand for absolutism. Moreover, by suggesting that the first amendment rightly sponsors dissent, I should not be taken to suggest that dissent should be encouraged to the same extent in all social contexts. That an independent spirit should generally be supported does not imply that the military is required to encourage dissent as a routine practice on the battlefield. At the same time, I do not mean to suggest that the first amendment has no role to play in the military context,[62] just that the value of dissent there is often diminished.

Some readers may think that these observations may be sensible but that some substantial backing and filling seems to be going on, and that appreciation for the value of dissent is beginning to mean less and less. I mean to make things worse in this respect before they get better.

Even if dissent were the only value of importance in first amendment decisions, it would often not be clear how concrete cases should be decided. For example, some cases present a conflict between group rights of dissent and individual rights of dissent. Suppose a dissenting member of an exclusive bargaining unit represented by a union complains that the union is expressing a political view contrary to that held by the dissenter. The dissenter argues that her contributions should not be used to support ideologies to which she is opposed.[63] To intervene on behalf of the dissenting individual, however, might be to limit the effectiveness of the dissenting group. Commitment to the value of dissent in the abstract does not resolve such issues.

Similarly, it may be difficult to figure out how the value of dissent relates to particular categories of speech. Pornography is a good example. On the one hand, pornography can be characterized as a form of dissent. It rebels against the puritanical outlook of an uptight society.[64] On the other hand, it can be regarded as a form of domination. Pornography can be thought of as the graphic, sexually explicit subordination of women. It can be thought of as a multibillion dollar industry that serves to continue the suppression of an already suppressed group. By perpetuating domination, it can be thought of as a means of isolating women in the role of servants and sex objects. On this understanding, pornography is a part of a social system that silences women.[65] Even if dissent were the only value to be considered, dissenters can be found on both sides of the pornography question.[66]

The same can be said for the law of libel. On the one hand, one could characterize defamatory speech as an exercise of dissent. Libel, by definition, is always critical, and dissenters' attacks are often caustic, biting—and defamatory. On the other hand, libel can involve a powerful media conglomerate attacking a social outcast—a dissenter. Moreover, trials of the press often hold up to public scrutiny the methods employed by influential individuals and institutions, influential individuals and institutions that are not well scrutinized by the media. That is, if there is one thing we know for sure about the quality of the press, it is that the press does a poor job of scrutinizing itself. If protecting dissent were the only goal of defamation law, the question of how it should be structured would remain difficult.

Thus, I not only argue that there are values other than speech that should be considered in specific contexts such as defamation, but also I cheerfully concede that dissent is not the only speech value. To place my claim in perspective, imagine a large Roman Catholic church. In Catholic theology, the Son of God is present in the tabernacle. I imagine the first amendment as a church with many tabernacles. Dissent is one of those tabernacles. To focus on one tabernacle is not to deny the importance of other tabernacles or values.[67]

Indeed, recognition of other first amendment values helps to mitigate what might otherwise be insuperable problems with the use of dissent as a value in first amendment adjudication. It would be hard to swallow, for example, if it turned out that dissenters were free to speak under the first amendment, but others were not. Moreover, even if that principle were acceptable, it would be risky to trust ad hoc decisionmaking about what was dissenting and what was not.

A number of responses to these related concerns are worth considering. First, one could try to solve it by tautology. The notion might be that if government were attempting to censor a particular form of speech, the speech should be considered dissenting by that fact alone. For many, if not most, cases it may well be that the speech targeted for suppression would be uniformly regarded as dissenting in character. But, as we have previously discussed, some categories of speech do not yield up an easy application of the dissent value. In some respects, just to cite one example, pornography might be regarded as dissenting; in other respects not. Moreover, government often attempts to suppress speech that would be hard to classify as dissenting in character. Particularly when government invokes time, place, and manner regulations (e.g., no handbills on the streets), it sweeps in much speech (consider commercial advertising) that few would think of as dissenting in character. To treat all speech as dissenting, therefore, is to engage in definition or tautology; it is to stray rather far from the judgments we would make on an individualized basis. Moreover, it would rob the dissent value of any significant role in the decisionmaking process. Indeed, that would be the point of adopting such a tautological device.

An alternative would be to shun the making of ad hoc decisions in individual cases about whether a particular form of speech is dissenting, but take the impact on dissenting speech into account in the formulation of rules. This alternative promises to allow a significant role for the dissent value while minimizing the disadvantages associated with ad hoc adjudication. So conceived, however, the alternative promises more than it can deliver. Rules are formulated and reformulated in concrete contexts. It is inevitable, if dissent is considered to be a first amendment value, that arguments will be made that people like Carlin and Myers are or are not dissenters for first amendment purposes, and judgments about those arguments will affect the formulation of rules. But a pluralistic approach to first amendment values mitigates the costs associated with using the dissent value in the adjudicatory process. Schenck, Abrams, and Gitlow were dissenters in ways that an advertisement for an automobile is not, even a relatively unpopular automobile. But so long as the approach to adjudicating first amendment issues recognizes multiple values, the consequences of not characterizing speech as dissenting are not drastic. Dissenting speech gets a plus, and the failure to get a plus may prove decisive on some issues, but using dissent as a value in the decisionmaking process is a far cry from adopting the principle that only dissenters get first amendment protection.

Finally, by suggesting that dissent gets a plus, I do not mean to suggest a move toward mathematical precision.[68] To be sure, there are clear cases where "we know it [dissent] when we see it." But there are many gray areas, and lots of room for argument in individual cases. Speech can be dissenting at one level and utterly conformist at another. It can be innocuous at a national level, but powerfully threatening at a local level. Clearly, the nature and purpose of the government regulation may be of fundamental importance in determining whether dissent is or is not threatened.

The extent to which the value of dissent is implicated in a particular context is unlikely to be determined by a mode of inquiry involving the application of abstract criteria to particular facts.[69] For example, consider the facts of *Rankin v. McPherson*.[70] McPherson, a nineteen-year-old black clerical employee in a county constable's office, hears on the radio of an attempted assassination of President Reagan. She remarks to a close friend in the office that Reagan has been cutting back on various welfare programs and that "if they go for him again, I hope they get him." Someone overhears the remark; it is reported to Constable Rankin; and McPherson is fired.

Is the value of dissent implicated? Some would argue that it is not because the remark was made in private and was not intended to be overheard. My reaction is that when a person states opposition to the President serious enough to countenance his death, dissent is clearly implicated. Moreover, broader dissenting associational activity frequently begins in private conversations.

Suppose McPherson had said that the boss drives a lousy car. Many would say this is not dissent, and again I disagree. It may be there is a difference in asking whether something is "dissent" (as if it had an essence) or whether the values associated with dissent are present. My approach would be to concentrate on the latter. But from either perspective to criticize those in authority (however private the criticism and however trivial it may be) implicates dissent values and, by my lights, is dissenting speech.

Another way to look at these examples is at a somewhat higher level of abstraction. What would be the implications for dissent if employees could be fired for criticism of authorities made in private conversations? I would argue that dissent in the workplace would be smothered if such a rule were adopted, and that a judicial decisionmaker ought to take that into account in deciding such cases.

In the *McPherson* case there are government interests that many believe should outweigh the free speech value. For example, a government office committed to law enforcement is embarrassed in its efforts when its own employees show lack of respect for law. In this respect, McPherson would have been in a worse position if her remark had been part of a public speech, even though its free speech value would arguably be even greater.

I give this example only to suggest that the analysis of dissent and its value will often be specific to diverse factual contexts and that reasonable people can differ about how it should be applied. To discuss its application in all free speech contexts, if not impossible, would fill many volumes. As has been the case with other first amendment values, it is likely that the perspectives associated with dissent will best be defined in the hard and continuing struggle of case-by-case adjudication.

The Difference Dissent Makes

If dissent is just one of many free speech values, and if speech values themselves can be outweighed by other values in vague and ill-defined ways and in vague and equally ill-defined contexts, should we not now admit that we have come all this way with precious little to show for it?

Consider two responses. First, to use another simple analogy, if one ingredient, such as garlic, is added to soup, the soup will be irretrievably changed. Similarly, if dissent were to be regarded as a major first amendment value, the course and direction of first amendment decisionmaking could be significantly affected and, in any event, the attitudes about free speech situations would be unalterably changed. If dissent were considered a major first amendment value, it would have been far more difficult to fire Sheila Myers, to "cleanse" the afternoon airwaves of the likes of George Carlin, to bar dissenters from access to important centers of communication, or to send Schenck, Abrams, Gitlow, Whitney, Dennis, or O'Brien off to jail. Even if the results of such cases were not changed, they could only have been accompanied by a frank recognition that important values had been compromised, that something substantial had been given up.

But I have a more pointed response to the general indeterminacy objection. The temperament that lies behind such an objection is hostile to the value of dissent in important ways. To put my response in positive terms, affirming the value of dissent has implications not only for the general direction of first amendment law, but also for its method, for the way we think about legal problems, for our patterns of justification, and for our modes of discourse. Our attitudes toward dissent are connected in important ways to our attitudes toward indeterminacy, toward balancing and social engineering. In short, our attitude toward dissent can have important consequences not only for what we decide in first amendment cases, but how we decide them. These assertions point us not only to the final chapters, but also to the ultimate claim of the book: to take a stand on the dissent value in first amendment discourse requires one to take a stand on the relationship between reason and romance.

4

The First Amendment and Method

A first amendment case can not be resolved without a method[1] to resolve it. Many commentators insist, however, that the method used to resolve first amendment cases has been ad hoc and subjective. The implication is that an improvement of method could significantly improve not only the decisionmaking process, but also the quality of decisions produced. Critics might suggest, for example, that it is not enough to be told that Schenck, Dennis, Whitney, O'Brien, Myers, and Carlin are dissenters, or that an act of dissent challenges existing habits, customs, traditions, or authorities. Certainly, they would not be satisfied with the suggestion that dissent could be further defined in concrete cases or that the weight given to the dissent value should depend upon the particular factual situation. They would insist on a more determinative method. By contrast, I maintain that the problem with first amendment decisionmaking is for the most part *not* with the method employed but with the values held by the decisionmakers. The path to first amendment safety lies not in the imposition of a particular method, but in a genuine cultural commitment to substantive first amendment values. If that commitment is not present, no "binding" method will hold.[2] If that commitment exists, method will take care of itself.[3]

The method employed in first amendment decisionmaking, however, has importance that transcends its capacity to determine results in individual cases. Aristotle defined rhetoric as the faculty of discovering in any individual case all the available means of persuasion. If the first amendment is to serve as an important cultural symbol, the modes of justification we use to persuade ourselves and others of its value and importance are themselves of special importance. If we are concerned about the kind of people the first amendment tends to encourage, we need to be as concerned with the rhetoric of first amendment discourse as with the details of its decisions. Our modes of justification themselves exhibit features of our character and appeal to features of our personality. If dissent deserves a stronger place in our first amendment discourse, it is fair to ask whether a commitment to the dissent value has any implications for the way we arrive at decisions and the way we justify them to others.

My contention is that the reigning first amendment method of decisionmaking deserves, for the most part, to be defended. But a substantial part of that defense must be by way of negation. Much of this book shows that alternative methods are unworkable. Chapter 1 shows that a distinction based on content is not only an implausible organizing strategy for existing doctrine, but also an excessively abstract and overly general basis for constructing a general theory of the first amendment even though the distinction may be of some doctrinal importance. Chapters 2 and 3 show that a political/nonpolitical distinction is an untenable foundation for a normatively acceptable general theory of the first amendment.

This chapter explores the weaknesses of a general theory that I label Kantian. The Kantian approach would promise to protect dissent (except when it does not deserve protection) by resort to a method that is more determinative than that employed in existing law. The Kantian approach posits that many of the most difficult questions in first amendment law can be most profitably addressed by abstraction from our different desires and preferences ("the passions").[4] Indeed, the Kantian approach posits that such questions can be resolved by deduction from or interpretation of a single aspect of the human condition, namely our moral autonomy or moral personality.

To some extent the model outlined here is fictitious; it is oversimplified, somewhat more extreme and ambitious than has been put forward by neo-Kantian advocates. Moreover, it emphasizes features that may only be moments of, or a subtext in, the argument of committed Kantians. The Kantian may be focused on the idea of justice or human freedom, but the model I will work with renders prominent the form and the rhetoric rather than the particular substance of justification. The model's purpose is not to present a rich, let alone the richest account of Kantianism,[5] nor is it to show that a sophisticated neo-Kantian approach must fail.[6]

Instead, its primary value is heuristic.[7] Whether or not the model I work with accurately captures moments in the total thought of Kantian theorists, the point is to emphasize the appeal of and limits of an appeal to a determinative abstract method, or the importance of clean lines,[8] or the determining power of particular concepts, or the sense of settling something once and for all. Sophisticated approaches must back and fill away from such appeals, and the extreme model helps to show the direction in which they must back and fill and some indication of why they must back and fill.

More important, despite its extremism, the model has substantial rhetorical and psychological appeal. The impulse to support or oppose it involves considerations not confined to substantive aspects of the first amendment or even to more general notions of freedom and equality. In particular, arguments about theory implicate considerations of temperament[9] that are related to substantive aspects only in subtle ways, if at all. Some of us are especially prone to exaggerate the limits of general theory; others tend habitually to lose sight of its limitations. The arguments about first amendment theory are deeply contested, then, not only because people have strong views about the first amendment, but also because many believe that how we think is as important as what we think. Each of us confronts, for example, the question of when and whether it is wise to abstract from the particularities of a given moral, legal, or political context, and the impulse toward abstraction both attracts and repels in ways that transcend particular contexts. This chapter explores the nature and character of that attraction and repulsion. It explores the ways in which some are driven toward the Kantian model and the ways in which others are driven away from it. My goal in discussing that appeal is less argument than exploration and provocation. I do not hope to persuade a single soul that the rhetorical appeal of a Kantian approach is better than its rivals (although my own biases will be all too clear). Indeed, my view is that the commitment to a particular type of method can be a major part of an individual's intellectual identity, and if I am right about that, persuasion in this area would be especially difficult. I do not even expect proponents of a Kantian perspective to think my "explanation" of the psychological and rhetorical appeal of Kantian approaches has been entirely fair, although I have not set out to be unfair. But I do hope for an understanding of the kinds of factors that might lead some to resist the appeal of Kantian theory.

The reigning method of first amendment decisionmaking resists that appeal. Those who would endorse the reigning method of first amendment decisionmaking (call them eclectic) are united in the view that social reality is too complicated and too diverse to support Kantian theory, indeed any general theory. Many eclectics find that disturbing, but realistic.

Still other eclectics find it comforting, not disturbing. One source of comfort is that positive value is placed on the diversity and complexity of social reality. Another source of comfort arises from a sense of freedom, a sense that nothing is forever fixed, a sense of freedom to break out of existing categories. These reactions find a home in the romantic tradition. Indeed, the romantic tradition grows out of and is a part of the conflict between the Kantian and the eclectic. The romantics opposed Kantianism and utilitarianism, and there was a connection between that opposition and the romantics' sponsoring of independence and dissent.

If the first amendment and democracy are bound up with dissent, so too is romanticism. For those with a temperament that takes comfort in the rejection of general theory, there may be an especially strong connection between the first amendment, democracy, and romance. But the first amendment appeals to people of diverse temperament, and the romantic movement emphasizes aspects of the human condition that are of importance to everyone. In the end, we are all rationalists, and we are all romantics. If we neglect the romantic aspects of the human condition, we will not understand the first amendment or democracy. In this chapter, I discuss the conflict between the Kantian and the eclectic. In the next, I turn to romance.

The First Amendment and Kantian Theory: Confronting Complexity

Kantian free speech theory has been put forward for the most part by American political liberals,[10] and its entry on the scholarly scene is somewhat recent. Twentieth-century American legal scholarship has been long dominated by pragmatists—by utilitarians, social engineers, and instrumentalists.[11] These scholars have been allied with an always-present group of (mainly constitutional) theorists who have emphasized the need to mix a bit of natural law in with the pragmatic calculations.

So it was. In 1971, a Harvard philosopher, John Rawls, offered a neo-Kantian theory of justice in response to the utilitarians;[12] later in the decade, Oxford philosopher Ronald Dworkin argued that if we were to "take rights seriously," we would have to ground rights in an approach to theory that owed much to Kant.[13] As Dworkin put it, "It is absolutely necessary for liberals now . . . to show that the true father of liberalism is not Bentham, who is in fact rather an embarrassment . . . but Kant, whose conception of human nature cannot be called impoverished."[14] In particular, Kant invoked the premise that human beings were to be distinguished from animals by their capacity to transcend the passions,[15] to make moral choices, to be autonomous.[16] Similarly, David Richards, for example, writes that a theory of equality demands equal respect for persons, respect for their autonomy, in large part because "'no animal other than man . . . appears to have the capacity for reflective self-evaluation that is manifested in the formation of second-order desires.'"[17] Although Kantians would invoke that premise (or a similar one) as the foundation of liberalism,[18] it is worth noticing that the same proposition has been invoked with almost equal fervor by some segments of the American right. The premise is general enough to service radically different conclusions.

The issue of obscenity illustrates the point nicely. Conservative[19] Irving Kristol argues, for example, that obscenity ought to be regulated because when "sex is a public spectacle, a human relationship has been debased into a mere animal connection."[20] He thus thinks that obscenity should be controlled for the same reason that bearbaiting and cockfighting are outlawed. These acts are prohibited, he suggests, "only in part out of compassion for the suffering animals; the main reason they were abolished was because it was felt that they debased and brutalized the citizenry who flocked to witness such spectacles."[21] What Kristol aims to preserve is the sharp divide between humans and animals. If sex is displaced from the private sphere to the public sphere, Kristol argues, human nature has been defiled: Obscenity, he says, emphasizes the base animality of our nature. It reduces the spirituality of humanity to mere bodily functions.

In contrast to Kristol's perspective, consider a Kantian perspective, a perspective which in some of its details is somewhat more simplified and more extreme than that taken by modern neo-Kantian writers. Like Kristol, the Kantian believes that autonomous humans should not be reduced to the level of animals.[22] But the Kantian would contest Kristol's conclusion. The Kantian argues that an appropriate interpretation of the respect for persons demanded by the requirement of equality leads to the conclusion that obscenity should be constitutionally protected so that humans can make their own autonomous choice as to what they shall or shall not read. Now it may well be, argues the Kantian, that persons should decide not to read obscene material. But, for the government to decide what people should read is to deny their capacity for moral choice. If human beings are to be afforded the respect that is their due, government should not limit human freedom unless the exercise of that freedom should interfere with the *freedom* of another.[23] Alternatively, a Kantian might argue that government should not interfere with any basic liberty or right unless its exercise would interfere with a *basic liberty* or *right* of another or if interference was otherwise necessary to protect basic liberties or rights.[24] But, on any version, the conclusion would be thought to follow from the primacy of moral personality and autonomous decisionmaking.

In any event, the Kantian argues that application of one or another such principle quickly resolves the obscenity question. Thus, freedom of speech is easily characterized as an exercise of human freedom, or as a basic human right, and freedom of speech embraces the right to read. Thus, in discussing obscenity, David Richards writes:

> The contractarian conception of equal respect for persons requires that the scope of free speech be assessed in terms of facts and values relevant to the independent exercise of our moral powers of rationality and reasonableness, a protection of critical conscience that rules out those state restrictions aimed at "dangerous" speech, which usurp one's right of conscience to assess these questions on one's own.[25]

The only way (again in the Kantian model I am describing)[26] to show that the right to read obscene material could be foreclosed would be to show that the exercise of that right interfered with the freedom of another or the right of another. Without some such showing, the right to read obscene material would be protected as a matter of principle.

But that is not all. A Kantian would contend that appropriate interpretation of the freedom or rights principle can support powerful conclusions about just societal arrangements across a range of issues, including most issues of interest in first amendment law. A Kantian interpretation is sometimes thought to resolve everything from defamation to advocacy of illegal action.[27] Moreover, it can claim to place dissent in just the right perspective. From the Kantian perspective, the right to dissent is protected just until it interferes with the freedom of another or the right of another.

But substantial difficulties plague Kantian principles both at the stage of their application and of their justification. One issue that brings many of the difficulties with Kantian theory rather quickly to the surface is the question of how government should treat defamatory speech.[28] The problem is to determine the rule or set of rules that should govern when freedom of speech or press unfairly threatens reputation. To what extent do Kantian principles assist deliberation about the issue? Does it help to start with the proposition that the freedom to speak obtains just until it interferes with another freedom or right?

That defamation is a difficult issue for Kantian theory is perhaps evidenced by the diversity of the outcomes proposed by those who work within the Kantian tradition. Kant, himself, for example, thought that reputation was a right, a part of freedom of property.[29] By his reckoning, defamation, even of the dead, was no part of freedom of speech.[30] From Kant's perspective, the polity had an obligation to safeguard reputation, and if one applied his position in the contemporaneous American context, the law of every state in the union would be considered defective for failure to go far enough in protecting reputation. By contrast, C. Edwin Baker has suggested that there is no "right" to reputation, that reputation is no part of anyone's freedom.[31] On that understanding, the law of every state in the union would also be considered defective, but not because of a failure to protect reputation. Quite the contrary, the defamation laws—all of them—would be defective, indeed unconstitutional, precisely because any protection of reputation at the expense of speech would go too far. Thus, on one interpretation of the Kantian principle quite stringent defamation laws are required; on another, no defamation laws are even permitted.

Ronald Dworkin invokes what amounts (for these purposes) to the same Kantian principle, but it leads him to yet another result:

> The law of defamation . . . limits the personal right of any man to say what he thinks, because it requires him to have good grounds for what he says. But this law is justified, even for those who think it does invade a personal right, by the fact that it protects the *right* of others not to have their reputations ruined by a careless statement.[32]

The initial challenge for Kantian theory is to explain how the concept of right or of freedom is to be filled in. To focus, for example, on Dworkin's analysis of defamation, we are led to ask where the "right" not to have a reputation ruined by a careless statement comes from. The law of defamation is itself more complicated than Dworkin's statement might be taken to suggest. Some plaintiffs can recover without a showing of carelessness;[33] some only if they show careless conduct;[34] others, only if they show more than careless conduct;[35] still others, not at all, even if they show that the defendant knowingly lied.[36] In no case is recovery a matter of constitutional right.[37] So Dworkin's statement should not be taken to describe existing law. All the more so because his project is designed to help us see how things ought to be. Where, then, does this "right" come from?

Interpretation of a Kantian conception of rights would naturally be guided by the initial premise that human beings have dignity because of their capacity for moral choice, and that to afford them appropriate respect requires recognition of their autonomy. The eclectic insists, however, that there are too many variables at stake *even in this single problem* to expect that a single principle could prove productive. One might want to know, for example, what the impact of any proposed rule might be on truthful speech. That impact might differ between media and nonmedia defendants; it might differ between types of media. The notion of what constitutes care might be more or less useful in different contexts. It might be well applied by juries; it might not.

One might, in assessing the application of the proposed right, want to know what remedies followed from the finding of a violation. Would compensation be available only for financial loss or would compensation be provided for the wounded feelings of victims? Would limits be imposed on such recoveries? Would insurance be permissible for such damages? Would it be available and in what amounts? Should a deprivation of the right give rise to punitive damages? Injunctions? Under what circumstances?

Most of these questions are routinely pursued by courts. They are more easily asked than answered, however. Defamation law involves complex institutions and far-ranging consequences in a multiplicity of social contexts. Courts must deal with complaints about statements made in letters of recommendation, in commercial credit reports, on the front page of the *New York Times,* or over the backyard fence. Those complaining include powerful public officials and not-so-powerful public officials, business leaders and those who would like to be business leaders, figures from the entertainment world or the world of sports (amateur and professional), people who have assumed a prominent social role in a large or small circle, and people who have assumed no prominence of any kind except to be the object of a defamatory statement. It may be that the same rule should apply without regard to the subject matter, the nature of the plaintiff, the nature of the defendant, or the character of the distribution of the utterance and without regard to any and all possible combinations of such factors. What seems unlikely is that rules should be formulated without detailed consideration of the *possibility* that quite different social contexts might appropriately be treated in quite different ways. What seems intuitively implausible is that we could make a lot of progress in approaching the defamation puzzle if we would agree not to focus on the consequences for our social and political institutions in adopting one approach or another, but instead should set out to achieve conceptual mastery of notions like respect, dignity, autonomy, freedom, or rights.

A flexible Kantian would urge that conceptual mastery of such concepts is not the issue. Rather the task is to *interpret* what respect, dignity, and the like would mean in a particular social context. No doubt, it would be possible to carry on a promising dialogue about social problems while using Kantian language. Indeed, a discussion of the defamation problem that omitted any reference to notions like dignity, autonomy, respect, or freedom might to that extent be impoverished. But Kantian theory demands more than the concession that such concepts should be considered. For the Kantian the fundamental issue is whether and to what extent one has a right to a reputation. No doubt, debate on the defamation issue could proceed with the argument being framed in Kantian terms. One could debate whether respect demands that reputation be a right or a freedom within Kantian theory.[38] But, if that debate took account of the multifarious consequences and contexts, if the analysis were in fact rooted in the particular and responsive to the possibly complicated demands of social reality, the principle itself would have become a vehicle for expressing a conclusion rather than a method for arriving at one. Its effectiveness would be rhetorical, not analytic.

From an analytic perspective, Kantian theory even in its most sophisticated versions has been unable to provide a persuasive account of what it takes to establish a right or how one resolves conflicts between rights.[39] It has been unable, if we might take another family of examples, to provide a methodology for determining whether, and in what circumstances, there is a "right" to be free of mental distress.[40] Of course, no one supports an absolute right to be free of mental distress, not even severe mental distress. If, for example, a competitor should set up a business across the street from yours, severe emotional distress might reasonably be triggered in you, but those facts alone could hardly found a claim to be free of the competitor who caused the distress.[41] The more interesting position (attractive to many in the Kantian tradition)[42] is simply to deny[43] that "mere" psychological harm is sufficient to justify limiting personal freedom.[44] But this form of argument also runs too many different examples together.[45] A person might be mentally distressed, for example, because of a public act of sexual intercourse on a street corner,[46] because an individual publicly burns a flag[47] or a copy of the Constitution, because a funeral parlor, or an adult theater, or a neon sign has been set up in the neighborhood, because socialists march, because Nazis march,[48] because a mob of people yell racist insults at a small child on the way to a newly integrated school,[49] because of an obscene telephone call, or because of a face-to-face hurling of racial, religious, or occupational insults.[50]

There is a strong case for allowing the exercise of liberty causing the mental distress in many of these examples, but few would
be comfortable with the claim that the mental distress in *every
one* of these cases is insufficient to support regulation in one form
or another. The only way one might get to a position quite that
extreme would be wholly to abstract from the social context.[51]
Once again, the problem with examples such as these is not one
of needing to figure out more about the nature of freedom or of
rights. That kind of thinking might provide a sturdy foundation
for a few of these examples. But some of these examples clearly
demand a more particularized inquiry. Without a basis for as-
signing rights or defining freedom, Kantian theory is strikingly
indeterminate.[52] And this family of examples,[53] like the defamation issue, strongly suggests that a methodology placing emphasis upon attention to the full range of factors at work in diverse
social contexts is likely to be a more promising approach to decisionmaking.

The Rhetorical Appeal of Kantian Theory

Modern Kantians would not deny that the theoretical aspirations
of Kantian theory are ambitious and that substantial difficulties
attend its development, and perhaps most of them would concede
that many of its difficulties may never be satisfactorily worked
out. Nonetheless, Kantian theory has substantial rhetorical
appeal[54] for many even in the somewhat extreme form I have presented it. What makes it attractive? Alternatively, beyond the
particular merit of its arguments, why might it evoke resistance
in others?

Rousseau wrote in *The Social Contract* that "Man was born
free, and is everywhere in bondage." If Rousseau inspired the romantics, he inspired Kant and the Kantians as well. Kantian
theory is born in a passion for freedom.[55] It yearns for a society of
morally autonomous individuals, a society in which diverse individuals can pursue their different passions, a society in which
people can follow their various conceptions of the good life and
achieve their dreams.[56] If the state is to use power to restrict any
individual's freedom, the Kantian demands that the state furnish
justification. But the different desires, preferences, and passions
present an enormous challenge. It is not enough for the Kantian

to provide a justification for the exercise of power over most people. The Kantian insists on respect for all and justification for all.[57]

The problem of legal and political argument from this perspective is to find a shared[58] principle that can transcend these passions.[59] As John Rawls puts it, "[T]he conflicts implicit in the fact of pluralism force political philosophy to present conceptions of justice that are abstract . . . ."[60] Moreover, he writes: "We should strive for a kind of moral geometry with all the rigor which this name connotes."[61] Thus, in building a theory of justice, Rawls and other modern Kantians would abstract from all our conceptions of the good life. They ask us how we would structure society if we had no notion of what our own conception of the good life might be. This device of abstracting from our passions would not necessarily be based on a denigration of the passions (though Kantians privilege reason over passion).[62] Indeed, some Kantians would argue that the passions are best celebrated by a device that in effect gives them representation without giving any of them a preferred place.[63] Moreover, the use of such a device of reasoning might itself be arrived at or justified by a mode of reasoning that itself might be highly contextual and not abstract.[64] So understood, this device of abstraction and an accompanying regulative ideal of moral geometry might prove attractive in a number of ways.

Part of the attraction is aesthetic. As William James puts it:

> The facts of the world in their sensible diversity are always before us, but our theoretic need is that they should be conceived in a way that reduces their manifoldness to simplicity. Our pleasure at finding that a chaos of facts is the expression of a single underlying fact is like the relief of the musician at resolving a confused mass of sound into melodic or harmonic order. . . . The passion for parsimony, for economy of means in thought, is the philosophic passion *par excellence* . . . . [65]

The attraction of moral geometry is not merely aesthetic, however. If society could just agree on a principle to guide its conduct, then it could reason from or interpret that principle. It is feared that society, in the absence of principle, will be without a basis for the legitimate exercise of power and will be mired in the passions of the day. Kantians need not pretend that sweeping conclusions about social reality follow with necessary deductive force from a small set of premises.[66] They can concede that their premises call for interpretation and for difficult judgments in concrete contexts.[67] They may strive for moral geometry, but may well be prepared to recognize that their aspirations for theory may never be fully realized.[68] But the establishment of a governing principle (or a small set of lexically ordered principles) is thought to be an important move if one is squarely to confront the diversity of passions in a complex society. Unless a governing principle is established to transcend the passions, effective and just governance seems altogether unlikely.[69] Thus, an important appeal of Kantian theory is the implied promise of legitimate and effective[70] governance, the promise of an alternative to getting lost in the diversity of human passions.[71]

By contrast, the eclectic believes that there are too many principles that interact in too many complicated ways in too many concrete contexts to warrant any realistic hope that any general theorist's project could succeed. The eclectic could not claim an ability to "prove" this negative assertion. The best the eclectic can do is to point to the ways in which the general theorist's project encounters difficulties and to refute specific principles as they are proposed.[72] This, of course, is exactly what I tried to do in the last section.

To date, no general theory including Kantian theory has won anything close to general acceptance.[73] Indeed, for the most part, first amendment discourse has been populated by many leaders and relatively few followers. One might be tempted to object that the relative lack of popularity of a general theory is by no means a reliable indication that the theory is flawed. Theories are surely not to be judged by popularity polls.[74] The failure of Kantian theory in any of its versions to win anything close to general acceptance, however, is of some importance. That failure undercuts an important part of its appeal: it can not credibly claim to provide a premise or small set of premises that can effectively transcend the passions of a diverse society. Right or wrong, Kantian theory has yet to afford any likely possibility of effectively bringing the society substantially closer to consensus.[75]

Nonetheless, Kantian theorists would each claim to have provided the best methodology for first amendment decisionmaking, and could also contend (allowing for various attitudes toward precedent) that judges would do well to adopt such a methodology even if the academic community had not joined happy hands in uniform endorsement. Indeed a major appeal of all general first amendment theorists rests on the supposition that the path of first amendment safety lies in keeping the amendment clear of the vagaries of public opinion.[76]

Consonant with that appeal, the Kantian theorist promises a rational[77] basis for decisionmaking. The method appeals to the desire for objectivity,[78] for rationality in a seemingly irrational world. By transcending the passions, the Kantian theorist not only hopes to provide a manageable premise for decisionmaking, but also seeks to avoid unreliable alternatives. The passions are regarded as unreliable, subjective, inferior.[79] In this respect, the appeal of Kantian theory is similar to that of the positivist or scientist. The positivist or scientist strives for a value-free, objective methodology. The goal is to avoid subjectivity, to assure that scientific experiments can be replicated. Although Kantian theory does not purport to provide a value-free methodology, the theory, like all general theory, has the appeal of limiting subjectivity,[80] of being able to point to a binding principle outside of one's own variegated passions[81] that can, at worst, cabin discretion and, at best, actually dictate the outcome in specific cases. In making decisions, the goal is to place the focus on the object—the principle—rather than the intuitions of the subject.

Closely allied to appealing to a desire for rationality and objectivity[82] is an appeal to our sense of integrity.[83] Action on the basis of the passions is easy to characterize as narrowly parochial and self-serving. Those who act instead on the basis of principle can think of themselves as being controlled by what is right, rather than being controlled by what they might selfishly desire.[84] They can think of themselves as having the integrity to stand by principle.[85]

Moreover, Kantian theory manifests an explicit appeal to a sense of human dignity. To rely on the passions is to reduce people to their preferences. It transforms people into pleasure centers. It animalizes and dehumanizes humanity. By reasoning from principle, Kantianism not only honors the human capacity to reason, it affords a sense of respect for human beings.[86] It affirms our moral capacity and thereby affirms a sense of human dignity.

Finally, Kantian theory seems to offer a firm basis for criticism.

To rely on the passions is to risk that prevailing intuitions will be respected and thus to privilege the status quo.[87] What is thought to be needed is an Archimedean point[88] outside the passions, if criticism is to be made possible.[89] By transcending the passions one hopes to avoid the corrupting bias of self-interested perception. Kantian theory, therefore, carries a progressive promise. It hopes to trade ideology for justice.

Taken together, the arguments for Kantian theory carry an appeal that goes beyond the details of any particular argument it puts forth. Accepting the methodology of the Kantian allows one to build a particular self-image. One can think of oneself as rational, objective, dignified, tolerant, critical, and progressive. By identifying with Kantian theory, one could regard oneself as having stood up for principle. One can believe that the choice to accept the Kantian methodology is to take a stand on behalf of moral integrity. The desire to identify with characteristics such as these can make one want to accept Kantian theory—to hope that it can work, even if it may not.

By contrast, the eclectic method has its own unique rhetorical appeal. It too has attractions that can gain it supporters it might not deserve. In assessing its appeal, however, we may find it useful to explore why some of its most fervent supporters might actually be repelled by the prospect of any general theory.

Certainly a major difference between the Kantian and the eclectic concerns the relationship between reason and emotion. The core of Kantian theory is the effort to transcend the passions.[90] By contrast, the eclectic emphasizes that prudential decisionmaking in general, and first amendment decisionmaking in particular, depends upon thorough immersion in the concrete details of social reality and that human beings and their desires and passions are a vital part of social reality. The eclectic emphasizes[91] that first amendment decisions are not mere analytic puzzles. At the forefront of the eclectic's concern is that first amendment decisions have important social and individual consequences. From this perspective, free speech decisionmaking requires the capacity to imagine how different people now feel and how they might feel in different circumstances.[92] It requires exploration of the passions, not transcendence, and it insists that rational decisionmaking must recognize the mutually interdependent relation of reason with desire. From this perspective, rationality depends upon integrating and reintegrating reason with desire, principles with passions, and theory with practice. As such the eclectic method emphasizes dialogue[93] and debate, not moral geometry.[94] It draws attention to the concrete,[95] rather than the abstract.[96] Thus, it sides with those who have made appreciative comments on the advantages of thinking small.[97]

From the perspective of the eclectic, Kantian theory is an instance of irrationality, not rationality. To transcend the passions is just to detach oneself from social reality. Feyerabend puts the point in terms that would entertain the eclectic and outrage the Kantian: "Schizophrenics very often hold beliefs which are as rigid, all-pervasive, and unconnected with reality, as are the best dogmatic philosophies. However, such beliefs come to them naturally whereas a [general theorist] may sometimes spend his whole life in attempting to find arguments which create a similar state of mind."[98] Although no serious eclectic would press the point in such severe terms (except in a fit of pique), for the eclectic, it does seem peculiar to rally around abstraction as a recommended method for resolving social problems.

From the perspective of the eclectic, it would be insufficient for a Kantian to respond by emphasizing the extent to which principles can be flexibly interpreted or applied. The greater the emphasis on flexibility, the greater the tension with the Kantian's claims to objectivity and integrity.[99] Those claims depend upon fidelity to principle. But if principle is continually adjusted to meet the needs of social reality—if the desire for particular outcomes defines and redefines the principle—then it is the social reality and the perception of social reality that is generating prescriptions, not the principle.

Nietzsche once observed that to have a system is to lack integrity.[100] In the same vein, the eclectic maintains that Kantians must choose between integrity and flexibility. Either they actually transcend the passions and stick doggedly to principle or they must manipulate principle to avoid reductionism. The eclectic insists that flexibility and integrity can coexist only if the requirement of abstract principle be liquidated. There is another alternative. The Kantian can embrace a general principle but decline to claim that it does determinative work in the analysis. In this respect, the Kantian keeps integrity and flexibility while moving some distance from the Kantian project and toward the eclectic perspective. The eclectic does not deny the importance of principle; the eclectic denies that first amendment decisionmaking can usefully be reduced to one or a small number of principles and further insists that principles conflict in concrete contexts. For the eclectic, principles are important, but reasoning is not principled.[101]

Similar considerations influence the eclectic to doubt the critical capacity of general theory. If Kantian theory is flexible enough to be adapted to changing circumstances, it is also flexible enough to be manipulated on behalf of intuitions favoring the status quo. The critical capacity of Kantian theory thus depends upon, indeed can be seen as coextensive with, its successful detachment from social reality. For Kantian theory to be successful, it would command integrity when its principles called for appropriate criticism of the status quo and would elicit "flexibility" when its principles pointed in undesirable directions. But this would require resort to the very subjective judgment the theory was set up to avoid.

Alternatively, it might just be that the principle would lead by itself to optimal results. This, after all, is what much general theory claims to do.[102] If genuine critical capacity is claimed, however (a critical capacity that transcends the passions), eclectics ask how the principle could be accepted by the status quo or maintained when the status quo was threatened. Kantians could fairly respond that the worth of a theory does not depend upon its political appeal. Even so, the eclectics would doubt the coherence of any theoretical attempt to escape the passions. Recall the contention that criticism of existing passions is possible only if an Archimedean point is established outside the passions. Argument is otherwise too often a mask for ideology. But this contention requires a showing of where the Archimedean point comes from, if not from the passions of the particular theorist.[103] Kantians here typically turn to a conception of human nature or to the idea of moral agency, but eclectics insist that these notions can not themselves lead as far as the Kantians claim and, in any event, that such notions are themselves dependent upon the very passions they are designed to criticize.[104] Ultimately, even if one could or should accept the consequences required by any particular Archimedean point, there are grounds to doubt that an Archimedean point can be justified without resort to the passions.[105]

Finally, the eclectic would claim that the notion that criticism depends upon the establishment of points outside the system is itself dubious. Many of the most effective critics of social and political systems have engaged it from within.[106] The conflict between the ideals of a system and its daily practice form the raw materials[107] of effective criticism.[108] To be sure, in some cases the ideals may be too detached from any achievable reality. But often the practice has been the product of force or power. Its justification is frequently a thin veneer. Exposing the corruption of practice may not produce results. Those who benefit from the arrangements may have the power to keep them. But the possibility of criticism does not depend upon an Archimedean point. And the force of criticism has created powerful consumer and environmental groups, threatened gender roles, toppled Presidents, and daily affects the art of what is considered possible in politics. At the same time, the eclectic would concede that passions are socially formed and often self-serving. Our intuitions are frequently corrupt; our experience is finite, and our vision is partial. These factors inevitably and invariably will limit the capacity for criticism. But the eclectic sees no escape from these limitations. We can broaden our vision; in the end it will still be partial.[109] We cannot escape finitude.

It is just at this point that differing political postures affect the nature of one's commitment to methodology and the nature of the appeal it may or may not have. A Burkean conservative might oppose general theory (and would certainly oppose Kantian theory) in part out of fear that it might be applied with integrity and be used to upset settled and cherished customs, habits, and traditions. By the same token, it is possible to construct general theory that is likely to preserve the status quo. Part of the attraction for conservatives of the constitutional theory developed by Robert Bork is that it would foreclose the introduction of new constitutional rights. Complicating the picture still further is that it would oversimplify the sociology of conservatism to impose a Burkean model upon it. Many conservatives want to challenge existing habits, customs, and traditions. Consider those, for example, who would inter the New Deal.

Indeed, it is the stance of those eclectics who value dissent and the possibility of change (in whatever political direction) that is most relevant for our purposes. There is a strong sense in which many such eclectics[110] could be genuinely repelled by general theory. If it be fundamental for general theorists that an ideal methodology would generate a principle powerful enough to dictate results in concrete cases, the same prospect could seem claustrophobic to many eclectics.[111] Those eclectics particularly prize the flexibility to break out of existing categories;[112] they resist the authority of principle and its static, frozen character.[113] For them, to be locked in, now and forever, into an uncompromisingly binding principle is an eclectic nightmare. From this perspective, substantial irony attends the posture of the Kantian theorist in the first amendment area. If a major purpose of the first amendment is to protect those who would break out of existing categories, it seems odd to argue for freedom of speech by resort to a methodology that relies on locking categories in. So perceived, the method is in tension with values such as open-mindedness, flexibility, and tolerance. By seeking to prove that freedom of speech is right—once and for all—the method of the Kantian can be perceived as in psychological contradiction[114] with the substance of the first amendment. Its authoritarian appeal[115] is in tension with an amendment that prizes resistance to authority.[116] With this gloss,[117] the greater the centrality of the dissent value to the first amendment, the greater the psychological attractiveness of a methodology that itself prizes openness, diversity,[118] and flexibility.[119] But this particular version of the eclectic stance has its own irony. By forging a strong connection between first amendment method and first amendment substance, by committing to a method that places a premium on tolerance, flexibility, and open-mindedness, these eclectics allow first amendment values themselves to be assessed and reassessed. That version of eclecticism may needlessly endanger the very values by which it seeks to live. Indeed that is typically a central concern of the general theorist.[120] These eclectics in turn deny, but fear, the possibility of general theory, and so it goes.

Kantian Theory: A Final Assessment

Notice that most of the criticisms the eclectic might launch against Kantian theory, and indeed, against any general theory, depend upon the contention that the working principle or principles of the Kantian are in fact too detached from social reality to be workable. However psychologically attractive some eclectics might find it to *believe* that system building will be confounded by the variety and diversity of social reality, it might seem downright irrational to oppose general theory if it turned out to be solidly grounded in the necessities of the society. However claustrophobic one might fear such a system to be, presumably the most fanatical first amendment eclectic would concede that there could be enough space left in life—even after general theory—for spark, spice, vitality, and verve. On the other hand, if one believed that the rhetoric of first amendment decisionmaking was of major symbolic importance or that it otherwise might play an important role in shaping and encouraging a certain kind of people, one might be faced with a choice between the efficiency of general theory in dictating sound results and the perceived negative authoritarian aspects of the rhetoric of justification. But the discussion in this and prior chapters, however, suggests that the eclectic to date has little to fear. That discussion at least supports the view that some of the leading principles offered in support of Kantian theory and other general theories are in fact *too* general to provide an adequate foundation for a workable first amendment. To be sure, that discussion does not show that a case could never be made, nor does it show that some other general theory might not prove productive; still less does it show that a general political theory containing a small set of principles might not support important conclusions in which a pluralistic first amendment would play a role. The examples I have discussed have only a suggestive quality. In no sense do they prove a case against Kantian theory or other forms of general theory. But they should at least make one pause before taking it as a given that either a general first amendment theory or a general political theory is located right around the corner.

A realist might suppose that such examples are beside the point. No other methodology is going to yield up any easy solutions or any easy methods for arriving at solutions. Moreover, the realist might argue in particular that Kantian theory's relative emptiness permits wise adjudicators to achieve justice by manipulating conceptions of rights or freedom. Nonetheless, Kantian theory has potentially serious costs. By privileging abstract and general principles over more detailed, fact-specific solutions, it discourages pragmatic trial-and-error approaches and points decisionmakers in what could well turn out to be the wrong direction. Moreover, it encourages decisionmakers to give cryptic attention to complicated social questions. I am struck by the fact that otherwise distinguished scholars have been led by Kantian methodology to think that a quick and conclusory paragraph about rights or freedom is enough to justify sweeping solutions to complicated problems. Finally, even if decisionmakers gave such problems the nuanced attention they deserve, and even if they were able to manipulate Kantian concepts to achieve socially desirable results, it is hard to understand what would be achieved by having decisionmakers explain their results in language that might be quite removed from their actual processes of deliberation. Kantian theory is in large part built on a concept of integrity, and if it is to retain appeal, it must be defended on the ground that it would be applied with integrity.[121] The realist provides no assistance for Kantian theory.

Indeed, Kantian theory's lack of realism is its greatest weakness. In the final analysis, it is excessively optimistic to expect that social problems can be profitably and uniformly addressed by abstracting from the passions. Moreover, it is at least arguable that Kant's underlying conception of human nature is defective. For Kant, what distinguishes human beings from animals is the capacity to reason or the capacity to make autonomous choices. The basic insight is that the notion of autonomy is a necessary hypothesis[122] to ground any notion of human beings as moral creatures. One might accept that insight without accepting the argumentative apparatus that ordinarily accompanies it. For one thing, it is not clear that the basis of moral and political theory best proceeds from reflections about why we humans are better than animals. Robert Nozick has wondered, for example, how we would react if a more intelligent, perhaps more autonomous, species came to this planet. Would this "superior" species be *entitled* to exercise dominion over humans because of its superiority?[123] Inquiries like Nozick's[124] lead some toward vegetarianism, others toward animal liberation. My point is less ambitious. It just questions the underlying assumption that a perceived superiority to animals should come to be regarded as a meaningful source of human dignity. Indeed many find dignity in the sharing of life and nature along with animals. If dignity were the issue, there would at least be grounds to question the privileging of the animal superiority perspective over the life and nature sharing perspective.

Alternatively, one might not argue for Kantian premises (although Kant did) by comparing humans with animals. But it does seem indispensable to a Kantian perspective to claim that the capacity to reason or the capacity to make autonomous choices (which is taken to be central to moral personality) is the most important thing about human beings.[125] And that supposition tends toward a confined conception of human nature. As Dworkin puts it, citing Rawls with approval, the right of persons to equal respect is "'owed to human beings as moral persons,' and follows from the moral personality that distinguishes humans from animals."[126] As Rawls puts it, "The parties regard moral personality and not the capacity for pleasure and pain as the fundamental aspect of the self."[127] The tendency is to assume that because reason or autonomy is of ultimate importance, human life, which consists of the rational and the passionate, must exclude, or at best downplay, the passionate.[128] There is thus a greater tendency to tolerate an artificial separation of reason from the passions[129] by failing to appreciate the symbiotic relationship between the two. In its worst form, Kantianism compartmentalizes the self. As Robert Solomon writes, "To divide the human soul into reason and passion, setting one against the other in a struggle for control, one to be master, the other the slave, divides us against ourselves, forcing us to be defensively half a person . . . ."[130] This is what Sheldon Wolin means when he asserts that "[P]sychoanalysis is the science necessitated by the liberal ethos."[131]

Kantian theorists, however, need not be taken to support bloodless, shriveled, emotionally starved imitations of humanity. No one favors empty autonomy or meaningless lives. Their hope, however unrealistic, was to build general theory from concepts that all might share.[132] Moreover, they hoped that a polity built on such concepts could support and encourage a rich variety of approaches to life. What they were against were lives slavishly devoted to selfish pursuit of the passions or lives pursued in a nonautonomous way. They refused to accept the notion that public policy should try to maximize all preferences (consider racist preferences) or that it should be enacted according to the arbitrary or wholly subjective preferences of whatever person happens to be in place with the power to make a decision.

Ultimately, the driving force of Kantianism is an opposition to utilitarianism. Kantians simply cannot accept the notion that human beings are nothing more than pleasure centers; they cannot accept the notion that all preferences are equal; ultimately, they sponsor the notion that "moral personality and not the capacity for pleasure and pain [is] the fundamental aspect of the self."[133] The drive for general theory is fueled by the conviction that utilitarianism robs humanity of human dignity.

The rejection of Kantianism, however, need not involve any opposition to human dignity or to moral lives. It need not endorse selfish hedonism; it need not nourish an egalitarian tolerance for all preferences no matter how mean-spirited; it need not worship subjectivity, let alone arbitrary decisionmaking. Alternatives to Kantianism can build on the insights and aspirations for humanity found in Kantianism itself. But Kantianism may never prove to be realistic, and, at least for the present, alternatives are unavoidable.

Eclectic Theory and the First Amendment

If first amendment decisionmaking is to proceed without the benefit of general theory, a number of choices will inevitably be made. Actually, a number of choices *have* been made. We need not approach the subject from a hypothetical stance. First amendment decisionmaking has proceeded throughout the century without resort to Kantian theory or general theory of any kind. Although I label the traditional approach "eclectic,"[134] nothing turns on that label. Much does turn, however, on the character of the choices that have been made. Recognizing the character of the choices made is, of course, a first step to an evaluation of whether some of those choices should be *un*made.

The traditional eclectic approach has several significant features. First, it takes balancing to be a significant aspect of the decisionmaking process. Balancing assumes that social reality is too complicated[135] to justify the belief that speech values are always more important than the values with which they conflict. In the first amendment context, the eclectic approach has assumed that free speech problem-solving should consider the nature and importance of the state interest, the extent to which the regulation of speech advances that interest, the extent to which the state interest could be advanced by means less restrictive of free speech values, together with the impact of the regulation on free speech values. Commitment to such consideration, however, is not a commitment to ad hoc adjudication. Consideration of such factors will frequently lead to the conclusion that particular rules are required in particular contexts. In other contexts, ad hoc adjudication may be considered preferable to any conceivable rule. The question of whether to adopt a rule is not itself predetermined by the method.

Second, the traditional approach is in fact eclectic. Most obviously, it has been eclectic in the sense that it has produced a variety of tests and approaches to deal with discrete factual contexts. Moreover, it has been eclectic in the sense that it has refused to limit the first amendment to a single value or even to a small set of values. But it has been eclectic in a much more general sense.[136] It has been pragmatic,[137] pluralistic,[138] and nonreductive. It has habitually employed a contextualized approach to decisionmaking.[139] It has been more intuitionistic[140] than systematic; it has resorted to practical reason,[141] not abstract reason. Thus, it has refused to endorse the notion that any single or small set of principles could justify sweeping solutions to first amendment problems. It has shunned not only Kantianism, but also utilitarianism. This does not mean that human happiness, for example, is not of fundamental importance in eclectic decisionmaking. But an eclectic approach rejects the assumption that all conflicts of values should be resolved by determining what will produce the most happiness. It does not assume that justice, truth, beauty, freedom, and equality are all nothing more than proxies for human happiness. Certainly nothing about a commitment to balancing requires any such belief.

Third, the traditional balancing approach balances not two opposing principles but a multitude of claims. To be sure, if one were to take the balancing metaphor literally (or if one were to purge the traditional approach of its eclectic aspects), one might assume that all conflicts were reduced to a single measure.[142] On a scale, apples and oranges can be weighed; their different tastes, textures, and appearances do not affect the outcome. The jurist who "weighs" or balances reputation against speech, however, takes many variables into account and does not purport to reduce them to a single measure. Thus, the jurist is making judgments about values for which there is often no "scale." Moreover, the balancing metaphor connotes a dualism that is frequently belied by the multifaceted character of the variables considered in resolving a problem.

The balancing metaphor is in part responsible for the tendency of some to equate first amendment jurisprudence with utilitarianism. In its most extreme Benthamite form, utilitarianism insisted that all human values could be reduced to a single phenomenon—pleasure. The goal of the Benthamite utilitarian was to maximize pleasure; all pleasure was considered equal.

Now the accommodation of values in first amendment law has many difficulties, but it need not be haunted by the ghost of Bentham. First, nothing in first amendment jurisprudence assumes that all preferences are equal. In accommodating values, one is entirely correct to say that the pleasure of the sadist or of the person who would reenact the Holocaust is entitled to no weight.

Second, nothing in first amendment jurisprudence need assume that the existing preferences are to be taken as given. In the process of accommodating values, the Court can depart from existing values and can criticize the process by which values are formed. Nothing in first amendment *method* requires the Court to accept government, corporate, or press domination of the intellectual marketplace. To be sure, in criticizing preferences the Court would depart from Benthamite neutrality regarding preferences. But nothing about accommodating values requires that neutrality.

Third, nothing in first amendment jurisprudence requires the assumption that persons are nothing more than their preferences or that the most important moral, social, legal, and political fact about a person is his or her preferences. Opponents of Benthamite utilitarianism object that *persons* are not taken seriously. The notion is that conceptions of dignity, integrity, and meaning in human life are demeaned by a philosophy that reduces people to their naked (or clothed) desires. There is absolutely nothing in the notion of accommodating values that connotes such cynicism about the way we should think about human beings.

Opposing utilitarianism, however, does not entail ignoring the impact of decisions on human lives.[143] Although balancing cannot fairly be equated with utilitarianism, the traditional eclectic approach takes an assessment of the consequences of the government regulation into account as an enormously significant factor in the decisionmaking process. The eclectic approach is deeply committed to social engineering.

Finally, the traditional approach is not just balancing or even eclectic balancing. It is interpretive, and an understanding of that aspect is important not only to an understanding of the eclectic approach but also to an understanding of the adjudicative process. The adjudicative process is not the legislative process even though both judges and legislators take policy consequences into account in their decisionmaking and despite the fact that both judges and legislators are unavoidably involved in interpretation.

A contemporary movement in the humanities and social sciences regards all moral, political, social, aesthetic, and legal thought as inescapably interpretive in character.[144] From the perspective of this intellectual movement, understanding of social reality is invariably affected by the finitude of human beings located in a particular time in a particular place, by their needs and their desires. Their interpretation of facts is always value-laden. Historically situated beings maintain values, beliefs, and perceptions that have been structured by their social environment, by their very language. Thus they are always situated in the present, looking at the past with an eye to the problems they face in the future. From the perspective of method, their task is hermeneutic. Like those who read literary texts or biblical texts, those who would make historical, moral, or political judgments must interpret the text of social reality. As Clifford Geertz observes, "The woods are full of eager interpreters."[145]

There is much to be said for the perspective advanced by the hermeneutics movement. In particular, it is always worth contemplating that our outlook at any and every moment is far more likely to be the product of the totality of our social environment than we are ordinarily likely to credit. Moreover, it is worth emphasizing the extent to which our normative judgments are influenced by our interpretation of the social environment. On the other hand, it is also important to appreciate the limits of understanding the process of policymaking through the filter of a reading or text analogy. To begin with, if social reality is to be regarded as a text, it is at least an unusual text. That is, the text we interpret is constantly changing around us. This feature, however, is less odd than it might appear. From a hermeneutic perspective, the text of Shakespeare is also constantly changing. That is, the subject reading the text brings new beliefs and attitudes to the text. The words of Shakespeare's text may stay the same, but they can be taken to mean different things in different historical contexts.[146] Moreover, our perception of the characters, of their motives and ethical stance, can change as we change over time. The notion of a changing text is paradoxical, but not problematic. Nonetheless, the text analogy has two biasing features that limit its utility, particularly if one were to focus on legislators. First, the text analogy is backward-looking. There may be some advantage to this even for legislators. Americans are an antihistorical people.[147] They take Emerson seriously.[148] They are too ready to believe that we are the American Adam.[149] But a method gripped by a metaphor that forces us always to look backward in order to go forward has a methodological bias against novelty.[150] Second, the text analogy emphasizes the object rather than the subject.[151] To be sure, this can be countered by emphasizing the crucial role of the subject in the interpretive process. That is, the text means different things to different subjects who come to it with different problems at different times. But it is the text that is being interpreted. Social engineers might do well if they would recognize the extent to which they are historical beings. But social engineers need not adopt the text analogy as the central part of their work—unless they are judges.

And that distinguishes judges from legislators. Whatever the limits of the text analogy for general social theory, first amendment decisionmaking is inevitably hermeneutic. Here the reference to text is not an analogy. There is a text, and in interpreting that text judges are not the American Adam. They do not write on a clean slate. They can not without limits mold first amendment law in the precise ways their own subjective views tell them would be best for the polity. They may think, for example, that Republicans are moral lepers and that political arrangements that work to the detriment of Republicans would maximize justice, freedom, equality, and human happiness. One might expect a Democratic legislator to think in just those terms when deciding how to vote on newly proposed lines for an election district. But no lawyer in America would think of arguing to a judge that a set of political arrangements was justified by the fact that it helped one political party over another, and any judge who took that fact into account would have abandoned the judicial enterprise. Judges make decisions in a cultural context that places some policy arguments beyond the pale. And, in any event, the cultural context of adjudication requires them to fit their decisions into a complicated matrix of prior law.

At the same time, judges are not ribbon clerks, nor are they "vehicles of revealed truth."[152] The interpretive task is by no means narrowly bounded. Law school casebooks ordinarily contain the words of the first amendment, numerous precedents, and some legal commentary as representative materials bearing on the interpretive process. If judges were limited to those materials, they would possess considerable discretion. But the notion of freedom of speech in our culture has not been confined to judicial writings or legal commentary.[153] I would argue that two pages of Emerson or Whitman in the free speech context may be worth more than any dozen volumes of the *Harvard Law Review.* That argument may or may not be persuasive, but it is clearly an admissible legal argument. The understanding of freedom of speech has long been a vital part of the self-understanding of the American culture, including the legal culture. When Justice Holmes interpreted the first amendment in 1921, he interpreted it in the context of American tradition, and he saw it as a commitment to a burgeoning marketplace of ideas. Decades later, when Justice Brennan interpreted the first amendment, he also interpreted it in the context of American tradition, and he saw it as a commitment to self-government. The language of the first amendment is embedded in a rich social context that changes over time. In interpreting the first amendment, in deciding the character of its values and their importance, historically situated judges must look at the past with an eye to the future. Their consequentialist decisionmaking is not unrestrained; it functions in a bounded but capacious context.

Eclectic methodology is capacious, but is it not empty or vacuous. To adopt an eclectic methodology is itself to make a number of choices, choices to exclude, for example, (a) any theory that would exclude one or more of the values of speech; (b) any theory that would value speech over all other values; (c) any theory that would always require the accommodation of speech and other values to take place at high levels of abstraction.[154]

Given choices such as these, an eclectic theory of free speech would have to be enormously complicated if it were to account for its results across a broad range of cases. An eclectic would take into account the nature of the state interest or interests in a given context and would, in comparing contexts, recognize that interests vary in their importance. The regulations at issue in particular cases would each advance the interests in different degrees, and those distinctions in degree might make a difference. So too the possibility of advancing the state interests in ways less restrictive of speech (in different degrees) while at the same time restricting other interests of more or less importance (in different degrees) could affect the regulation or protection of speech in individual contexts. Again, any restriction on speech would have different meanings for different first amendment values and those values could themselves conflict. Layered on top of all this in the context of adjudication would be the necessity of explaining how those considerations fit with sources of interpretation such as language, intent, precedent, policy, and power. These sources might themselves conflict in concrete contexts, and an eclectic might well contend that no clear hierarchy could be discerned among these sources.

What we know for sure is that the substance of free speech theory would vary dramatically from eclectic to eclectic. Eclectic methodology, as I have described it, is wildly capacious, capacious enough to include persons with markedly different values about freedom of speech. One could flesh out the accommodation of values in concrete contexts in many different ways, ways that could range from the radical to the reactionary. Although eclectic methodology is indeterminate and incomplete, we do not operate in a complete vacuum. While using an eclectic approach, the Court has produced a vast body of substantive accommodations between speech and other values. I disagree with many of those accommodations; so does every member of the Court, and—I would guess—so does every reader of this book. To the extent that we would all argue for change (and the changes "we" would argue for would be conflicting), I think we are better off arguing within the confines of an eclectic methodology. But there are many brands of eclecticism—in the end, all eclectics must choose—and I want to put a particular gloss on the traditional eclectic method.[155] More precisely, I aim to connect the general themes of this book with the romantic tradition. I favor a form of "romantic eclecticism."

5

The First Amendment and Romance

In *The Creation of the American Republic,* Gordon Wood writes that the American Constitution "marked an end of the classical conception of politics and the beginning of what might be called a romantic view of politics."[1] This romantic view of politics, according to Wood, emphasizes "the piecemeal and the concrete in politics at the expense of order and completeness,"[2] or as he also says, "The Constitution represented both the climax and the finale of the American Enlightenment, both the fulfillment and the end of the belief that the endless variety and perplexity of society could be reduced to a simple and harmonious system."[3]

The terms *romance, romantic,* and *romanticism* have been used somewhat gingerly by American scholars at least since Arthur Lovejoy declared that there was no one fundamental "romantic" idea to be gleaned from the many movements that had been loosely given the name.[4] From Lovejoy's perspective, it was preferable to speak of a "plurality of Romanticisms,"[5] and even then it was important to note that many of these movements stood for quite different, even contradictory things. Although Lovejoy's discussion of romanticism was illuminating, his general point needs some perspective. The terms *liberal, conservative, Kantian, Hegelian, feminist, Marxist,* and the like have also been used in many different ways by many different people;[6] many of those ways have been contradictory; but intellectual discourse would surely have been less rich and less energetic if these terms had been purged from the scholarly vocabulary.[7] So far as romanticism is concerned, Frederic Baumer is on sound footing when he writes that "[T]here can be no real doubt that there was a Romantic Movement and, what is more, that it effected a real transvaluation of Western values."[8] Without purporting to capture the beliefs of any and all who have been described as romantic (indeed, recognizing that some romantics do not fit parts of this picture at all), let us understand romantics as those who have sought to emphasize the passions against abstract reason; the subjective against the objective; the concrete and the particular against the general and the universal; activity, dynamism, and movement against the frozen, static, and eternal; creativity, originality, imagination, and spontaneity against mechanical calculation, rote analysis, or artificial, bloodless routine; invention over discovery; and struggle over victory.[9] As Isaiah Berlin puts it, the romantics stand for the "celebration of all forms of defiance directed against the 'given'—the impersonal, the 'brute fact' in morals or in politics or against the static and the accepted and [for] the value placed on minorities . . . as such, no matter what the ideal for which they suffer."[10]

Like Berlin, I too want to emphasize those romantics who celebrated dissent and defiance, those who, as John Stuart Mill put it, revolted "against the narrownesses of the eighteenth century."[11]

To place an argument or a set of arguments within a tradition frequently necessitates choices about which aspects of the tradition to sponsor and which to leave behind. Those who argue within the Kantian tradition leave many of Kant's formulations behind, for example, his notions about the distribution of wealth, his absolutist views about the duty to obey the law, or his stern conceptions of punishment.[12] So too with romanticism, there is much to leave behind. The romanticism I encourage is only one of the pluralism of romanticisms,[13] and there is much in the romantic tradition that deserves to be forthrightly discarded. Romanticism has been used to support convention as well as to oppose it.[14] Supporting passion against abstract reason risks placing romanticism without standards "at the disposal of every sentiment."[15] And there is no doubt about it: Romanticism has had its dark side. To glorify the subjective is to flirt with narcissism,[16] with self-absorption,[17] with elitism,[18] and worse. To glorify the passions begs the question of the ends to which the passions will be put,[19] and some romantics have stored their passions in hopes of retrieving an unretrievable past; others have poured their energies into the glorification of militarism[20] or of totalitarian states.[21] If the iron steel of "reason" led to Stalin, misdirected elitist passion paved a path for the Führer.

The celebration of dissent, however, is at the heart of the romanticism I am sponsoring. I am siding with those romantics who sought to make it possible to criticize existing habits, customs, and traditions; and I mean specifically to oppose forms of romanticism that do not regard dissent as central. No guarantees are possible, but if a citizenry is committed to protecting and encouraging dissent as a major part of its tradition, then romanticism of that character carries no special risks of totalitarianism. Indeed, romanticism with such an emphasis would not only regard such regimes as especially evil, but also would stand specially opposed to the authoritarian mind set. But, it might be asked, who rallies around "the authoritarian mind set"? Who among us, to take another example, favors a life of "mechanical calculation, rote analysis, or artificial, bloodless routine"? In these respects, isn't everyone a romantic? My answer is no. One can tell a great deal about a tradition by the particular demons it sets out to exorcise. Everyone is opposed to a life of bloodless routine, but everyone does not make it a point of their tradition to combat it, and those who do are more likely to find it and to fight it. Everyone is in favor of the specific in some contexts and the general in others, but some traditions stress the need for theory and others stress the need for context and specially look after it.

Romanticism inevitably functions in a social context, and there are social contexts in which some of the priorities of romanticism are upside down. If we could go back in a time machine to the Haight-Ashbury scene in the late 1960s, I doubt that many of us would be arguing that the people we saw there needed to put *more* emphasis on the passions, on the advantages of spontaneity, or on the desirability of challenging conventions. In that context, we might be looking for a touch more order, a bit more routine, a little less dynamism.

But in the context of American culture and particularly its legal culture, the romantic tradition has much to offer. Those who have attempted to translate their progressive aspirations through notions such as pragmatism, practical reason, hermeneutics, deconstruction, eclecticism, feminism,[22] or contextual-ism can find much to appreciate in their own connection with the bright side of the romantic tradition.[23]

So too there is much to be nurtured in the bright side of the Emersonian tradition.[24] In Chapters 2 and 3 I invoked Emerson as speaking with special resonance on the importance of dissent, intellectual independence, and democracy. Those claims do not depend on any particular connection with the modernized conception of the romantic tradition I am presenting; nonetheless Emerson is intimately related to that tradition. Romanticism in America received its most influential expression in the form of transcendentalism,[25] but any *firm* judgments about Emerson's relationship to what I have called the bright side of the romantic tradition would be difficult to support. Emerson is sufficiently paradoxical that scholars spend a healthy intellectual life contesting where his real sympathies lie[26] and, of course, those sympathies themselves may have changed over time.[27] Few, however, would doubt Emerson's commitment to activity, dynamism, movement, creativity, originality, imagination, spontaneity, invention, and struggle. And, most important, no one should doubt his encouragement for those who would dissent against existing customs, habits, and traditions. In these respects he powerfully represents the characteristics of the romantic tradition emphasized here.[28]

With respect to some of the dichotomies, however, Emerson spoke eloquently on both sides. In the contest between the particular and the general, for example, Emerson frequently spoke of the necessity for finding the general in the concrete and the particular, but many would say he was prepared to find the general all too fast. Emerson stressed our common humanity. He emphasized the ways in which we are all alike, and, as he well understood, this theme is of substantial importance when one is considering our national commitment to equality. But Emerson's emphasis upon our common humanity must be placed in perspective. That emphasis followed from Emerson's religious focus, but it did not deny our diversity. As Emerson remarked in his journal: "A man, I, am the remote circumference, the skirt, the thin suburb or frontier post of God but go inward & I find the ocean; I lose my individuality in its waves. God is Unity, but always works in variety. I go inward until I find Unity universal, that Is before

the World was; I come outward to this body a point of variety." [29]
As Sherman Paul writes, "Like William James after him, [Emerson] found the multiplicity of life too rich to be impoverished by
the metaphysician's sentiment of rationality. That multiplicity
. . . could . . . not be simplified, but it could be used in all its potentialities as the stuff of analogy by which to achieve the unity of
vision." [30] Or as Paul also writes, Emerson "intended to assert a
multi-dimensional universe of spiritual possibilities rather than
to overcome the restraints and trivialities of everyday prudential
life." [31] Thus, in discussing free speech, Emerson rejected any totalizing unity. He spoke against conformity, against the tendency
to be like the others. His consistent message was that our oneness must emerge through individuality, not through imitation.

Most intriguing of all, however, is Emerson's conception of reason and its place in Kant's work. There is a double irony. Irony
one: many romantics have fought against Kantian abstract reason but, at the same time, in important ways they have owed to
Kant the notions of individualism, freedom, and the sovereign
ego that they have used in various ways to undermine abstractionism. Kant in many ways made romanticism possible. His emphasis on freedom, dignity, and autonomy—his opposition to utilitarianism—his epistemological emphasis on the importance of
mind and its connection to objectivity—all these themes were
enormously influential in the romantic movement. Just as Kant
could owe much to Rousseau without being a follower, so too the
romantics owed much to Kant; but Kant was not a romantic, and
the romantics were not Kantians.

Irony two: Emerson thought his conception of reason was Kantian, and he sometimes trumpeted transcendentalism as if it
were Kantian. But Emerson's understanding of Kant was mediated through Coleridge, and as John McAleer has observed,
"Actually, though Emerson knew it neither then nor later, Coleridge . . . had misread Kant." [32] Emerson stressed the importance
of reason, but Emerson's conception of reason was intuitionistic.
He ran reason together with insight, imagination, and vision.
For example, Emerson described reason as "the highest faculty of
the soul—what we mean often by the soul itself; it never *reasons,*
never proves, it simply perceives; it is vision." [33] In addition, as
Michael Gilmore puts it, "[Emerson] argues that Reason or intuition enables men to apprehend the spiritual element that per-

vades the universe and heals the breach between mind and matter."[34] On the latter point, Emerson's views were closer to post-Kantians like Fichte than to Kant.[35] As Peter Thorslev explains, Fichte placed "the Ego, in its infinite striving, among the noumena. The Ego becomes the constitutive principle not merely, as with Kant, of phenomenological reality, but of all reality . . . ."[36]

More important, for our purposes, Emerson's notion of reason emphasized intuition, not conceptualization, not formalism, and certainly not categorical imperatives. As F. O. Matthiessen wrote in *American Renaissance:* "The revolution in which Emerson shared was primarily the one that was waged against the formulas of eighteenth-century rationalism in the name of the fuller resources of man."[37] Emerson favored experience over book learning and insight over experience. For Emerson, reason was insight gained from confrontation with the particular. To be sure, this is some distance from an emphasis on the passions: insight and vision are not desire or feeling. Indeed Emerson tended to steer away from the individuating aspects of the passions because of his emphasis on the shared aspects of our humanity.[38] But Emerson was driving us toward a moral sentiment,[39] one that followed from our appreciation of the harmony and beauty of the universe. As Leon Chai puts it in *The Romantic Foundations of the American Renaissance:* "The perception of this beauty of harmony or correspondence inspires the mind with the *intuition* of the moral sentiment, the recognition that the beauty of the correspondence derives from its perception by the mind, which through its *experience* of that perception becomes one with the divine consciousness."[40]

For Emerson, passion precedes, is present in, and follows from that experience. It precedes it because through experience—through laughing, weeping, loving, being commended or cheated or chagrined—through life, we come to the truth of the moral intuition.[41] That intuition is not merely a perception; it is an experience and a sentiment. "A more secret, sweet, and overpowering beauty appears to man when his heart and mind open to the sentiment of virtue."[42] That sentiment is a "reverence and a delight."[43] Passion follows from that experience. It makes for "our highest happiness. Wonderful is its power to charm and to command."[44] For Emerson, the moral intuition leads to benevolence, love, association, and justice. If Kant grounded morality in duty to the law, Emerson grounded morality in love for the law. If Kant's law was stern, Emerson's was liberating. If Kant emphasized the authority of the law, Emerson emphasized that morality could not flow from obedience to authority, but had to flow from fullness of the heart. Although Emerson avoided public autobiographical displays of his own individuating passion,[45] his basic philosophy stressed the importance of passion[46] and recognized the symbiotic connection between reason and desire.

At the same time Emerson's emphasis on the moral sentiment with its attendant emphasis on harmony and beauty in the universe sits side by side with quite different "Emersonian moments," moments of doubt and skepticism, moments of sadness and disquiet. For all of his emphasis on the unifying capacities of the moral sentiment, Emerson's writings reveal a person of many moods, of quite different consciousness and emphasis. As with Tolstoy, Emerson's understanding of the diversity of the human condition often overwhelmed the strength of his metaphysical commitments. Like Tolstoy, Emerson was a fox—trying desperately to be a hedgehog.[47]

My object, of course, is not to urge acceptance of transcendentalism, let alone any of Emerson's specific formulations. Influenced by his strong religious commitment that inquiry into the self was a manifestation of the "eternal One,"[48] for example, Emerson too often spoke as if insight were unerring.

The Emersonian perspective of use to us must be more general; it must transcend different religious perspectives and be less confident. But there is instruction to be gained even from this aspect of Emerson's optimism. First, neither Emerson nor the romantics in general were nihilists. Their emphasis on subjectivity and intuition did not lead them to deny the existence of truth. In finding the truth, however, they stressed insight gained from confrontation with experience. Second, Emerson is a considerable distance from "postmodernism." Emerson does not promote the kind of "anti-romance . . . I've-seen-it-all"[49] cynicism that "dissolves commitment into irony."[50] At his best, in essays like "Fate,"[51] Emerson is prepared, as Hegel put it, to "look the negative in the face and live with it."[52] For Emerson, "living with it" is not resignation. As he said in his great lecture on protest: "The old, halt, numb, bedrid world must ever be plagued with th[e] incessant soul [of protest]. . . . By resistance to this strong Custom and strong Sense—by obedience to the soul, is the world to be saved."[53] Moreover, what Marshall Berman says of modernism can as well be said of Emerson: "The fact that 'all that is solid melts into air' is a source not of despair, but of strength and affirmation. If everything must go, then let it go: modern people have the power to create a better world than the world they have lost."[54]

Of course, Emerson's writings are complicated, multifaceted, and often paradoxical. But his tie to the romantic tradition and his influence ranges well beyond his emphasis on dissent. Without abandoning a commitment to our common humanity, Walt Whitman gave renewed life to diversity and passion within an Emersonian perspective. Beyond Whitman, Emerson's eloquent emphasis on the concrete and the particular,[55] his hostility to systemic formalism,[56] and his willingness to challenge authority and convention anticipated the pragmatists,[57] and thus the romantic tradition of supporting dissent broke into the twentieth century, albeit without some of its transcendental ties.[58] Emerson's influence has been important, but selective. And Emerson would have had it no other way. He did not encourage slavish following.[59] Indeed one of his strongest religious commitments was to accept the Bible as inspiration, but to reject its authority. And this perspective he followed across the board. In "The American Scholar," for example, he counseled us to be inspired by some "past utterance of genius," but not to be pinned down; he advised us to look forward, not backward; he invited us to search for "creative manners . . . creative actions, creative words; manners, actions, words, that is, indicative of no custom or authority . . . ."[60] We can be inspired by Emerson; we need not be pinned down. His work strongly connects with the bright side of the romantic tradition.

The Relevance of Romance to Dissent and Democracy

When Gordon Wood argues that the American Constitution inaugurated a romantic conception of politics, he emphasizes the extent to which the Constitution is a creative experiment. The Founders worked in a bounded context, to be sure, but they did not believe they were discovering a preexistent model; theirs was a work of invention. The Founders did not believe that they had set up any frozen categories indelibly to be preserved, now and forever. They knew that they had formulated a set of tensions and compromises to be struggled over, again and again. Their greatest achievement was the provision of a structure flexible enough to contain but also to accommodate continuing struggle. Wood's apt characterization of the Founders' work as romantic calls up no images of narcissistic self-indulgence or nationalistic totalitarianism. It does helpfully remind us of the role of subjective invention, and of the renunciation of the abstract and the frozen from the very inception of the Constitution.

Just as Wood believes that illumination is provided by looking at the founding of the Constitution through a romantic lens, so too romanticism is uniquely relevant to first amendment analysis. One way of characterizing this book is as an extended argument for the proposition that first amendment decisionmaking is more romantic than generally understood, but still not romantic enough.

There are important respects in which first amendment discourse can already be characterized as responsive to the side of the romantic tradition I am highlighting. Like Wood's Founders, the Court does not pretend that first amendment decisions uncover a preexistent meaning. There is no claim that the results in free speech cases were dictated from records left by the Founders. Justices are "molders of policy, rather than the impersonal vehicles of revealed truth."[61] Invention triumphs over discovery.[62]

The eclectic approach used in first amendment decisionmaking recognizes the futility of systemic approaches designed to transcend the passions. It recognizes that abstract reason alone cannot generate a satisfactory first amendment theory; it recognizes that first amendment values conflict[63] in complicated ways with numerous other values in complicated contexts.[64] A principal attraction of balancing as a mode of discourse is that it invites candor about how conflicts between important values[65] are resolved (at least so long as it does not retreat to formulaic standards of review). In this respect the arguments for balancing, dissent, and romanticism run together. The underlying hope is for candor and integrity.

So too balancing rejects any notion that first amendment law could ever be molded into a frozen form. And it stresses that first amendment decisions are not just puzzles, and not just symbolic exercises, but that first amendment decisions have important human consequences. Indeed first amendment methodology arguably gives a strong role to the passions. By its modes of justification the Court has suggested that free speech problems call less for an understanding of the concept of autonomy and more for recognition of the need for empathy.[66] Free speech balancing requires the capacity to imagine how different people feel and how they might feel in different circumstances. It requires exploration of the passions, not transcendence. As such the eclectic method encourages dialogue, debate, and flexibility,[67] not moral geometry. It draws attention to the concrete, rather than the abstract. In each of these respects first amendment decisionmaking is responsive to the romantic tradition. If romanticism stands against the abstractionist methods of the eighteenth-century enlightenment, so does first amendment methodology.

More interesting is whether first amendment decisionmaking can be charged with the sort of mechanistic utilitarianism so often denigrated by the romantics. In an uninteresting respect, of course, it can be. To make first amendment decisions is to govern a real society. The romantic so alienated by the governing process as to demand poetry *in place of government* will surely find first amendment decisionmaking unduly hidebound and mechanistic.[68] But romanticism need not take the form of anarchism. As Morse Peckham has argued: "Since the logic of Romanticism is that contradictions must be included in a single orientation, but without pseudo-reconciliations, Romanticism is a remarkably stable and fruitful orientation. For the past 175 years the Romantic has been the tough-minded [person], determined to create value and project order to make feasible the pure assertion of identity, determined to assert identity in order to engage with reality simply because it is there and because there is nothing else, and knowing eventually that his orientations are adaptive instruments and that no orientation is or can be final. [Romantics do] not escape from reality; [they escape] into it."[69]

Like Peckham and Wood, I do not equate romanticism with touching the leaves or with starry-eyed evasions of reality. There is no war between realism and romanticism. Even placing romantic anarchism to the side, however, there are aspects of first amendment decisionmaking that appear mechanistic and might seem offensive to the romantic spirit. Specifically, I have in mind the recent tendency of the Court to resort to "standards of review" in first amendment cases. The mechanism and artificiality of that device was explored at some length in Chapter 1 and we need not rehearse it again. At least from the romantic perspective, standards of review can be criticized as clumsy vehicles for expressing conclusions even if they are not necessarily indicative of a mechanistic decisionmaking process. At least with respect to standards of review, the argument here has been that the Court's frequently stated methodology is insufficiently romantic.

More generally, the romantics could object to the emphasis on rules in first amendment methodology.[70] Indeed the conflict about rules, standards, and open-ended decisionmaking implicates many of the same rhetorical and psychological appeals that envelop the debate for and against general theory.[71] The romantic would worry, for example, that rules would be insufficiently responsive to the complexity and the diversity of social reality. Those who argue for rules point to the need for certainty, predictability, and the like. Contemporary first amendment methodology could be characterized as antiromantic in the sense that it displays a preference for rules.[72] Moreover, the argument of this book could be characterized as antiromantic in that it respects and applauds that preference.[73]

On the other hand, what does or does not fall within the romantic tradition is inevitably a question of context. From the perspective of the culture of first amendment scholarship, the argument of this book has been antirule. The traditional wisdom has expressed concern over the extent to which first amendment methodology has failed to produce rules. What I argued in Chapter 1 against Nimmer and others is that first amendment methodology displays a preference for rules, but rightly leaves open the question of whether a rule is appropriate for a particular context. What is too often assumed is that rules are *always* needed in first amendment law. Indeed, it is often casually assumed that without clear rules a pernicious chilling effect will invariably ensue. Yet many persons speak without the slightest attention to the law books. How many speakers consult the law books before racing out to curse their local policemen? Even in those cases where the objects of the law's attention do consult the law in advance of speaking, the "chilling" effect may not be pernicious. In the libel context, despite a complicated body of "rules," it is often impossible to know at the time of a prospective publication whether a particular utterance is defamatory or, for example, whether the potential plaintiff is a "public figure" or a "private person." Often the effect of that uncertainty is that writers or "fact checkers" investigate further and, in the process, find information that ultimately adds to the richness and accuracy of the original story. I think that some of the uncertainty in the libel law is productive. Some of it is quite pernicious, but, even there, the pernicious uncertainty might be preferable to the effects of a clear but repressive rule. What seems certain to me is that attention to the particular effects of rules or the lack of them is more constructive than slogans about chilling effects or any mind-numbing insistence on clarity. Whether this aspect of the argument is understood as romantic or not, the point is that first amendment methodology is on sound ground when it entertains an open-minded, flexible perspective on the status of rules.

A romantic perspective affords support not only for particular methodological features of first amendment law, but also for important aspects of substantive first amendment law. For example, it has strong implications for the treatment of commercial advertising. As Raymond Williams observes in *Culture and Society,* romanticism is best understood in light of the social context in which it emerged.[74] Thus in the English context:

> The emphasis on a general common humanity was evidently necessary in a period in which a new kind of society was coming to think of man as merely a specialized instrument of production. The emphasis on love and relationship was necessary not only within the immediate suffering but against the aggressive individualism and the primarily economic relationships which the new society embodied. Emphasis on the creative imagination, similarly, may be seen as an alternative construction of human motive and energy, in contrast with the assumptions of the prevailing political economy.[75]

Reacting against the background of the industrial revolution, the English romantics spoke out against materialism, the power of the machine, mechanical calculation, utilitarianism, the treatment of human beings as objects, and the general crushing of the creative spirit of humanity.

If the English romantics sometimes exhibited nostalgia for the way things once were, Emerson welcomed the introduction of the machine into the American landscape.[76] He described himself as "gay as a canary bird" over the prospect that America would become a manufacturing country, and he exulted at the promise that the hungry might be fed.[77] But Emerson was no ego-maximizing, calculating, materialistic, utilitarian. Emerson expected and hoped that Americans would "renounce the values of a commercial society."[78] He posited an ideal in which Americans would settle for economic sufficiency rather than a "lust for wealth."[79] Like Emerson, Whitman also welcomed the business energy, and indeed, the "almost maniacal appetite for wealth."[80] But Whitman also warned of the need to cabin the "materialistic and vulgar" aspects of our culture.[81] He argued that the "tremendous and dominant play of solely materialistic bearings upon current life in the United States" had to be "confronted and met."[82] To argue that efforts to place limits on the excessive commercialization of American society should be encouraged, and to argue that the Court rightly relegates commercial advertising to a low position in the hierarchy of first amendment values, is to invoke a perspective that has deep roots in the romantic tradition.[83]

Similarly, from the romantic perspective, it is easy to understand why powerful business corporations could be subjected to burdensome regulations when they seek to dominate political campaigns. Such corporate activity has been subjected to substantial regulation because of "concern over the corrosive influence of concentrated corporate wealth" and in an effort to restrict the influence of "'political war chests funneled through the corporate form.'"[84] The romantics I have in mind fought to break free of classical forms. They sponsored dissent, the breaking "away from the acceptance of caked wisdom and toward the exploratory development of the individual . . . ."[85] From the romantic perspective, the regulation of the wealthy, the powerful, and the large corporate conglomerate does not ordinarily inspire concern that those who would break out of classical forms are in danger of being stifled or that individual self-expression is at risk. Instead those concerns become acute when government moves to attack the unconventional—the Schencks, the Carlins, the O'Briens. From the romantic perspective, it is clear: the powerful rarely need protection; dissenters too often do.

The exceptions prove the rule. Some powerful corporate conglomerates get uniquely special protection. Consider the owners
of *Time,* CBS, and the like. Like other business corporations,
broadcasters and national magazines are out to make a profit.
But the press is deemed to be a source of criticism and that distinction makes a difference.

Indeed it is precisely at the point that business corporations
begin to look like dissenters that regulation of their speech becomes more controversial. When tobacco companies take on the
scientific establishment by challenging the received wisdom that
cigarette smoking causes cancer, their first amendment case becomes more appealing. If they should lose, it would not be because they are moral lepers. The first amendment protects moral
lepers.[86] What counts against them is not only the extent to
which their speech is verifiably false, the undesirability of making ad hoc judgments about the editorial or political character of
commercial advertisements (which in the main are not editorial
or political), and the significance of the threat to public health,
but also the lack of connection between their speech and genuine
self-expression. The corporate tobacco speaker seeking to maximize profits just does not exhibit the kind of independence and/or
rebellion that we ordinarily associate with dissent or the romantic tradition. Nonetheless, it has to be recognized that such
speech in taking on the scientific establishment implicates some
of the values associated with dissent and the romantic tradition.
If such speech were not protected, it could not plausibly be maintained that there was a total absence of first amendment value.
The romantic perspective assists in clarifying the nature of the
first amendment values at stake.

A focus on the romantics also makes it easier to understand
how *some* might perceive a strong connection between first
amendment substance and first amendment method. Recall that
in discussing the rhetorical appeal of Kantian theory, I mentioned that some—by no means all—eclectics could find Kantianism unappealingly claustrophobic. *Those* eclectics—I being
one—stand solidly in the romantic tradition. The romantics attacked the stifling characteristics of enlightenment rationalism
precisely because they believed that there was a connection between substance and method. The fixed abstractions of Kantian
rationalism provided insufficient room for the recognition of the

vitality, the versatility, and the diversity of human experience.[87] By contrast, the eclectic methods of first amendment methodology seem to instantiate the very candor[88] and flexibility[89] prized by the romantics. A contextualized approach to decisionmaking insists that all factors be considered and thus furthers the romantic desire to avoid being locked in.[90] By emphasizing the concrete rather than the abstract, first amendment methodology allows for the possibility of change. It can be characterized as valuing tolerance, flexibility, and open-mindedness, not only as a part of the substance of the first amendment, but also as an important part of its method. It could be that these methodological commitments could provide less (or more) first amendment freedom than would adherence to a Kantian perspective. And that itself points to an interesting irony. The Kantians are usually associated with an antagonism to utilitarianism and consequentialism. But, when arguing against eclectics, the Kantians (and others inclined toward absolutism) frequently announce that the trouble with eclectic approaches is that judges could use them to limit first amendment values. They want an approach that will prevent that from happening. In other words, they give a consequentialist justification for their approach to method. Would it not be surprising to discover that underlying the Kantian approach is a profoundly strategic temperament? On the other side, the eclectics have often been associated with utilitarianism. But romantic eclectics when presented with the charge that their methodology threatens first amendment values respond that alternative methods are dishonest. In other words, they invoke integrity against consequences. Would it not be intriguing to learn that underlying the eclectic approach is a valuing of Kantian-like integrity over beneficial consequences?

Of course, the romantic eclectics deny that alternative methods will better protect first amendment values.[91] In this context, they deny the conflict between integrity and consequences. Moreover, from their romantic perspective, the social engineering of the eclectic method is more faithful to the underlying premises of a first amendment that would claim to prize dissent. Indeed, from this perspective, social engineering is romantic.

I entertain no illusion that readers will uniformly share the romance, however. Many readers, including some eclectics and some romantic eclectics, would resist any connection between engineering of any type and romance. That resistance might proceed from an understandable romantic resistance to mechanism and calculation. If the social engineering metaphor were replaced by a trope emphasizing the dialectical character of first amendment methodology, many of those readers might have greater sympathy for the perspective.[92] Still other readers, and here I am particularly[93] thinking of those attracted to the republican tradition, would balk at the metaphor of social engineering even if it were purged of any pretense of scientism,[94] and even if the prudential, pragmatic, practical, and dialectical aspects of reason were emphasized. For writers like William Sullivan, the notion of social engineering is part and parcel of a scheme of liberal individualism that accommodates individual and group interests but can provide no "convincing conception of a common good."[95] Instead, he and others would urge us to revive a civic republicanism that envisions politics as an end, as the realization of the common good.[96] This, I would argue, however, is a part[97] of republicanism that should not be revived.

Classical republicanism assumed a local and homogeneous population. That population, it was thought, could reason together to arrive at solutions that would transcend the parochial concerns of any individual. We live, however, in a nation of more than 240 million people. In many circumstances there is no *common* good.[98] To start out with the assumption that the end[99] of decisionmaking is the common good runs the risk of suppressing difference and minimizing the tragedy of choice. A social engineer need not be a utilitarian; a social engineer can be fully committed to an understanding of practical reason. A social engineer is not an egoist;[100] a social engineer strives to decide what will be best for the polity.[101] A social engineer need not promote hedonism or materialism and need not denigrate the importance of participation, justice, dignity, virtue, or responsibility.

A social engineer must strive to make decisions that are best for the polity, but in any such attempt must recognize that competing conceptions of the common good may well transcend parochial concerns, that "parochial" concerns, in any event, may be legitimate, and that frequently there may be no solution that transcends the accommodation of individual and group interests. Implicit in the metaphor of social engineering is the necessity of resolving conflict. There need be no connotation that the resulting decision is anything other than a good-faith effort to accommodate the competing concerns. An effort will have been made to serve the public interest, but no one need pretend[102] that what has emerged is *the* common good. In short, space is left for politics.[103]

Admittedly, social engineering is not a concept calculated to inspire enthusiasm; it does not generate feelings of warmth.[104] But social engineering has advantages as a metaphor. It focuses attention on the consequences of decisionmaking; it recognizes that decisions affect people in significant ways, in ways that require care and that necessitate attention and dialogue.[105] Perhaps, most important, social engineering accepts difference; romance celebrates difference.

From the romantic perspective, it is significant that social engineering functions within and is mitigated by an eclectic framework that is constrained to interpret the past as it looks toward the future. Decisions can not be made without a sense of where we have been or where we are going. From the romantic perspective, the social engineering aspects of first amendment methodology can proceed only with some general vision of the kind of society to which one aspires. Vision, even utopian vision, is a necessary fuel to keep eclecticism dynamic and alive. But the need for social engineering prevents any such vision from serving as a flight from tragedy. Emersonian moments of vision are not only a necessary source of inspiration and vitality, but also a continuing reminder of what should be or might be. Those moments inspire us even as they offer painful reminders of how far we have fallen short and as they challenge us to do better. From the romantic perspective, then, the eclectic method can combine social engineering with vision and fuse realism with romance. Chapter 1 concluded with the observation that we want more than social engineering, and we do. Moreover, it is not enough to be told that social engineering functions within an eclectic framework. We want more than mere eclecticism. But the remedy for whatever first amendment ills that might plague us is not a new method, but a different vision of first amendment priorities, a better sense of values, a different romance. There is no quick-fix method waiting in the wings. Indeed, the current modes of justification are for the most part compatible with the best of the romantic tradition.

Whatever metaphors are used, however, be they social engineering, eclecticism, the "common good," or some other tropes, first amendment methodology will be what it is, and still other readers will insist that any strong connection between *romance* and first amendment methodology should speak against first amendment methodology, not for it. As we have seen, the attraction for general theory in first amendment law is widespread, and many eclectics do not regard themselves as romantics at all, let alone romantics in the sense I have used in this section.

One need not be a romantic eclectic, however, to recognize that dissent is of important first amendment value. One need not be a dissenter or a romantic dissenter to value dissent. General theorists can value dissent; indeed, American general theorists usually do. Utilitarians can value dissent; American utilitarians usually do. Aristotelians can value dissent; American Aristotelians usually do. Nonromantic eclectics can value dissent; American eclectics usually do.

The fact is Americans value dissent. That fact is of importance to general theorists, and it is of importance to anyone who would apply the eclectic method. I now want to place that fact in perspective by situating it in a vision or interpretation of the place of the first amendment in the American culture. It is an interpretation that should have appeal for those eclectics who can not identify with the romantic tradition as it has been discussed and defined in this section, and it has much to offer even for those who are committed to one or another general theory.

It is an interpretation, however, that this time *insists* on the relevance of romance to the first amendment in a number of different senses, some of them more limited than I have used in this section. I will claim that in a limited sense everyone is a romantic, but my interpretation does not depend on that claim. The interpretation does not require that anyone *be* a romantic, but it *insists* that the first amendment, democracy, and romance are interdependent. Finally, I also mean to make good on the claim that it is possible to have social engineering (or, if you prefer, "pragmatism") *and* romance. And I hope to make good on the claim without resort to the contention that social engineering *is* romance.

"Solving" the Romantic Puzzle

Harold Bloom has written that, "All romance, literary and human, is founded upon enchantment."[106] For many readers of this book, however, what it means to think like a lawyer is to be able to resist enchantment. Many of them believe with Freud that without "the great disenchanter, reason, [and] the scientific attitude, . . . [no] civilized values are possible."[107] But as Geoffrey Hartman observes, "[T]he intellectual effort is always against enchantment, but that doesn't mean that every enchantment must be rigidly resisted, as a matter of Superman-like honor. Then the cure is worse than the disease."[108]

In the end, in a limited sense, we are all romantics and we are all rationalists. No particular can be perceived without a general category or set of categories.[109] No one perceives categories without reference to particulars.[110] The rationalist can not make decisions without some reference to the passions, and the romantic must ultimately *select* what to be enchanted about. Reason must control the passions, but reason requires the "anchorage and earthy wisdom of the passions."[111]

Human beings are meaning-creating animals.[112] They need to feel that their lives have meaning and that they play a role in defining what that meaning might be. At the same time, the social and political structure of the country in which they mature plays an enormous role in creating and shaping their desires, preferences, and values. One of the most important issues for any polity, whether or not it is squarely faced, is the question of what kind of citizens it hopes to foster. From the perspective of Constitution-making, it is desirable that, at a minimum, citizens take pride in the document. From that perspective, it would be hoped that citizens might feel some emotional bond with the country in which they live and with the Constitution that seeks to bind the country together. The nurturing of such emotional bonds does not require that citizens be thoroughly conversant with the details of constitutional doctrine. Cherished constitutional values may come to be cherished precisely because they are understood as part of a general picture[113] rather than as an "analytically" defined concept. Indeed, Kenneth Karst has argued, with characteristic eloquence, that "[I]t is no accident that our most cherished constitutional values . . . are diffuse rather than specific. Their very lack of specificity helps them to serve as symbols of community. The part of the brain that houses intuition and whole-pattern ways of knowing is also the home of dreams, and tears, and laughter. For a value to endure, to do its work in building a community, that value must not merely appeal to our interests but touch our emotions. Diffuse loyalty is the essence of community. There are no footnotes on the flag."[114]

Perhaps I have been wholly misled by my own interests in the first amendment, but it seems to me that American citizens not only feel a deep emotional attachment to the country, but also that an important source of that attachment is a sense of pride about the first amendment.

The first amendment speaks to the kind of people we are and the kind of people we aspire to be. In a sense it affords a national solution to a persistent romantic puzzle. Romantics have perennially flirted with two contrary ideals.[115] On the one hand, they have wanted to be bound up with something larger than themselves. Romantics have sought a rendezvous with destiny. When they have found their destiny, however, they find it claustrophobic.[116] And so they trade destiny for freedom. In choosing freedom, however, they feel alienated and alone. They crave union with something larger than themselves.[117]

The cultural genius of the first amendment is that it promotes a certain kind of people without inducing a sense of claustrophobia. It plays an important role in the construction of an appealing story, a story about a nation that promotes an independent people, a nation that affords a place of refuge for peoples all over the globe, a nation that welcomes the iconoclast, a nation that respects, tolerates, and even sponsors dissent. So understood, it is a nation whose citizens can come to regard themselves as a part of something larger than themselves without losing a sense of freedom. Moreover, the image called up by this national picture trades on the values of romanticism.[118] It encourages us to picture Walt Whitman's citizenry—vibrant, diverse, vital, stubborn, and independent. It encourages us to believe with Emerson that "America is the idea of emancipation."[119]

First amendment cases come and go. They are ordinarily dispatched without any serious consideration of what might bind us together as a country. But there is one leading case in which that sort of inquiry could not be put aside, and that case manifested a strong appreciation for the Emersonian and Whitmanesque vision of America. The case, *West Virginia v. Barnette*,[120] held that our constitutional conception of free speech barred a school board from compelling a school child to salute the American flag. The

Court did not pretend the case was routine. The Court understood that the flag is an important national symbol and that compulsory flag salutes require fundamental choices about the meaning of the first amendment and American democracy: "The case is made difficult not because the principles of its decision are obscure but because the flag involved is our own."[121] To decide the case was to decide the meaning of the flag, and to decide that was to proceed from a particular conception of what the country stood for. Three years before *Barnette,* in *Minersville School District v. Gobitis,* the Court had stated that compulsory flag salutes were "phases of the profoundest problem confronting a democracy—the problem which Lincoln cast in memorable dilemma: 'Must a government of necessity be too *strong* for the liberties of its people, or too *weak* to maintain its own existence?'"[122]

But the *Barnette* Court saw no such democratic dilemma: "To enforce [free speech] rights today is not to choose weak government over strong government. It is only to adhere as a means of strength to individual freedom of mind in preference to officially disciplined uniformity for which history indicates a disappointing and disastrous end."[123] The Court continued:

> Struggles to coerce uniformity of sentiment in support of some end thought essential to their time and country have been waged by many good as well as by evil men. . . . Ultimate futility of such attempts to compel coherence is the lesson of every such effort from the Roman drive to stamp out Christianity as a disturber of its pagan unity, the Inquisition, as a means to religious and dynastic unity, the Siberian exiles as a means to Russian unity, *down to the fast failing efforts of our present totalitarian enemies.* Those who begin coercive elimination of dissent soon find themselves exterminating dissenters. Compulsory unification of opinion achieves only the unanimity of the graveyard.[124]

The reference to our totalitarian enemies is telling. *Barnette* was written in the midst of World War II, a time when America's self-understanding was that it was fighting to preserve democracy. It is illuminating that the Court would call forth the idea of protecting dissent as fundamental to what the society stood for. So too the opinion speaks of the importance of fostering free minds,[125] intellectual individualism,[126] as well as intellectual diversity,[127] spiritual diversity,[128] and rich cultural diversity.[129]

In the end, *Barnette* exhibits an Emersonian understanding of the individual and the society. If individuals are to bind themselves to the cultural symbols of the society, they are encouraged to do so out of reverence, as a voluntary and spontaneous act,[130] not out of authority, not as "compulsory routine."[131] The very notion of citizenship,[132] suggests *Barnette,* must leave space for an autonomous decision about how closely to bond with one[133] of our most important national symbols.[134] Thus, if there is to be any central constitutional understanding, it proceeds from a profound national commitment to preserving dissent, encouraging free minds, and basking in the rich cultural diversity that follows from such preservation and encouragement. If there is to be any "fixed star in our constitutional constellation,"[135] it reaches beyond politics to a broader "sphere of intellect and spirit."[136] In short, the national picture drawn by *Barnette* is Whitmanesque and Emersonian: it resonates strongly with the romantic tradition.

But this national picture is also romantic in an aspirational sense; and some might describe it as downright quixotic. The story, it might well be said, depicts an utterly idealized social conception. It would be just as easy to spin a story showing that the United States has not really valued dissent in its actual practice.[137] A realistic social historian might show that the eccentrics and the iconoclasts have been perennially ostracized as social outcasts and victimized by abusive governmental action. That tale could focus on the nation's treatment of Native Americans, its general racism, its sexism, its marginalizing of difference, and its thoroughgoing hypocrisy. The realistic social historian would contend that his or her tale is a truer picture of American social reality than any sunny Whitmanesque portrayal. And I would agree with the social historian.

But the "realistic" picture is also reductionist. All stories—certainly all national stories—are reductionist. All stories blink a portion of reality.[138] The question we have been pursuing is what constitutional story to tell[139] from the perspective of the nation,[140] and, certainly, any story told from that perspective will portray the country in its best light. From the constitutional perspective—a perspective that is necessarily skewed in a conservative way—it makes sense to tell an aspirational story. What would make no sense, however, would be to tell a story so far removed from the self-understanding of the nation as not to be credible. But the Emersonian and Whitmanesque story has been widely told. The nation's claims to respect freedom of speech and to value dissent[141] have been persistently proclaimed from every political pulpit. That vision has been a vital part of the nation's self-understanding.[142] By consciously blinking reality, this romantic understanding of the first amendment has the merit of forcing a confrontation between American theory and American practice.[143]

On the other hand, it might be objected that the invocation of tradition in support of challenging tradition is paradoxical,[144] if not self-contradictory. Reliance on an argument from tradition might be thought to be unnecessary and undesirable: unnecessary, because if supporting dissent is desirable, no tradition is necessary; undesirable, because such reliance promotes the very authoritarianism the "tradition" is out to combat. There is force in this objection, but it ignores too much. As to necessity, the first amendment is embedded in the legal institutions of the nation, and legal interpretations are more acceptable when they grow out of, rather than break from, the past. More important, the objection trades on excessive individualism. We are situated in the present in a particular time and place and country. An interpretation that makes us feel that we can combat our institutions from within allows us to be more than a nation of combatting strangers; such an interpretation builds solidarity and meaningful individuality—both at the same time.[145] A tradition may be cherished and contribute to a sense of self without a sense that one has submitted to authority. Indeed, however much one sponsors dissent, the fact of our embodiment in a particular place at a particular time has an enormous stabilizing effect.[146] As Gadamer has written: "Even where life changes violently, as in ages of revolution, far more of the old is preserved in the supposed transformation of everything than anyone knows, and combines with the new to create a new value."[147] Thus, we reaffirm tradition even as we change it. Finally, if arguments from tradition have some tendency to support authoritarianism (and I concede that they do), they have not stifled dissent. Indeed they have long been the staple of those who would dissent from existing institutions.[148] Thus Myra Jehlen has observed a

> remarkable consistency in the self-presentation of American dissenters[:] . . . Typically, it is claimed that the measures advocated are already implicit in the founding idea and/or the Constitution, and that therefore (this from the left) the effect will be to complete the Revolution, or (from the right) to return to it. This fundamentalism adds a significant dimension to the more common pattern of associating change with old verities. In this case, the old ways not only are cited as the basis for a new historical construction, but are said already to contain the new. So that, unlike [Melville's] Pierre, who leaves his paternal estate, unhappy American sons historically have answered the challenge to "love it or leave it" with the transcendent claim that they *are* it.[149]

Of course, if arguments from tradition are admissible, there are other[150] constitutional stories that might be told about the first amendment. More conservative renditions are available as well as more radical interpretations. For some, the Emersonian or Whitmanesque version of American culture is itself claustrophobic—nowhere near the kind of ideal we ought to hold up against our practice. Both conservatives and radicals might press for a less individualistic and more communitarian interpretation though they would, of course, disagree about the nature of the community they would regard as ideal. It is easy, for example, to see how the conservative could construct a story about the first amendment that would be decidedly less "romantic" than the rendition I have offered. That story might emphasize the construction of a "public morality" that has repressed various forms of subversive speech, obscenity, fighting words, vulgarity, and the like. That rendition would emphasize the place of order, civility, and morality in first amendment interpretation.

One of the radical stories might emphasize the value of participation in the American idea of democracy, connect it to the first amendment, and press for yet a different tension between first amendment ideals and first amendment practice.

It would be foolish to deny a lack of grounding in the materials of American history or culture for either of these stories though it would be possible to argue that some stories "fit" better than others.[151] Instead of an extended critique of these perspectives, I will settle for a few observations about the process of choosing between and among various accounts.

First, although there is grounding for many stories about American culture and history, the question of which to accept is by no means entirely arbitrary. The question in large part turns on a notion of what will help human lives flourish,[152] and some parts of what we think about that are not socially constructed. A nuclear bomb dropped upon us will kill us. Period. This is a fact. It is not a product of our language; it is not a social construction.[153]

Second, if a bomb were dropped upon us, it would prevent the flourishing of our lives. It would not "make" our day. This conclusion may be socially constructed, but in an uninteresting way. It might be that we could be socialized to long for the bomb to drop upon us, that we could be socialized to regard it as a source of pride, a great way to end a life. One would have to be a thoroughgoing relativist to regard such socialization as anything other than irredeemably sick. Indeed, if we encounter otherwise healthy individuals who are bent on suicide, we tend to regard them as in need of treatment. Our values against death and suffering are so widely shared that their social construction ordinarily goes unnoticed. If there is a line between nature and nurture here, it would be hard to find.

On the other hand, many of the interesting issues about how human beings flourish in a particular society depends on evaluating how human beings think they flourish, which in part will be connected to what society has encouraged them to think will make for a flourishing existence. If one is trying to determine which types of lives a society should encourage, an element of circularity is unavoidable. Moreover, those who make such decisions will invariably[154] be influenced by the partiality of their own perspective no matter how hard they try to empathize with the perspectives of others.

At the same time, even a partial perspective has been formed through social interaction, and perspectives are constantly being revised and enlarged[155] by continued interaction. Thus, in any culture there is much to promote a common sense of what makes human beings flourish, and progress can often be made in arranging rules, structures, and institutions the more one pays attention to what people have found undesirable about the current arrangements. But even assuming perfect information, the best of intentions, and extraordinary acumen, there will never be agreement about how human lives flourish or what social arrangements are appropriate to any particular conception of the good life.

Although the question of how human lives flourish inevitably stimulates controversy, one of the strengths of the romantic perspective is that it places the issue at the forefront. A powerful theme running through the work of romantics in general and Emerson in particular is that human beings must be free to express their true nature.[156] The criticism of customs and institutions, for example, must ordinarily proceed from some vision of how it might be better, of what new social arrangements might do a better job in meeting the genuine needs and interests of human beings. In determining whether to criticize customs and institutions, Emerson urged us to consult our intuitions. Underlying that encouragement is the belief that there are genuine human needs and interests discoverable if we would think deeply about our real needs and aspirations. Thus, for Emerson, the subjective and the objective run together.

But there is more. The romantic perspective encourages the view that freedom of expression is a crucial part of human flourishing, that to realize one's nature one's life itself must be an interpretation of what it means to be a human being.[157] Moreover, the romantic vision itself can encourage a clustering of views that tie together around the notion of freedom or liberation.[158] As Charles Taylor has written in commenting on the romantic perspective: "The battle against political domination, and against the constricting forms of bureaucratic capitalism,[159] is also bound up with the aspiration to free the richness of nature from the bonds of abstract reason."[160]

Whether or not a romantic perspective were entertained and whatever clusters of views might emerge from such a perspective, the concept of human flourishing (or something like it) must be an important part of human decisionmaking. Yet, it is unlikely that the concept (or anything like it) could fairly be said directly to exhaust the sources of decisionmaking criteria. If some people believe, to take an easy example, that holding hands in public is disgusting (the example would be a little more interesting if the objection were to *males* holding hands in public), they might phrase their objection in terms easily reducible to a claim about what makes humanity flourish. They might say that a decision to permit public handholding would undermine their sense of the proper boundaries between the public and private sphere and inflict mental distress upon them. Similarly, public handholders might object to a prohibition of public handholding on the ground that it would undermine their sense of the proper boundaries between the public and private spheres and would inflict mental distress upon them. But public handholders might invoke a conception of rights that they might deem to override claims of interference with human flourishing, and opponents of public handholding might invoke conceptions of morality that might be deemed to override any claims of human flourishing. Perhaps both of these approaches ultimately reduce to a deeper grounding based on assumptions of human flourishing alone. Perhaps not.[161] Both, however, might well deny the *right* of the state to make a decision different from that ordained by their conception of rights or morality.

What would be incoherent would be for either of them to suppose that the state could do anything other than make a decision about the issue. Not to prohibit public handholding is to make a decision to permit public handholding. Thus, complicated as the process of decisionmaking might be, lengthy as any defense of such a decision might turn out to be, the one choice unavailable to the state is to make no decision about what kind of people its institutions will encourage its citizens to be. The state must decide to have public education or not to have public education and in so deciding it will affect the character of its citizenry. To be sure, it could proceed with a total lack of regard for the impact of its decisions on the kind of people encouraged by its institutions, but that would also be a decision and it could rightly be held responsible for the natural and foreseeable consequences of its conduct.

Similarly, society must choose between an Emersonian vision or some other version of the culture or some combination. Thus, conservatives might object that the privileging of dissent in first amendment discourse would impinge on their conception of human flourishing, and they might be right. But the failure to privilege dissent would impinge upon a romantic conception of what would make for human flourishing. The question is not whether to make a choice but what choice to make.

But a final choice will never be made. The contest between liberal independence and conservative order is a continuing dialectic in American society. Even if all citizens spontaneously decided to embrace an Emersonian picture of American culture, and even if that decision were clung to now and forever, such a decision would not erase the dialectic. It would just move the tension to a different place.

The other stories usually told about the first amendment are primarily flawed by their failure to be comprehensive. To focus on liberty or self-realization, for example, puts too much emphasis on the self at the expense of associational values. The marketplace metaphor calls up ego-maximizing connotations of buyers and sellers, ironically at the same time that it unnecessarily privileges truth over self-expression. Like the checking value, marketplace values tend to take the speaker out of speech and to cast the first amendment in a purely instrumental mold. The image of the citizen as an autonomous ruler in a democratic society is so far removed from the reality of American politics as to lack credibility, and it has the additional disadvantage of unnecessarily privileging political speech.

The advantage of a focus on dissent is that it serves to consolidate the values contained in the other stories. A focus on dissent does not liquidate liberty, freedom, equality, justice, tolerance, respect, dignity, self-government, truth, marketplace values, the checking value, associational values, cathartic values, or any other value that has been tied to freedom of speech or press. By emphasizing dissent, one focuses on an activity that serves as a repository of first amendment values.

There are also strategic reasons to build romance around the dissent concept. In what Vincent Blasi has called the pathological periods of our nation's history,[162] it has been precisely the problem that the values associated with dissent have been slighted and that dissenters have been repressed. There are no guarantees in this world, but if dissent were placed at the forefront of the romance-building work of the first amendment, it would be more difficult to send the Schencks off to jail.

But it would be hard to make a stronger claim than that. For example, if the country genuinely feels threatened, it is hard to muster any confidence about the judicial capacity to stand in the way for long.[163] It is not that judges are cowards, it is that judges are themselves a part of the culture they seek to interpret. If judges are often[164] hostage to the culture of which they are a part, judges will stop sending the Schencks off to jail only when our culture's democratic self-understanding is that the Schencks are not supposed to go to jail. Even when people prize dissent in the abstract there can be no assurance that they will respect it in the concrete.[165] Surely, academics as much as any group in society could be said to value dissent in the abstract. Many of them would characterize their life's work as valuing tolerance, open-mindedness, and the challenging of assumptions. Yet academics otherwise committed to the liberal tradition have a distinctly checkered record when the time has come for them to exhibit toleration in their own workplace. Consider, for example, the behavior of university academics during the McCarthy era and their treatment of both the right[166] and the left in more recent times.[167] It is important to press for genuine commitments to dissent as a first amendment value, but the battle over abstractions will be fought again in the concrete situation.

Without embracing any pie-eyed expectations, I submit that it is not unreasonable to suppose that one's general attitudes toward values like toleration and dissent would have a significant impact on many of the decisions one might make. Even in those cases where the values of dissent are perceived as being outweighed by other more pressing concerns in a particular context, in a dissent-focused regime it is more likely to be recognized that important constitutional values have been compromised. It would no longer work to say that there was *no* first amendment loss; it would no longer be a knockout blow to discover that the speech was not "political" or not a marketplace "idea." Decision-makers would be forced to experience the tragedy of choice.

At least, for a while.

If dissent came to be seen as a treasured first amendment value, it too would become a contested concept and, over time, it could become as twisted and distorted as the concepts of "political speech," or "speech," or "ideas" have been twisted and distorted in first amendment law. For this reason alone, I regard "dissent" as a potentially *temporary* romance.[168] And, in any event, even now,

I favor a deliberately schizophrenic approach. For purposes of rhetoric and romance, I believe courts, commentators, and Fourth of July speakers would best serve the interests of the country by associating the first amendment with the metaphor of dissent, with dissenters and the dissent value. For purposes of first amendment decisionmaking and social engineering, dissent should be afforded a far more prominent place in the Court's understanding of the first amendment and should be afforded substantially greater protection. But the Supreme Court and the lower courts should follow a thoroughly eclectic approach. When social engineering is the issue, the first amendment needs all the help it can get. It deserves the support of any and all values that can be mustered in its support whether singly or in combination.

Whatever the Court's methodology, the dissent value should play a more prominent role in the Court's rhetoric and its decisionmaking than has previously been the case. Although the general citizenry does not read the opinions of the Court, many lawyers do. Moreover, the Court has the ears of many other powerful opinion leaders, including a self-interested press and broadcast industry. What the Court says about speech and its values continues to be of cultural significance. The romance-building power of the court is not insubstantial.

It does seem unduly speculative, however, to suppose that the complexity[169] of first amendment doctrine (or lack of it) bears any substantial relationship to the extent of cultural support for the first amendment.[170] No doubt, there are areas where first amendment law could usefully be simplified. But if the first amendment is to serve the human needs of a complicated society, first amendment doctrine will inevitably be too complicated for anyone but specialists to understand.

Our citizenry does not understand first amendment doctrine, and it never will. But citizens understand what the FIRST AMENDMENT means. And that is why we need not trade freedom for destiny or destiny for freedom. If we play our cards right, we can have social engineering *and* romance. But from time to time, we may have to change the romance.

Notes

Index

Notes

Introduction

1. R. W. Emerson, "An Address," in *Ralph Waldo Emerson: Essays and Lectures* 80 (J. Porte ed. 1983).

2. G. Allen, *Waldo Emerson* 320 (1982).

3. R. W. Emerson, supra note 1, at 80.

4. Id. at 81.

5. Id.

6. Id. at 82.

7. Id.

8. Id. at 81.

9. Id.

10. Id. at 82.

11. Id. at 84.

12. R. W. Emerson, "The Protest," in III *The Early Lectures of Ralph Waldo Emerson: 1838–42* at 85, 102 (R. Spiller & W. Williams eds. 1972).

13. Id. at 94.

14. Id. at 89.

15. J. Porte, *Representative Man: Ralph Waldo Emerson in His Time* 104 (1988).

16. Rehnquist, J., dissenting in Smith v. Goguen, 415 U.S. 566 (1974) and yet again dissenting in Texas v. Johnson, 57 U.S.L.W. 4770 (U.S. June 22, 1989), both cases involving flag desecration and free speech, refers to Emerson's mention that the farmers' flag had been unfurled at Concord when "they fired the shot heard 'round the world," but does not refer to Emerson's views about freedom of speech. Nor does he acknowledge that Emerson's references to the American flag were sometimes contemptuous. See *Emerson in His Journals* 421 (J. Porte ed. 1982).

Emerson is not cited in any other Supreme Court case involving a free speech claim.

17. See generally Pound, "The Theory of Judicial Decision, Part III," 36 *Harv. L. Rev.* 940 (1922–23).

18. Id. at 954.

19. Id. at 954–955.

20. Id. at 956.

21. For the suggestion that Pound had first amendment influence, nonetheless, see Lahav, "American Influence on Israel's Jurisprudence of Free Speech," 9 *Hastings Const. L.Q.* 21, 24, 37–38 (1981).

22. Cf. Schauer, "Codifying the First Amendment," 1982 *Sup. Ct. Rev.* 309 (citing conversation with Professor Van Alstyne regretting the resemblance between the Internal Revenue Code and the first amendment).

23. T. Emerson, *The System of Freedom of Expression* 15 (1970).

24. But see Karst, "The First Amendment and Harry Kalven: An Appreciative Comment on the Advantages of Thinking Small," 13 *UCLA L. Rev.* 1 (1965).

25. For criticism of the "fortress model," see L. Bollinger, *The Tolerant Society* 76–103 (1986).

26. I. Berlin, *Four Essays on Liberty* 118–172 (1969).

27. Emerson strongly influenced Holmes (see, e.g., S. Bent, *Justice Oliver Wendell Holmes* 42–45, 127 (1969)), but Holmes set his own path (see C. Bowen, *Yankee From Olympus* 199–201 (1944)). Indeed Holmes sent Emerson one of his first essays on the law, remarking that Emerson "more than anyone else first started the philosophical ferment in my mind." M. Howe, *Justice Oliver Wendell Holmes: The Shaping Years* 203 (1957). My argument suggests that Emerson was not influential enough.

1. The First Amendment and Social Engineering

1. I. Berlin, *Russian Thinkers* 24 (1978). The apparent originator of the fox-hedgehog metaphor is the Greek poet Archilochus. See id. at 22.

2. Id. at 51.

3. I. Kant, "Critique of Judgment," in *The Philosophy of Kant* 265, 280 (C. Friedrich ed. 1949).

4. There are important variations on this distinction, particularly one that distinguishes between regulations that are content-based and those that are content-neutral. See text accompanying note 130 infra.

5. Nimmer, "The Meaning of Symbolic Speech under the First Amendment," 21 *UCLA L. Rev.* 29 (1973).

6. Ely, "Flag Desecration: A Case Study in the Roles of Categorization and Balancing in First Amendment Analysis," 88 *Harv. L. Rev.* 1482, 1497 (1975).

7. L. Tribe, *American Constitutional Law* §12-2, at 582 (1978).

8. M. Nimmer, *Nimmer on Freedom of Speech* (Student ed. 1984).

9. If the pronouncements of Nimmer, Ely, and Tribe are read with care, they amount to a statement that these two ways *ought* to make a difference

and that the Court's pronouncements were evolving in that direction. As Ely put it, "The Court has made a clear start in this direction, and it is a good one." Ely, supra note 6, at 1502. Moreover, if the pronouncements of Nimmer, Ely, and Tribe are read with care, it is obvious that they had slightly different directions in mind.

10. Nimmer, Ely, and Tribe themselves each were at pains to avoid distinguishing between speech and conduct. As Ely puts it, "[B]urning a draft card to express opposition to the draft is an undifferentiated whole, 100% action and 100% expression." Ely, supra note 6, at 1495. More generally, as Tribe says, "All communication except perhaps that of the extrasensory variety involves conduct." L. Tribe, *American Constitutional Law* §12-7, at 827 (2d ed. 1988). Thus, in order to avoid the speech-conduct distinction, Tribe resorts to numbers and talks of Track One and Track Two.

I use the labels *content track* and *conduct track* (because I think they are less clumsy than the alternatives) despite their potential for confusion and certainly not because I doubt that the use of content is a form of conduct.

11. Nimmer's terminology was somewhat different. If state action regulated a nonmeaning effect, Nimmer called the state's interest a "nonspeech" interest; if it regulated a meaning effect, he labeled the interest an "anti-speech" interest.

12. M. Nimmer, supra note 8 §2.05[A], at 2-28.

13. Id. §2.05[B], at 2-29.

14. In particular, see id. §2.03, at 2-15 to 2-24.

15. Id. at 2-18.

16. See id. §2.02, at 2-9 to 2-14. But see L. Tribe, supra note 10 §12-2, at 794: "On track two, when government does not seek to suppress any idea or message as such, there seems little escape from this quagmire of ad hoc judgment, although a few categorical rules are possible."

17. M. Nimmer, supra note 8 §2.06[A], at 2-85.

18. 391 U.S. 367 (1968). The case involved a draft card burning as a protest against the draft. For a discussion of the case, see Chapter 2, text accompanying notes 171 to 176 infra.

19. 391 U.S. at 377, discussed in M. Nimmer, supra note 8 §2.06[A], at 2-85 to 2-93.

20. But see notes 35, 37 & 46 infra.

21. See Konigsberg v. State Bar, 366 U.S. 36, 61 (1961) (Black, J., dissenting).

22. M. Nimmer, supra note 8 §2.01, at 2-2 to 2-8.

23. See id. §2.03, at 2-16.

24. See generally id. §2.02, at 2-9 to 2-14.

25. See generally id. §2.03, at 2-15 to 2-24.

26. Id. §2.02, at 2-10.

27. Id. §2.05[C], at 2-41 to 2-55.

28. Branzburg v. Hayes, 408 U.S. 665 (1972).

29. See generally Goodale, "Branzburg v. Hayes and the Developing Qualified Privilege for Newsmen," 26 *Hastings L.J.* 709 (1975).

30. See M. Nimmer, supra note 8 §4.09[C], at 4-60 & 4-64 (but distinguishing the defamation context from the grand jury context).

31. 418 U.S. 323 (1974).

32. Rosanova v. Playboy Enterprises, Inc., 411 F. Supp. 440, 445 (S.D. Ga. 1976), *aff'd*, 580 F.2d 859 (5th Cir. 1978). The point is not merely that an ad hoc judgment is necessitated, but that the rule defining a public figure necessitates ad hoc balancing in application. For example, it sometimes makes a difference whether the alleged "public figure" was involved in a "public controversy." To determine whether a controversy is public apparently requires a normative weighing of the importance of the speech—its public value—against public and private interests in privacy. In any event, to the extent rules leave room for discretion, any distinction between ad hoc judgment in applying rules and ad hoc balancing will not be sharp.

33. See M. Kelman, *A Guide to Critical Legal Studies* 44 (1987): "The open invocation of an apparently vague standard . . . may be reasonably predictable in practice because even relatively detailed tacit community norms so converge that application of vague policy sentiments to cases poses little danger of disagreement." As Thomas Grey notes, a major strain of argument in the realist movement was the criticism that rules were often less predictable than standards: "In many situations decisions would be both more predictable and more acceptable if the ruling norm were a vague standard that allowed judges or juries to apply their intuitive sense of fairness case-by-case, rather than a clear rule that was sporadically and covertly evaded." Grey, "Langdell's Orthodoxy," 45 *U. Pitt. L. Rev.* 1, 45 (1983). For additional insight concerning the myriad ways in which rules and standards collapse into each other, see Schlag, "Rules and Standards," 33 *UCLA L. Rev.* 379 (1985).

34. What the proxy has been created for depends upon who is regarded as the creator. In the text, I focus on the one factor that everyone seems to agree is at least a large part of the story. For discussion of other factors, see notes 37 & 46 infra.

35. See, e.g., Cass, "Commercial Speech, Constitutionalism, Collective Choice," 56 *U. Cin. L. Rev.* 1317, 1352 (1988): "The root concern for first amendment prohibitions on abridgement of speech and press freedom is official bias. There is widespread agreement that limitation of official bias is the principal aim of the first amendment, historically and as amplified over the past half-century by the courts." Professor Schauer has attempted a philosophical justification for freedom of speech not based on any positive aspects of speech, but based on the premise that governments are "less capable of regulating speech than they are of regulating other forms of conduct." F. Schauer, *Free Speech: A Philosophical Enquiry* 81 (1982). See also Schauer, "Must Speech Be Special?" 78 *Nw. U.L. Rev.* 1284 (1983). He suggests that bias, self-interest, and a general urge to suppress that with which one disagrees are significant reasons for this incapability. See *Free Speech*, supra, at 80–86. As he interprets the first amendment, therefore, its "focus . . . is on the motivations of the government." Schauer, "Cuban Cigars, Cu-

ban Books, and the Problem of Incidental Restrictions on Communications," 26 *Wm. & Mary L. Rev.* 779, 780 (1985). But see note 49 infra (citing sources in which Professor Schauer acknowledges a role for positive aspects of speech in decisionmaking). In the "Cuban Cigar" article, Schauer takes a short pass at a showing that his "negative perspective on the first amendment" (as opposed to one that emphasizes the positive values of speech) is more or less congruent with the doctrine.

Professor Cass too is an exponent of negative first amendment theory. His views are impressively detailed in "Commercial Speech," supra, and in Cass, "The Perils of Positive Thinking: Constitutional Interpretation and Negative First Amendment Theory," 34 *UCLA L. Rev.* 1405 (1987) (emphasizing official self-interest and, to a lesser extent, intolerance as the principal motives of concern).

I use the term *bias* in the text to embrace any sort of iniquitous motive, while recognizing that there are some contexts in which distinguishing between self-interested, paternalistic, and ruthlessly suppressive motives may be important and that distinguishing between acceptable and unacceptable self-interested, paternalistic, or ruthlessly suppressive motives may also be important. What the emphasis on motive downplays or rules out is any notion that the *effect* of government conduct on the quantity or quality of speech is of independent first amendment value. In the text, I ultimately deny not only that a focus on content regulation is an efficient method of getting at motive, but I also deny that motive is the *sine qua non* of first amendment violations or that an exclusive focus on government incompetence—which I take to be broader than motive—is the best approach.

In short, I take an eclectic perspective, believing that both negative and positive first amendment approaches need to be synthesized. In this position I am joined by Nimmer, Ely, Tribe, and Stone. The chief difference between their positions and mine concerns the relative value and importance of the content distinction for first amendment analysis. To believe that the content distinction or some similar distinction is valuable, however, in no way commits one to the view that the first amendment is ultimately reducible to a concern about motive. See, e.g., note 46 infra.

Finally, it is, of course, possible to collapse most "positive" approaches into negative approaches and vice versa. However much one emphasizes the positive values of speech, it can be argued that the ultimate concern is the government's incompetence for not figuring it out. Moreover, however much one emphasizes the government's incompetence, it must at least be conceded that speech has positive value for otherwise one would not be concerned about the government's conduct. This deconstructive move should not obscure that a genuine dispute exists and that the outcome of important cases could turn on whether a judge was an eclectic, positive, or negative theorist.

36. See, e.g., U.S. Postal Service v. Council of Greenburgh, 453 U.S. 114, 132 (1981), quoting Consolidated Edison Co. v. Public Service Comm'n, 447 U.S. 530, 536 (1980): "[I]f a governmental regulation is based on the content

of the speech or the message, that action must be scrutinized more carefully to ensure that communication has not been prohibited 'merely because public officials disapprove the speaker's view.'" See also Bogen, "The Supreme Court's Interpretation of the Guarantee of Freedom of Speech," 35 *Md. L. Rev.* 555, 557 (1976) (arguing that the essence of the first amendment is an antipathy to content control, in particular that "The government may not penalize speech because it is opposed to the ideas expressed.").

37. The character of that concern may nonetheless raise first amendment concerns. Government may not disagree with a message but may, nonetheless, have a paternalistic objection to its being received. It may think, for example, that people will place too much emphasis on the information. See, e.g., Virginia Pharmacy Bd. v. Virginia Citizens Council, 425 U.S. 748, 770 (1976) (invalidating state prohibition on the advertising of drug prices; rejecting argument that people will emphasize price over quality of the pharmacist as "highly paternalistic"). See generally Stone, "Content Regulation and the First Amendment," 25 *Wm. & Mary L. Rev.* 189, 228 (1983) (comparing and contrasting animus against speech with paternalistic justifications for suppressing speech).

38. The laws themselves in a significant sense are neutral regarding point of view. In application, however, factfinders must find a statement to be false before it can be considered perjurious or fraudulent.

39. Bogen, supra note 36, at 557 n.19. Cf. Cass, "Perils," supra note 35, at 1485–1486 nn.237–238 (discussing extent to which apparent focus on effects may ultimately be motive-based analysis and that the focus on effects may be prompted by the difficulty of proving iniquitous motives).

40. 308 U.S. 147 (1939).

41. Most commentators including Nimmer argue that this regulation should fail the *O'Brien* test either because the anti-leafleting statute is not essential to the furtherance of the government interest or because the anti-littering interest is not sufficiently substantial. See M. Nimmer, supra note 8 §2.06[A], at 2-92.

42. One might be suspicious of this, for example, in those circumstances where leafleting is banned within airport terminals.

43. Stone, supra note 37, at 232: "[T]he critical motivational inquiry is not whether the government officials would have adopted the restriction even if they did not disfavor the restricted speech, but whether they would have adopted it even if it had been directed at speech that they themselves supported."

44. 308 U.S. at 161.

45. Indeed, the *Schneider* Court relied in part on Lovell v. Griffin, 303 U.S. 444 (1938), observing that the *Lovell* Court had stated that "*whatever the motive,* the ordinance was bad because it imposed penalties for the distribution of pamphlets, which had become historical weapons in the defense of liberty, by subjecting such distribution to license and censorship .... " 308 U.S. at 162 (emphasis added). Of more recent vintage, see Minneapolis

Star & Tribune v. Minnesota Commissioner of Revenue, 460 U.S. 575, 592 (1983) (Court striking down legislation but expressing reluctance to "impugn the motives of the Minnesota legislature . . . . Illicit legislative intent is not the *sine qua non* of a violation of the First Amendment."), citing *Lovell* and *Schneider*.

46. Dean Stone argues that one of the reasons to support a distinction between the degree of scrutiny afforded to content-based and content-neutral regulations is an interest in preventing the distortion of public debate. See, e.g., Stone, supra note 37, at 217–227. He would concede that many content-neutral regulations distort public debate and that very strict scrutiny would often be required. At the same time, he would also concede that many content-based regulations do not deserve strict scrutiny. His general position is discussed later in this chapter. For the moment, it is first worth noting something Stone would also cheerfully concede. The regulation in a case like *Schneider*—falling on the content-neutral side of the dichotomy— threatened substantially to interfere with public debate despite the fact that no particular point of view was singled out for special treatment. Insofar as effect on public debate is concerned, the content-based/content-neutral distinction is overinclusive and underinclusive.

Even if in the general run of cases one were persuaded that one type of regulation was on average likely to be more threatening than the other, that would not necessarily justify the invocation of a differential standard of review. Stone ultimately places heavy emphasis on the inability of courts to sort out which content-based regulations distort public debate and which do not. But his own analysis provides strong reason to doubt the courts' ability to fathom which content-neutral regulations inappropriately distort public debate. Even if one were to accept the patchwork of exceptions Stone supplies to hedge against the overinclusiveness and underinclusiveness, the starting point rests on a judgment about judicial competence that is strongly contestable. For a powerful argument that the content-based/content-neutral distinction is an inadequate proxy for iniquitous effects on public debate, see Redish, "The Content Distinction in First Amendment Analysis," 34 *Stan. L. Rev.* 113, 130–131 (1981).

47. New York Times Co. v. Sullivan, 376 U.S. 254, 270 (1964).

48. H. Kalven, *The Negro and the First Amendment* 204 (1966).

49. Cases like *Schneider* and the defamation line of cases speak against a negative theory of the first amendment. See note 35 supra. There and elsewhere the language of the cases is hostile to negative theory, i.e., the Court routinely extols the affirmative values of speech and acts as if those values make a difference. No negative theorist would deny this. If negative theory has descriptive power, it has to be as a guide to results, not to what the Court has historically thought it has believed.

As to results, in response to a case like *Schneider*, Professor Schauer would concede that it is part of a long line of cases involving speech on property controlled by government that together constitute a "public forum" exception to any descriptive power a negative theory might have in explaining first amendment law. See Schauer, "Cuban Cigars," supra note 35, at 788–789. Although it might be possible to defend constitutional protection for defamation with a strong emphasis on the capacity of decisionmakers to go wrong, it is unlikely that protection for defamatory utterance would proceed without belief in and reliance upon affirmative appreciation for the value of speech. Interestingly, Professor Schauer, in considering constitutional protection for defamation, has advanced a tentative justification that relies upon the affirmative value of speech, rather than the bias of the decisionmaker. See Schauer, "The Role of the People in First Amendment Theory," 74 *Calif. L. Rev.* 761, 785–787 (1986) (suggesting that a system of open commentary on public officials may be the best way to guard against government abuse). See also id. at 782 n.81 (recognizing that any such argument is a part of positive theory not negative theory: "A true negative theory finds its negatives in the process of regulating speech, rather than in the dangers that speech specially prevents."); Schauer, "Public Figures," 25 *Wm. & Mary L. Rev.* 905, 929–935 (1984) (commentary about public officials generally more valuable to society than commentary about certain classes of public figures—and recognizing that the argument does not belong to negative theory). Compare Cass, "Perils," supra note 35, at 1485 n.237 (recognizing that one of the leading defamation cases (*Gertz*) is at odds with negative theory and suggesting that it should be reconsidered). Cass also suggests that affirmative values may be at stake in some defamation cases (see id. at 1459) (discussing the "public goods" aspects of seditious libel though his general discussion of defamation remains firmly rooted in negative theory).

The *O'Brien* test itself further embarrasses the power of any descriptive claim for negative theory (see note 97 infra).

50. 408 U.S. 92, 96 (1972).

51. See generally M. Yudof, *When Government Speaks* (1983); Shiffrin, "Government Speech," 27 *UCLA L. Rev.* 565 (1980).

52. Assessments about the value of speech can be distinguished from point of view discrimination depending, of course, on the definition of point of view discrimination. See note 57 infra.

53. Chaplinsky v. New Hampshire, 315 U.S. 568, 571–572 (1942) (emphasis added).

54. 413 U.S. 49 (1973).

55. 413 U.S. at 61 n.12.

56. Miller v. California, 413 U.S. 15 (1973).

57. See Brockett v. Spokane Arcades, Inc., 472 U.S. 491 (1985). The treatment of such appeals thus discriminates on the basis of point of view. For examples of other exercises of legally permissible point of view discrimination together with a perceptive discussion of determining what should count as point of view discrimination, see Sunstein, "Pornography and the First Amendment," 1986 *Duke L.J.* 589, 609–617.

58. See, e.g., Schauer articles cited in note 59 infra; Stephan, "The First Amendment and Content Discrimination," 68 *Va. L. Rev.* 203 (1982).

59. For perceptive discussion of many of the issues involved at this stage of first amendment analysis, see Schauer, "Categories and the First Amendment: A Play in Three Acts," 34 *Vand. L. Rev.* 265 (1981); Schauer, "Codifying the First Amendment," 1982 *Sup. Ct. Rev.* 285.

60. FCC v. Pacifica Foundation, 438 U.S. 726, 762–763 (1978) (dissenting).

61. Renton v. Playtime Theatres, Inc., 475 U.S. 41, 49 n.2 (1986).

62. Ohralik v. Ohio State Bar Association, 436 U.S. 447, 456 (1978).

63. FCC v. League of Women Voters, 468 U.S. 364, 380 n.13 (1984).

64. Id.

65. M. Nimmer, supra note 8 §2.06[A], at 2–85 to 2–93. In addition, Nimmer argued that "overnarrow" statutes should be invalidated, at least if they did not meet the standards appropriate to the content track. Id. at 2-94 n.36. In part, Nimmer argued for this position because overnarrow statutes (those which regulate expressive conduct, but not regulating non-expressive conduct implicating the same purported governmental interest) may better be placed on the content track than on the conduct track.

66. See also the discussion of *Schneider,* supra, text accompanying notes 40–46.

67. 458 U.S. 747 (1982).

68. Id. at 759–760.

69. Id. at 760.

70. Id.

71. This was not Nimmer's terminology. He called content track restrictions "anti-speech" restrictions.

72. M. Nimmer, supra note 8 §2.04, at 2-25 (emphasis added).

73. See 458 U.S. at 759 & n.10.

74. But see Schauer, "Codifying the First Amendment," supra note 59, at 302 (1982) ("[W]here, as in *Ferber*, the state interest is not with the effect of that content on viewers, the special dangers of content regulation are absent, and the case is one more of format discrimination than content discrimination.").

75. 458 U.S. at 757 n.8

76. Nonetheless, the Court emphasized that the government action in *Ferber* implicated no "question . . . of censoring a particular literary theme." Id. at 763. See Stone, "Comment: Anti-Pornography Legislation as Viewpoint-Discrimination," 9 *Harv. J. L. & Pub. Pol'y* 461, 471–472 (1986) (emphasizing the viewpoint-neutrality of the restriction).

77. There are strong reasons, for example, to doubt the Court's willingness or capacity to unearth hostility when facially content-neutral regulations are at issue. (See, e.g., discussion of *O'Brien,* infra). See generally Redish, supra note 46, at 132–133; cf. Karst, "The Costs of Motive-Centered Inquiry," 15 *San Diego L. Rev.* 1163 (1978) (discussing reluctance of courts to find improper motives by governmental actors in equal protection context).

78. Adderley v. Florida, 385 U.S. 39 (1966).

79. 408 U.S. 104, 116 (1972).

80. Id. at 116.

81. Perry Educ. Ass'n v. Perry Local Educators' Ass'n, 460 U.S. 37, 45 (1983).

82. Hague v. CIO, 307 U.S. 496, 515 (1939).

83. 466 U.S. 789 (1984).

84. Alternatively, it might have assumed that the street was the relevant public forum and that placing signs on utility poles was one *manner* of communicating in a public forum. It could then have proceeded to inquire whether the manner of regulation was reasonable. See Quadres, "Content-Neutral Public Forum Regulations: The Rise of the Aesthetic State Interest, the Fall of Judicial Scrutiny," 37 *Hastings L.J.* 439, 451 n.64 (1986). For various phrasings of tests applicable to manner regulations, see note 122 infra.

Finally, it might have asked whether the manner of communication was compatible with the use to which the property had been lawfully dedicated and declined to ask whether any particular property was a public forum. For a powerful argument for the view that asking whether property is a public forum is the wrong question, see Farber & Nowak, "The Misleading Nature of Public Forum Analysis," 70 *Va. L. Rev.* 1219 (1984).

85. But see note 90 infra.

86. *Perry,* 460 U.S. at 46.

87. *Vincent,* 466 U.S. at 804.

88. Id.

89. No pun intended.

90. *Vincent,* 466 U.S. at 815 n.32. If the issue were to be characterized in such terms, the Court declared that the right of access to utility poles was not "comparable" to that previously "recognized" for public streets and parks. Id. at 814. If the concept of tradition is susceptible to narrow or capacious readings, the *Vincent* rendition surely counts as an instance of reading tradition in a narrow fashion. Cf. Stone, "Content-Neutral Restrictions," 54 *U. Chi. L. Rev.* 46, 97 n.204 (1987) (Court denial of a traditional right to post signs on utility poles is "both off-hand and questionable"). See generally Quadres, supra note 84, at 451 n.64.

91. See id.

92. Karst, "Equality as a Central Principle in the First Amendment," 43 *U. Chi. L. Rev.* 20, 42 (1975) (referring in a different first amendment context to Court pretense that particular state justifications were to be taken seriously).

93. Those uninitiated to Supreme Court discourse might suppose that the *O'Brien* test would be applied in future contests over access to government property. The question was presented the very next year in *Cornelius v. NAACP Legal Defense and Educational Fund, Inc.,* 473 U.S. 788 (1985). The Fund argued that its exclusion from a federal charity drive aimed at federal employees constituted a violation of its first amendment rights.

Among other things, the Fund argued that a crazy patchwork of "charitable" organizations had been allowed to participate including the Moral Majority. The Fund claimed a right of access to government property to solicit funds for its organization in the regular charitable solicitation drive. In approaching the question, the Court did not do two things: first, it did not mention the *O'Brien* test; second, it did not mention the *O'Brien* case. Rather it asked whether the charitable solicitation drive was a traditional public forum, determined that it was not, further determined that the exclusion of legal defense and political advocacy organization appeared reasonable, but concluded that it did not have enough facts to know whether the government had discriminated on the basis of point of view, and remanded the case to the lower courts for further litigation on that issue. The *O'Brien* test simply disappeared; *Vincent* was cited in passing (only in support of the proposition that an otherwise reasonable state interest in barring access to a nonpublic forum will not suffice if that interest is a "facade for viewpoint-based discrimination"; id. at 811).

94. Sometimes the test applied is less stringent. See, e.g., Arcara v. Cloud Books, Inc., 478 U.S. 697 (1986) (*O'Brien* test would be too stringent under circumstances where building housing bookstore was ordered closed for one year because of illicit sexual activities on the premises). See notes 97 & 122 infra, addressing notion that *O'Brien* is toothless. Sometimes the test applied is more stringent than *O'Brien*. See, e.g., Roberts v. United States Jaycees, 468 U.S. 609 (1984) (alleged infringement on right of expressive association requires showing of compelling state interests by means that could not be achieved in less restrictive way). Sometimes the test is close to the *O'Brien* test. See note 122 infra.

Dean Stone has catalogued seven standards that have been articulated with respect to content-neutral regulations. See Stone, supra note 90, at 48–50. Even those seven have many variations in linguistic formulation, variations that as worded would make a difference if taken seriously. See note 122 infra. Dean Stone argues that the seven can be reduced to three: deferential review, intermediate review, and strict review. See id. at 50–54. The variety and grossness of those categories suggests that to know that a regulation is on the conduct track is to know very little about how the regulation will be treated.

95. Zacharias, "Flowcharting the First Amendment," 72 *Cornell L. Rev.* 936, 968 n.170 (1987). For the point that this form of balancing follows from the Court's failure to determine whether cognizable expressive interests were present in *O'Brien*, see Werhan, "The *O'Brien*ing of Free Speech Methodology," 19 *Ariz. St. L.J.* 635, 642 (1987).

96. 466 U.S. at 805 (emphasis added).

97. Professor Schauer argues that the *O'Brien* test in application is in reality a form of toothless scrutiny even though it is "open linguistically to the possibility of some bite." Schauer, "Cuban Cigars," supra note 35, at 787–788. This conclusion was important if his negative theory of the first

amendment (see note 35 supra) was to have any descriptive power. Indeed, he also believes that the normative value of a theory depends in part upon its descriptive power. See Schauer, "The Role of the People," supra note 49, at 773–774. The challenge presented by the *O'Brien* test to negative theory is that it purports to apply first amendment review to government regulations that have an *incidental* impact on speech without regard for a showing of illicit motive. But see note 39 supra. The difficulty with Schauer's characterization of the *O'Brien* test as toothless (a characterization shared by Stone—see note 122 infra) is that it focuses on the Supreme Court and does not take into account the application of the test in the lower courts. It thus generalizes from a small and unrepresentative sample of cases. It might be possible to argue that the lower courts have just not caught on, but it is doubtful that the Court intends the *O'Brien* test or the related time, place, and manner test in its various incarnations (see note 122 infra) to be toothless. First, if it intends no or next to no scrutiny it knows how to say so (see *Arcara,* cited in note 94), though admittedly carelessness and the absence of candor can not be ruled out. Second, if it so intended it might have more regularly policed the lower courts' handling of the test than it has. Third, if it intended the test to be genuinely toothless, it would be difficult to understand why it would struggle so hard in a case like *Arcara* to avoid the invocation of the test. In any event, as a descriptive matter, at the moment, the very existence of the *O'Brien* test challenges negative theory, and first amendment law as it functions in the lower courts gives more teeth to the *O'Brien* test than is revealed by the few cases handled by the Supreme Court. See note 122 infra.

98. Some commentators think the wording of the test does not match the real message which they think is to do nothing. See notes 97 supra & 122 infra. My reading is somewhat different. The Court is saying: do not apply strict scrutiny, but beyond that we have nothing to say except that saying nothing sounds more lawlike when we accompany it with an incantation of some obvious all-purpose factors to consider.

99. J. Ely, *Democracy and Distrust* 114 (1980).

100. Id. at 110 (emphasis in original).

101. Id. at 113–116.

102. 418 U.S. 323 (1974).

103. Id. at 325.

104. The Court indicated that it would not lightly abandon the interest in protecting someone's good name or the state interest in compensating individuals for defamatory falsehoods (id. at 341), and it also indicated that it was "especially anxious to assure to the freedoms of speech and press that 'breathing space' essential to their fruitful exercise." Id. at 342.

105. New York v. Ferber, 458 U.S. 747, 756 (1982). *Ferber's* language is rare. The Court had previously been reluctant to admit that free speech values had been compromised in the obscenity context. *Ferber's* description of the relevant state interests, however, is somewhat incomplete. Although concern about unwilling recipients was the most prominent concern in the

case in which the current obscenity standard was announced (see Miller v. California, 413 U.S. 15 (1973)), a broader array of state interests were said to be indicated in the companion case (see Paris Adult Theatre I v. Slaton, 413 U.S. 49 (1973)), and the presence of unwilling recipients is not a necessary prerequisite for an obscenity prosecution. See id.

106. *Paris Adult Theatre I,* 413 U.S. at 62.

107. See id. at 60–61. In particular, see id. at 60 n.11.

108. Consolidated Edison Co. v. Public Serv. Comm'n, 447 U.S. 530, 540 (1980).

109. See, e.g., Central Hudson Gas & Elec. Corp. v. Public Serv. Comm'n, 447 U.S. 557, 566 (1980) (regulation must directly advance a substantial state interest in a way that is not more extensive than necessary to meet that interest). Recall that *O'Brien* required that a regulation "further" (without a directness requirement stated) a substantial or important state interest with restrictions on freedom of speech no greater than essential to the furtherance of the interest. For discussion of the relationship between the *O'Brien* test and the commercial speech cases, see Werhan, supra note 95, at 663–673.

110. FCC v. League of Women Voters, 468 U.S. 364, 376, 380 (1984) (restriction must be narrowly tailored to meet a substantial state interest; compelling state interest not required).

111. See *Central Hudson,* supra note 109 (invalidating conservation ordinance).

112. Posadas de Puerto Rico Associates v. Tourism Co., 478 U.S. 328 (1986) (upholding regulation that prohibited advertising of casino gambling to Puerto Rican residents, but permitted advertising of horse racing, cockfighting, and the state lottery to such residents and permitted advertising of casino gambling to nonresident tourists).

113. 424 U.S. 1 (1976).

114. Id. at 16–18.

115. Id. at 25.

116. Id. at 25.

117. See, e.g., Nicholson, "Buckley v. Valeo: The Constitutionality of the Federal Election Campaign Act Amendments of 1974," 1977 *Wis. L. Rev.* 323.

118. See Farber, "Content Regulation and the First Amendment," 68 *Geo. L.J.* 727, 747 (1980).

119. In fact, it is even more complicated because the Court also has to attend to its prior precedents and any evidence of the framers' intent. I do not regard the listing of general factors to evidence an exclusively instrumental approach to decisionmaking. I ultimately argue that how we decide free speech cases in part turns on who we think we are as a people and what kind of people we want to be. I consider that to be both a part of first amendment values and a part of the judgment as to their importance in particular contexts. That is, we daily constitute and reconstitute ourselves.

Standards of review themselves connote in even stronger ways an instrumental cast of mind. Even there, those who use standards of review may themselves recognize that the identification of ends and the determination of their importance in deciding who we are as a people is often the most important aspect of the decisions made. For criticisms of instrumental rationality from quite different stances, compare Tribe, "Technology Assessment and the Fourth Discontinuity: The Limits of Instrumental Rationality," 46 *S. Cal. L. Rev.* 617 (1973), and Tribe, "Policy Science: Analysis or Ideology?" 2 *Phil. & Pub. Aff.* 66 (1972), with Nagel, "Rationalism in Constitutional Law," 4 *Const. Commentary* 9 (1987), and Nagel, "The Formulaic Constitution," 84 *Mich. L. Rev.* 165 (1985).

120. Such factors may be of less significance in particular cases and not be mentioned. That they are not referred to in a particular case would not necessarily warrant the judgment that they had been forgotten or ignored.

121. It is all too easy to slip into mathematical metaphor in discussing the consideration of multiple considerations in decisionmaking. As Owen Fiss states in a related context, "The terms used have an attractively quantitative ring. They make the task of judicial judgment appear to involve as little discretion as when a salesman advises a customer whether a pair of shoes fit. . . . [But, in] contrast to the case of shoes, the concept . . . has no quantitative content. It only sounds quantitative—as do the words 'how much' when used to describe the intensity of affection." Fiss, "Groups and the Equal Protection Clause," 5 *Phil. & Pub. Aff.* 107, 120–121 (1976).

122. Another revealing example of this phenomenon is the line of cases which have purported to state the test for judging the constitutionality of time, place, and manner restrictions, at least when public forums such as parks and streets are concerned. For example, Heffron v. International Society for Krishna Consciousness, Inc., 452 U.S. 640, 648 (1981), quoting Virginia Pharmacy Board v. Virginia Citizens Consumer Council, 425 U.S. 748, 771 (1976), stated such restrictions to be permissible if they are "'justified without reference to the content of the regulated speech, that they serve a significant governmental interest, and that in doing so they leave open ample alternative channels for communication of the information.'" But the test is differently stated in different cases. For example, U.S. Postal Service v. Council of Greenburgh, 453 U.S. 114, 132 (1981), spoke of "adequate" as opposed to "ample" alternative channels of communication, and City of Renton v. Playtime Theatres, Inc., 475 U.S. 41 (1986), transcended the difference by requiring that the restriction not "unreasonably limit" alternative channels of communication. Beyond these terminological shifts, a number of cases stated that the regulation must be "narrowly tailored" to serve a significant government interest as opposed to just serving a significant government interest. See, e.g., Perry Educ. Ass'n v. Perry Local Educators' Ass'n, 460 U.S. 37, 45 (1983); U.S. v. Grace, 461 U.S. 171, 178 (1983).

An interesting puzzle for those schooled in this form of casuistry (for example litigants and judges in the lower courts) was to wonder how the time, place, and manner test differed from the *O'Brien* test and to determine which test applied when. Only one prepared to learn that the Emperor had no clothes would have summoned the temerity to ask *why* these different sets of tests had developed in the first place. To be sure, if the concern is with a regulation's "incidental" impact on free speech, it makes sense to inquire whether means less restrictive of free speech are available. So too, if a place restriction on free speech is in question, it makes sense to wonder about alternative possibilities for communication. Nonetheless, if a place restriction limits speech, it would also make sense to inquire whether the state objectives could be achieved by means less restrictive of speech. Similarly, depending on what the "incidental" restriction might be, it could make sense to consider alternative channels of, or possibilities for, communication as one means of evaluating the severity of the restriction.

One of the many maneuvers in City Council v. Taxpayers for Vincent, 466 U.S. 789 (1984), was casually to conflate the "narrowly tailored" version of the reasonable time, place, and manner test together with the *O'Brien* test—as if they were the same—and Clark v. Community For Creative Non-Violence, 468 U.S. 288, 298 (1984), explicitly stated that the standard applied to time, place, and manner restrictions is "little, if any, different" from the *O'Brien* test. All this, among other things, despite the fact that the time, place, and manner test requires a showing of "ample" (*Clark*) or "adequate" (*Vincent*) alternative channels of communication and *O'Brien,* by its terms, at least, does not.

Dean Stone, for one, argues that the two tests are functionally similar in that when either test applies, the government regulation is upheld. Stone, supra note 90, at 52 (1987). This is a plausible reading of the small number of Supreme Court cases that have applied these tests, but Stone's conclusion has nothing to do with the law as it has functioned in the lower courts. Not only have restrictions been struck down under both of the tests, but the lower courts have frequently struggled with the Court's meanderings in an attempt to figure out which test to apply, sometimes with the view that determining which test or version of the test to apply might matter. For a sample, see Century Communications Corp. v. FCC, 835 F.2d 292 (D.C. Cir. 1987), *cert. denied,* 108 S. Ct. 2014 (1988); Olivieri v. Ward, 801 F.2d 602 (2d Cir. 1986); City of Watseka v. Illinois Pub. Action Council, 796 F.2d 1547 (7th Cir. 1986), *aff'd,* 479 U.S. 1048 (1987); Wisconsin Action Coalition v. City of Kenosha, 767 F.2d 1248 (7th Cir. 1985); Avalon Cinema Corp. v. Thompson, 667 F.2d 659 (8th Cir. 1981); Women Strike For Peace v. Morton, 472 F.2d 1273 (D.C. Cir. 1972); Breen v. Kahl, 419 F.2d 1034 (7th Cir. 1969), *cert. denied,* 398 U.S. 937 (1970).

As I send this book to the publisher to meet a publication deadline, Ward v. Rock Against Racism, 57 U.S.L.W. 4879 (U.S. June 22, 1989), has arrived in Ithaca. There Justice Kennedy, speaking for the Court, reasserts that the *O'Brien* test is little different from the time, place, and manner test, and then states: "Lest any confusion on the point remain, we reaffirm today that a regulation of the time, place, or manner of protected speech must be narrowly tailored to serve the government's legitimate content-neutral interests but that it need not be the least-restrictive or least-intrusive means of doing so. Rather, the requirement of narrow tailoring is satisfied 'so long as the . . . regulation promotes a substantial government interest that would be achieved less effectively absent the regulation.'" Id. at 4884. Justice Marshall, dissenting, joined by Justices Brennan and Stevens, complains of the Court's "serious distortion of the narrowly tailoring requirement" and states that the Court's rejection of the less restrictive alternative test relies on "language in a few opinions . . . taken out of context." Id. at 4886.

Although *Rock Against Racism*'s rendition of the case law is an inventive piece of law office history, at least the Court paid attention to the test it was using.

123. See the commercial advertising cases cited in notes 109 & 112 supra.

124. See Ohralik v. Ohio State Bar Ass'n, 436 U.S. 447, 455–456 (1978).

125. Renton v. Playtime Theatres, Inc., 475 U.S. 41, 49 n.2 (1986).

126. See the several opinions exalting public speech over private speech in Dun & Bradstreet v. Greenmoss Builders, Inc., 472 U.S. 749 (1985). In particular, see id. at 758 n.5 (plurality opinion). See also Connick v. Myers, 461 U.S. 138 (1983).

127. CSC v. Letter Carriers, 413 U.S. 548 (1973). For powerful criticism, see Redish, supra note 46.

128. New York Times Co. v. United States, 403 U.S. 713, 714 (1971).

129. United States v. Progressive, Inc., 467 F. Supp. 990 (W.D. Wis. 1979) (preliminary injunction issued Mar. 28, 1979), *request for writ of mandamus den. sub nom.* Morland v. Sprecher, 443 U.S. 709 (1979), *case dismissed,* Nos. 79-1428, 79-1664 (7th Cir. Oct. 1, 1979). On a narrow reading, the decision to issue a preliminary injunction in the *Progressive* case was merely a decision to preserve the status quo pending final adjudication. Nonetheless, the District Judge went further, finding, for example, that the "objected-to portions of the article fall within the narrow area recognized . . . in which a prior restraint . . . is appropriate" (id. at 996) and finding the "likelihood of direct, immediate and irreparable injury to our nation and its people" (id. at 1000). Even beyond the *Progressive* case, political speech can be routinely subject to a system of prior restraints when it appears in the medium of film. See Times Film Corp. v. Chicago, 365 U.S. 43 (1961) (in order to prevent obscene films, all films can be subjected to a licensing scheme). Such schemes could result in the delay of wholly protected material (although some safeguards exist, see Freedman v. Maryland, 380 U.S. 51 (1965)), but should not result in a permanent restraint. This may make such schemes more palatable, but they do not justify a licensing scheme in my view. Finally, sweeping statements about the immunity of political speech from prior restraints are excessively confident about the ease of distinguishing between political speech and commercial speech. For a sample of the difficulties, see Shiffrin, "The First Amendment and Economic Regulation: Away from a General Theory of the First Amendment," 78 *Nw. U.L. Rev.* 1212 (1983).

130. Stone, supra note 37, at 189. See also Stone, supra note 90, at 46: "The content-based/content-neutral distinction plays a central role in contemporary first amendment jurisprudence."

131. Stone, supra note 37, at 196–197. But cf. Stone, supra note 90, at 54: "[I]t has been suggested that the emergence of the content-based/content-neutral distinction has produced 'a two-tiered approach' to first amendment cases: 'while regulations that turn on the content of the expression are subjected to a strict form of judicial review,' content-neutral regulations 'receive only a minimal level of scrutiny.' The Court's frequent use of the intermediate and strict standards belies this suggestion. Although the Court at times may underestimate the extent to which content-neutral restrictions threaten first amendment values, it does not test all such restrictions with a 'minimal level of scrutiny.'"

132. In addition, as Stone himself recognizes, content-neutral restrictions are frequently tested by demanding standards. See id.

133. Stone, supra note 37, 200–233.

134. See FCC v. Pacifica Foundation, 438 U.S. 726 (1978).

135. Stone, supra note 37, at 243.

136. Id.

137. Id. at 244.

138. See generally Stone, "Restrictions of Speech Because of Its Content: The Peculiar Case of Subject-Matter Restrictions," 46 *U. Chi. L. Rev.* 81 (1978).

139. Id. at 113.

140. Stone, supra note 37, at 244.

141. The extent of the burden of justification would depend upon the degree of interference with communication. "The greater the interference with effective communication, the greater the burden on government to justify the restriction." Id. at 190.

142. 475 U.S. 41 (1986).

143. Id. at 48–49.

144. Stone, supra note 138, at 111–112.

145. Stone, supra note 37, at 194–197.

146. Id. at 195–196.

147. Id. at 195 n.24.

148. Id.

149. Id. at 194–195.

150. Id. at 195.

151. Id. at 196.

152. Brandenburg v. Ohio, 395 U.S. 444, 447 (1969).

153. See Gitlow v. New York, 268 U.S. 652 (1925); Whitney v. California, 274 U.S. 357 (1927).

154. Whitney v. California, 274 U.S. 357, 372 (1957) (Brandeis, J., concurring); Gitlow v. New York, 268 U.S. 652, 672 (Holmes, J., dissenting); Abrams v. United States, 250 U.S. 616, 624 (1919) (Holmes, J., dissenting).

155. Stone himself may personally reject the views of Holmes and Bran-

deis and ally himself, at least to an extent, with scholars like Judge Bork (see Bork, "Neutral Principles and Some First Amendment Problems," 47 *Ind. L.J.* 1 (1971)), thus regarding the speech as of low value. In so doing, he would not need to go as far as Judge Bork (i.e., he need not deny any protection for advocacy of illegal action), and he could afford quite substantial protection for speech that did not advocate illegal conduct but which created a clear and present danger nonetheless. Even on this understanding, however, Stone's scheme, which would depend upon rejecting the views of Holmes and Brandeis, could not pass as a description of the Court's stated views in the area, at least in the past quarter of a century.

156. Time, Inc. v. Hill, 385 U.S. 374, 406 (1967) (Harlan, J., concurring in part and dissenting in part).

157. 418 U.S. at 339–340.

158. J. S. Mill, *On Liberty* 18 (D. Spitz ed. 1975).

159. 418 U.S. at 344 n.9.

160. See Stone, supra note 37, at 194 n.15.

161. Id. at 195.

162. Of course, that depends on what the orthodoxy is. Dean Stone has suggested to me in correspondence that: "The central meaning of the first amendment is that government may not suppress a point of view because the government fears its citizens will adopt that point of view in the political process. No category of low value expression comes even close to violating that principle." Letter of March 16, 1989. As I suggest in Chapter 2, however, any such "central meaning" would be too narrow.

163. I should emphasize that by this statement I do not mean to deny that some factors are more important than others or that some factors may not exercise particularly strong force in particular decisionmaking areas. For example, although there are exceptions, the principle against point-of-view discrimination is an important first amendment principle and the existence of that principle influences decisions. I do not mean to deny that first amendment doctrine has created a set of presumptions or that certain of those presumptions might not be very strong. I do insist that none of these principles (for a helpful list, see Blasi, "The Pathological Perspective and the First Amendment," 85 *Colum. L. Rev.* 449, 460 (1985)) can serve as an organizing vehicle for first amendment law, and I counsel suspicion that any general principle will function in an absolute way in all times and circumstances.

2. The First Amendment and Democracy

1. See New York Times Co. v. Sullivan, 376 U.S. 254, 273 (1964).

2. A. Meiklejohn, *Political Freedom* 27 (1960).

3. Id. at 20–27.

4. Id. at 37.

5. Id. at 79.

6. See, e.g., G. Anastaplo, *The Constitutionalist* (1971); BeVier, "The First Amendment and Political Speech: An Inquiry into the Substance and

Limits of Principle," 30 *Stan. L. Rev.* 299 (1978); Bloustein, "The First Amendment and Privacy: The Supreme Court Justice and the Philosopher," 28 *Rutgers L. Rev.* 41 (1974); Bork, "Neutral Principles and Some First Amendment Problems," 47 *Ind. L.J.* 1 (1971); Kalven, "The New York Times Case: A Note on 'The Central Meaning of the First Amendment,'" 1964 *Sup. Ct. Rev.* 191; Meiklejohn, "Public Speech and the First Amendment," 55 *Geo. L.J.* 234 (1966); Sunstein, "Hard Defamation Cases," 25 *Wm. & Mary L. Rev.* 891 (1984).

7. A. Meiklejohn, supra note 2, at 79.

8. Indeed the theory was so interpreted the year after Meiklejohn's first discussion of his theory appeared. Chafee, "Book Review," 62 *Harv. L. Rev.* 891, 896 (1949). The criticisms contained in Chafee's review (largely repeated here) have never been effectively answered. For other valuable critical commentary, see, e.g., L. Bollinger, *The Tolerant Society* 46–53, 145–158, 168–174 (1986); Blasi, "The Checking Value in First Amendment Theory," 1977 *Am. B. Found. Research J.* 523, 554–567; Redish, "The Value of Free Speech," 130 *U. Pa. L. Rev.* 591, 596–611 (1982).

9. Meiklejohn, "The First Amendment Is an Absolute," 1961 *Sup. Ct. Rev.* 245, 256.

10. This, of course, is not the exclusive basis for voter decisionmaking, but that it is a significant variable is a proposition few would deny. See generally M. Burgoon, *Approaching Speech Communication* 25–54 (1974); J. McCroskey & L. Wheeless, *Introduction to Human Communication* 350 (1976); D. Nimmo & R. Savage, *Candidates and Their Images* (1976); Andersen & Clevenger, "A Summary of Experimental Research in Ethos," 30 *Speech Monographs* 59 (1963).

11. See Nimmo & Savage, supra note 10.

12. See, e.g., T. Clevenger, *Audience Analysis* (1966); G. Miller & M. Burgoon, *New Techniques of Persuasion* (1973); P. Zimbardo, E. Ebbesen & C. Maslach, *Influencing Attitudes and Changing Behavior* (2d ed. 1977).

13. The best evidence of this intent is the address of the Continental Congress in 1774 to the people of Quebec, in which it is stated that the purpose of freedom of press, "besides the advancement of truth, science, morality, and arts in general, [lies] in its diffusion of liberal sentiments on the administration of Government, its ready communication of thought between subjects, and its consequential promotion of union among them, whereby oppressive officers are shamed or intimidated, into more honorable and just modes of conducting affairs." G. Anastaplo, supra note 6, at 537 n.100 (quoting 1 *J. Continental Congress, 1774–1789,* at 108 (1904)). Anastaplo, who argues that except for prior restraints, id. at 537 n.100, the Founders intended to confine first amendment protection to political speech, id. at 123, has his greatest difficulty with this passage. He submits that even this letter "puts the emphasis on the 'political,'" which, of course, does nothing to support the view that the first amendment is exclusively political insofar as subsequent restraints are concerned. He further suggests that perhaps the letter means that art is advanced because of the general politi-

cal freedoms, a suggestion which places insufficient weight on the use of the word "besides." Finally, he suggests that art is advanced by its protection from prior restraints. This is better, but it points to the principal weakness in the historical argument: It is one thing to show that the Founders focused on political speech; it is quite another to show they intended that only political speech be protected from subsequent restraints. Nor is it surprising that the Founders did not worry much aloud about threats to the protection of literature. Attempts to censor literature on obscenity grounds, for example, did not become significant until the nineteenth century. Kalven, "The Metaphysics of the Law of Obscenity," 1960 *Sup. Ct. Rev.* 1, 2.

14. More narrowly, the Court confined such showings to defamatory falsehoods relating to the public official's official conduct. 376 U.S. at 279.

15. Id. at 270 (emphasis added).

16. Id. at 273.

17. Id. at 291, citing City of Chicago v. Tribune Co., 139 N.E. 86, 88 (1923).

18. Kalven, supra note 6, at 194.

19. Id. at 209.

20. Id. at 221.

21. Id. at 221 n.125.

22. See Kalven, supra note 13, at 16.

23. See Kalven, "The Reasonable Man and the First Amendment: Hill, Butts, and Walker," 1967 *Sup. Ct. Rev.* 267, 294–295, 304–305.

24. See id.

25. Some closet—the pages of the *Supreme Court Review.* But, Kalven is a skillful advocate. Despite his rejection of the Meiklejohn theory, he was widely perceived as the foremost advocate of the Meiklejohn position and he defined what it was to mean in practice.

26. Kalven, supra note 6, at 205.

27. Id. at 209.

28. See id. at 214.

29. See id. at 214–216 (discussing particular forms of balancing and the idiom associated with it as well as "two-level theory"). See Shiffrin, "Two-Level Theory," in 4 *Encyclopedia of the American Constitution* 1930 (1986).

30. Kalven, supra note 6, at 221.

31. Brennan, "The Supreme Court and the Meiklejohn Interpretation of the First Amendment," 79 *Harv. L. Rev.* 1, 16 (1965), quoting Kalven, supra note 6, at 208.

32. Id. at 19, quoting Garrison v. Louisiana, 379 U.S. 64, 75 (1964).

33. Id. at 16, quoting Kalven, supra note 6, at 208.

34. 379 U.S. 64, 74–75.

35. Id. at 75 (emphasis added), quoting *New York Times Co. v. Sullivan,* 376 U.S. at 270.

36. See id.

37. In his plurality opinion in Rosenbloom v. Metromedia, 403 U.S. 29, 43–44 (1971) (emphasis added), Brennan stated that "We honor the commit-

ment to robust debate on public issues, which is embodied in the First Amendment, by extending constitutional protection to all discussion and communication involving *matters of public or general concern,* without regard to whether the persons involved are famous or anonymous." He made no distinction between matters of public or general *concern* and matters of general or public *interest.* See id. at 44–45.

38. 468 U.S. 364 (1984).

39. Id. at 375–376.

40. Id. at 381.

41. Id. at 381, quoting NAACP v. Claiborne Hardware Co., 458 U.S. 886, 913 (1982), quoting Carey v. Brown, 447 U.S. 455, 467 (1980).

42. Id. at 383, quoting Whitney v. California, 274 U.S. 357, 375 (1927) (Brandeis, J., concurring).

43. Id. at 393 (emphasis added).

44. 425 U.S. 748 (1976).

45. Id. at 763.

46. Id. at 765.

47. Id. at 764–765.

48. But see Stephan, "The First Amendment and Content Discrimination," 68 *Va. L. Rev.* 203, 206 (1982) (recognizing the tension between recognizing hierarchies of speech and a broad notion of content-neutrality and contending that any "broad content neutrality rule is indefensible").

49. Of course, in Justice Brennan's reckoning some speech was outside the scope of the first amendment altogether, e.g., perjury. If it got within the scope of the amendment, however, Brennan resisted distinctions based on the speech's value.

50. 427 U.S. 50 (1976).

51. Id. at 70.

52. Id.

53. See Rostker v. Goldberg, 453 U.S. 57 (1981) (Court, joined by Stevens, J., upholds draft registration of males but not females against gender discrimination claim).

54. 427 U.S. at 85–86 (Stewart, J., dissenting).

55. Id. at 87, quoting Winters v. New York, 333 U.S. 507, 528 (Frankfurter, J., dissenting).

56. Renton v. Playtime Theatres, Inc., 475 U.S. 41, 49 n.2 (1986).

57. FCC v. Pacifica Foundation, 438 U.S. 726 (1978).

58. 425 U.S. 748 (1976).

59. Dun & Bradstreet, Inc. v. Greenmoss Builders, Inc., 472 U.S. 749 (1985) (nonmedia defamation); Connick v. Myers, 461 U.S. 138 (1983) (public employee discharge).

60. J. Ely, *Democracy and Distrust: A Theory of Judicial Review* 5 & 7 (1980) (emphasis added).

61. J. Choper, *Judicial Review and the National Political Process: A Functional Reconsideration of the Role of the Supreme Court* 4 (1980).

62. I do not mean to suggest that Ely and Choper ignore that literature.

Indeed, one of the many contributions of Choper's book is its recognition of the importance of connecting democratic theory with the actual functioning of the political system, and in the course of his analysis, he relies heavily on political science literature. His analysis is much influenced by the pluralism of Robert Dahl, and Choper laments that the "empirical evidence is relatively sparse and undoubtedly more remains to be discovered than ever will be." J. Choper, supra note 61, at 38. Choper would be among the first to recognize that his conclusions and Dahl's conclusions are contestable. For some of the work criticizing Dahl's conclusions, see sources cited in note 94 infra.

63. In recent years important dissents to that perspective have finally appeared in the legal literature. See, e.g., Fiss, "Foreword: The Forms of Justice," 93 *Harv. L. Rev.* 1, 5–17 (1979); Brest, "The Fundamental Rights Controversy: The Essential Contradictions of Normative Constitutional Scholarship," 90 *Yale L.J.* 1063, 1096–1105 (1981); Sager, "Rights Skepticism and Process-Based Responses," 56 *N.Y.U. L. Rev.* 417, 441–445 (1981); Chemerinsky, "The Price of Asking the Wrong Question: An Essay on Constitutional Scholarship and Judicial Review," 62 *Tex. L. Rev.* 1207 (1984); Ackerman, "The Storrs Lectures: Discovering the Constitution," 93 *Yale L.J.* 1013 (1984); Michelman, "Foreword: Traces of Self-Government," 100 *Harv. L. Rev.* 4, 16 (1986); Elfenbein, "The Myth of Conservatism as a Constitutional Philosophy," 71 *Iowa L. Rev.* 401 (1986).

64. Alexander Bickel's *The Least Dangerous Branch* (1962) significantly influenced the terms of the debate in contemporary constitutional scholarship: "The root difficulty is that judicial review is a counter-majoritarian force in our system." Id. at 16. Bickel's understanding of politics was by no means unsophisticated. His crucial move, however, was by definitional fiat: "[A]lthough democracy does not mean constant reconsideration of decisions once made, it does mean that a representative majority has the power to accomplish a reversal. This power is of the essence, and no less so because it is often merely held in reserve." Id. at 17. If, of course, this is what democracy *means,* much discussion would be required to reconcile the institution of judicial review with democracy. There is, then, as Bickel put it, a "counter-majoritarian difficulty." Id. at 16.

65. Some American legal scholars, for example, Dean Sandalow, would simply dispense with judicial review if legislation reflected a "deliberate and broadly based political decision" such as an enactment by the Congress "after full debate" or an enactment recently passed by most states. Sandalow, "Judicial Protection of Minorities," 75 *Mich. L. Rev.* 1162, 1186–1187 (1977). See also Sandalow, "The Distrust of Politics," 56 *N.Y.U. L. Rev.* 446 (1981); Sandalow, "Racial Preferences in Higher Education," 42 *U. Chi. L. Rev.* 653 (1975).

66. See, e.g., Sager, supra note 63, at 441–445; Elfenbein, supra note 63, at 479–484.

67. But see Sandalow, "Judicial Protection of Minorities," supra note 65.

68. Neither would confine the rights enforcement aspects of judicial review to "minority rights." Choper, for example, states that "[t]he political theory ordained by the Constitution forbids popular majorities to abridge certain rights of individuals even when the latter may be part of the majority and even though their interests may be forcefully represented and carefully considered in the political process." J. Choper, supra note 61, at 64.

69. The emphasis on the discrete and insular character of minorities derives from dictum in United States v. Carolene Products Co., 304 U.S. 144, 152 n.4 (1938). Great emphasis upon it is placed in J. Ely, supra note 60. For sharp criticism of the emphasis upon discreteness and insularity, see Ackerman, "Beyond Carolene Products," 98 *Harv. L. Rev.* 713 (1985). For a powerful general attack on the notion that the representational character of legislative acts should be a major judicial concern, see Van Alstyne, "Interpreting *This* Constitution," 35 *U. Fla. L. Rev.* 209, 215–225 (1983).

70. J. Ely, supra note 60, at 93–94. See also J. Choper, supra note 61, at 71 (discussing Court's role in "affording all participants in the democratic process a full and fair opportunity to influence the promulgation and alteration of policies affecting them").

71. To make a substance/process distinction would, of course, itself constitute the making of a substantive choice, and no such choice could ever be implemented without an underlying—and perhaps (in the end) a full—conception of substantive rights and values. See generally Tribe, "The Puzzling Persistence of Process-Based Constitutional Theories," 89 *Yale L.J.* 1063 (1980).

72. Although Ely would not limit the first amendment to political speech even if the term could be determinately defined, he states that the attribution of nonpolitical functions to the first amendment "has the smell of the lamp about it" and has a "highly elitist cast." J. Ely, supra note 60, at 94.

73. U.S. Const. art. I, §2, cl. 1, states: "The House of Representatives shall be composed of members chosen every second Year *by the People* of the several States" (emphasis added).

74. In opposing election by the people to either branch of the federal legislature Roger Sherman of Connecticut, for example, insisted that election should be by the state legislature because the people "should have as little to do as may be about the Government. They want information and are constantly liable to be misled." Similarly speaking against the proposal, Elbridge Gerry of Massachusetts opined that the "evils we experience flow from the excess of democracy. The people do not want virtue; but are the dupes of pretended patriots." He observed that he had been too republican before, and although he still considered himself in favor of republicanism he "had been taught by experience the danger of the lev[e]lling spirit." In response George Mason of Virginia conceded that "we" had been "too democratic" but that rejecting popular election in one branch would be too extreme. He saw what was to become the House of Representatives as "the

grand depository of the democratic principle" of the government. Madison in this same exchange thought that direct popular election should obtain in *one* branch of the legislature, but opposed popular election for the rest of the federal government, i.e., for the Senate, the President, and the Judiciary. The exchange I describe (see 1 M. Farrand, *The Records of the Federal Convention of 1787* 48–50 (1966)) is one of many that took place at the Convention and at the ratifying conventions. I think it representative. No one would find it aberrational. Indeed, in Wesberry v. Sanders, 376 U.S. 1 (1964), Justice Harlan, dissenting, quotes Professor Hacker for the characterization that "[t]he assemblage at the Philadelphia Convention was by no means committed to popular government, and few of the delegates had sympathy for the habits or institutions of democracy. Indeed, most of them interpreted democracy as mob rule and assumed that equality of representation would permit the spokesmen for the common man to outvote the beleaguered deputies of the uncommon man." Id. at 31 n.15, quoting A. Hacker, *Congressional Districting* 7–8 (1963). See also, e.g., R. Hofstadter, *The American Political Tradition* 3–21 (1973). Hacker's characterization is quite plausible, but it does not really support Justice Harlan's contention that Article I, Section 2 was not intended to support a one person–one vote principle. Particularly in discussing the rotten boroughs of Connecticut, the framers evidenced a commitment to something quite close to a one person–one vote principle for the House of Representatives. Justice Harlan was on much stronger footing in his claim that Congress, not the Court, was intended to enforce Article I, Section 2. Even there, the evidence is not as overwhelming as a reading of Justice Harlan's opinion might lead one to suppose.

75. From a larger perspective, however, the House of Representatives was thought to be no more representative of the people than the other parts of the government. G. Wood, *The Creation of the American Republic, 1776–1787* 599 (1969).

76. As Cass Sunstein puts it, "Bicameralism thus attempted to ensure that some representatives would be relatively isolated while others would be relatively close to the people." Sunstein, "Interest Groups in American Public Law," 38 *Stan. L. Rev.* 29, 43 (1985). See also notes 74 & 75 supra. Sunstein makes the clever argument that, given the Founders' commitment to a mixed regime, the increasingly "democratic" character of the structure of the American polity (because of the Seventeenth Amendment and the decline of the deliberative character of the electoral college) argues for a stronger stance in favor of judicial review (to assure a "sober second look" at political outcomes). Id. at 43 n.62, responding to J. Ely, supra note 60, at 7.

77. Clearly the framers opted for a mixed regime rather than a democratic regime: "Like the reformers of the state constitutions in the decade after 1776 the Federalists were filled with 'an enlightened zeal for energy and efficiency of government' to set against 'the turbulence and follies of democracy' as expressed by the lower houses of the state legislatures, 'the democratic parts of our constitutions.'" G. Wood, supra note 75, at 474.

78. Consider id. at 502: "Indeed, it was this factious majoritarianism, an anomalous and frightening conception for republican government, grounded as it was on majority rule, that was at the center of the Federalist perception of politics. In the minds of the Federalists the measure of a free government had become its ability to control factions, not, as used to be thought, those of a minority, but rather those of 'an interested and overbearing majority.'"

79. A. Hamilton, J. Madison & J. Jay, *The Federalist Papers,* Number 10, at 77 (New Am. Library ed. 1961).

80. As Professor Sager writes in supra note 63, at 442: "[T]he Constitution, approached without a distinct perspective to guide its interpretation, is far too eclectic a document to be the basis of a claim that majoritarianism is the guiding principle of our governmental affairs. The numerous structural provisions of the Constitution that deflect and diffuse the public will, and more centrally, the rights-conferring constitutional provisions and amendments, suggest a much more complex set of goals than the direct translation of public will into official action." See also Chemerinsky, supra note 63, at 1231–1232.

81. C. Lindblom, *Politics and Markets* 356 (1977): "It has been a curious feature of democratic thought that it has not faced up to the private corporation as a peculiar organization in an ostensible democracy. Enormously large, rich in resources, the big corporations . . . command more resources than do most government units. They can also, over a broad range, insist that government meet their demands, even if these demands run counter to those of citizens expressed through their polyarchal controls. Moreover, they do not disqualify themselves from playing the partisan role of a citizen—for the corporation is legally a person. And they exercise unusual veto powers. They are on all these counts disproportionately powerful . . . . The large private corporation fits oddly into democratic theory and vision. Indeed, it does not fit." See also R. Dahl, *Dilemmas of Pluralist Democracy* 181–185, 197–198 (1982).

82. I. Kristol, *Reflections of a Neoconservative* 204 (1983).

83. Some might contend that compensation would be required. But that is exceedingly unlikely (every bit as unlikely as the possibility that it would become an issue to be decided). See L. Tribe, *American Constitutional Law* §9-4, at 595–599 (2d ed. 1988). For a variety of views on the takings clause, see B. Ackerman, *Private Property and the Constitution* (1977); R. Epstein, *Takings: Private Property and the Power of Eminent Domain* (1985); Michelman, "Property, Utility, and Fairness: Comments on the Ethical Foundations of 'Just Compensation' Law," 80 *Harv. L. Rev.* 1165 (1967); Sax, "Takings, Private Property and Public Rights," 81 *Yale L.J.* 149 (1971).

84. I. Kristol, supra note 82, at 216–217. But see R. Dahl, supra note 81, at 199: "It might be argued that by decentralizing decisions and political resources, an economic order of relatively independent firms gives support to the democratic process, and at any rate helps to prevent the concentration of power and resources that in the long run would probably undermine the

institutions of polyarchy. The argument is, I believe, valid. But it is an argument for decentralization and not necessarily decentralization to privately owned firms. In principle the argument would be met by decentralization to socially owned or employee-owned firms, either of which might in principle be democratically controlled." See generally R. Dahl, *A Preface to Economic Democracy* (1985) (citation omitted).

85. Varieties of this worry are entertained by "an odd mixture of welfare state liberals, muckrakers, Marxists, and free-market economists." Posner, "Theories of Economic Regulation," 5 *Bell J. Econ. & Mgmt. Sci.* 335, 335 (1974), quoted in Macey, "Promoting Public-Regarding Legislation through Statutory Interpretation: An Interest Group Model," 86 *Colum. L. Rev.* 223, 224 n.7 (1986) (citing much of the economic literature and emphasizing the auction features of the political process rather than a capture model). Thus, free market economists enlist such concerns in support of a governmental structure that would make governmental action difficult. See, e.g., Macey, "Competing Economic Views of the Constitution," 56 *Geo. Wash. L. Rev.* 50 (1987). Many welfare state liberals emphasize reforms that would seek to attenuate the connection between money and political clout. See, e.g., Lowenstein, "Political Bribery and the Intermediate Theory of Politics," 32 *UCLA L. Rev.* 784 (1985); Lowenstein, "Campaign Spending and Ballot Propositions: Recent Experience, Public Choice Theory and the First Amendment," 29 *UCLA L. Rev.* 505 (1982). Even more directly, some commentators would have courts distinguish between legislation that is the product of interest group capture and that which is not. See, e.g., Wiley, "A Capture Theory of Antitrust Federalism," 99 *Harv. L. Rev.* 713 (1986).

86. I do not mean by this statement to endorse the current arrangements. I do not have a fixed view of what the relationship between politics and the market ought to be.

87. Compare the system by which the FCC selects broadcast licensees and the accompanying controversy. See, e.g., B. Owen, *Economics and Freedom of Expression: Media Structure and the First Amendment* (1975); L. Powe, *American Broadcasting and the First Amendment* (1987); Bollinger, "Freedom of the Press and Public Access: Toward a Theory of Partial Regulation of the Mass Media," 75 *Mich. L. Rev.* 1 (1976); Ferris & Kirkland, "Fairness—The Broadcaster's Hippocratic Oath," 34 *Cath. U.L. Rev.* 605 (1985); Krattenmaker & Powe, "The Fairness Doctrine Today: A Constitutional Curiosity and an Impossible Dream," 1985 *Duke L.J.* 151; Lange, "The Role of the Access Doctrine in the Regulation of the Mass Media," 52 *N.C.L. Rev.* 1 (1973); Powe, "American Voodoo: If Television Doesn't Show It, Maybe It Won't Exist," 59 *Tex. L. Rev.* 879 (1981); Van Alstyne, "The Mobius Strip of the First Amendment," 29 *S.C.L. Rev.* 539 (1978).

88. For an especially clear exposition of this point, see R. Dahl, *A Preface to Democratic Theory* 124–131 (1956). As he puts it: "[O]n matters of specific policy the majority *rarely* rules." Id. at 124 (emphasis added).

89. See generally Ferguson & Rogers, "The Myth of America's Turn to the Right," 257 *Atlantic* 43 (May 1986).

90. See generally W. Kelso, *American Democratic Theory: Pluralism and Its Critics* 53–59 (1978).

91. Thus, in reporting about a strongly contested seat in the House of Representatives, a *Wall Street Journal* staff reporter remarked: "The race is a rarity for many reasons. It is one of the few in which a House member must fight to keep his seat. In 1986, the advantages of incumbency proved so powerful that 98.4% of those who sought to return to the House were reelected." Birnbaum, "Election [Contest]," *Wall St. J.* 42 (Sept. 12, 1988). This is not a new phenomenon. See, e.g., D. Leuthold, *Electioneering in a Democracy* 127 (1968); Sullivan & O'Connor, "Electoral Choice and Popular Control of Public Policy: The Case of the 1966 House Elections," 66 *Am. Pol. Sci. Rev.* 1256 (1972).

92. See J. Choper, supra note 61, at 38.

93. See Miller & Stokes, "Constituency Influence in Congress," 57 *Am. Pol. Sci. Rev.* 45 (1963).

94. For a brief survey of the mainline pluralist literature and a cogent response, see Wright, "Politics and the Constitution: Is Money Speech?" 85 *Yale L.J.* 1001, 1013–1021 (1976). See generally P. Bachrach, *The Theory of Democratic Elitism* 83–92 (1967); S. Lukes, *Power: A Radical View* (1974); W. Kelso, supra note 90; R. Wolff, *The Poverty of Liberalism* 122–161 (1968).

95. Consider Thomas Spragens's summary of the survey data in 1976: "The voters were found to be, on the whole, nothing like the 'rational' citizenry on which democracy was allegedly based. They did not know how candidates stood on the issues; they did not understand the issues themselves; and they seemed not too concerned to overcome their ignorance. Instead, they were content to vote as their parents had voted, or because they just habitually were attached to a certain party label. And finally, survey data seemed clearly to indicate that these politically ignorant and apathetic nonelites were not very devoted to some of the central democratic 'rules of the game'—such as free speech and universal suffrage." T. Spragens, *Understanding Political Theory* 123–124 (1976). On the latter point, see generally H. McCloskey & A. Brill, *Dimensions of Tolerance: What Americans Believe about Civil Liberties* (1983) (drawing on survey data from the 1970s). But cf. W. Kelso, supra note 90, at 47–48 (contending that if citizens are encouraged to participate in "group-oriented" fashion they could emerge as more civil libertarian in outlook).

96. Although I associate the Constitution with a preference for a Burkean mode of representation, I resist the association of Burkeanism with republicanism. But cf. Sunstein, "Beyond the Republican Revival," 97 *Yale L.J.* 1539, 1560–1561 (1988) (defending "Madisonian republicanism" as steering a "middle course" between pluralism and Burkeanism, but apparently assuming, as I do not, that Burkeanism is hostile to ensuring a measure of electoral accountability). Professor Sunstein associates Madison's *Federalist* 10 (with its strong Burkean notions) with "republicanism"—this despite the emphasis of republicans on participatory localism and despite the desire of many republicans to bind representatives to follow the ex-

pressed will of the people. Madison also attempted to forge such an association. See, e.g., Pocock, "Between Gog and Magog: The Republican Thesis and the *Ideologia Americana,*" 48 *J. Hist. Ideas* 325, 343 (1987) ("Madison found it necessary to redefine the republic as a system of representative rather than participatory government"). Sunstein accomplishes this appropriation by casting republicanism against a species of pluralism that *did not exist in the eighteenth century.* Sunstein paints the picture of pluralists in these terms: "The pluralist approach takes the existing distribution of wealth, existing background of entitlements, and *existing preferences* as exogenous variables. All of these form a kind of prepolitical backdrop for pluralist struggle. The goal of the system is to ensure that the various inputs are reflected accurately in legislation; the system is therefore one of aggregating citizen preferences." Sunstein, supra, at 1543 (emphasis added). My objection is not merely that no one in the eighteenth century would have phrased issues in these terms (regretfully today there are people who do— even outside the city of Chicago, and Sunstein is right in opposing any such species of pluralism); my objection is that opposition to this conception was in no sense a distinguishing feature of republicanism. *Both* Federalists and Antifederalists were united against any such conception. The Federalists wanted the federal government to have a lot more power than the Antifederalists did, and they were more suspicious of the virtue of the people than were the Antifederalists, but few people thought the federal government should run a system of education. Federalists and Antifederalists alike would have recoiled at the thought that preferences were exogenous variables. They hoped and expected that churches and/or schools would participate in the encouragement of virtue, civic and beyond. See Yarbrough, "The Constitution and Character: The Missing Critical Principle," in *"To Form a More Perfect Union": The Critical Ideas of the Constitution* (H. Belv, R. Hoffman & P. J. Albert eds., forthcoming, 1990). On the complications associated with assuming that the language of virtue is the language of republicanism, see Kramnick, "The 'Great National Discussion': The Discourse of Politics in 1787," 45 *Wm. & Mary Q.* 3, 15–23 (1988).

97. See generally Stern, "The Tin Cup Congress," 20 *Washington Monthly* 23 (May 1988); Easterbrook, "What's Wrong with Congress?" 254 *Atlantic* 57, 70–79 (Dec. 1984); Green, "Political Pac-Man," 187 *New Republic* 18 (Dec. 13, 1982).

98. Any judgment I would make would have to be a priori because I, like millions of others, know nothing about the representatives from Bakersfield or Orlando.

99. I do not mean to suggest that the case for judicial review should depend upon individual showings of the failure to exercise independent judgment. This is not a case of norm and exception with the norm being one of legislators making independent judgments. As Professor Fiss has observed, the best case for judicial review does not imagine a model of legislative failure parallel to a model of market failure. Fiss, supra note 63, at 10. But, an important part of the best case for judicial review depends on the judgment

that the legislature is characteristically ill-suited to make independent judgments.

100. See Easterbrook, supra note 97, at 84: "[H]aving lobbyists crowd outside the chambers of the House and Senate, flashing thumb signs to congressmen like coaches issuing orders to Little Leaguers, is a national disgrace." Unfortunately, as Easterbrook notes, "Photographers are forbidden to take pictures by the chamber doors, so they cannot capture this spectacle." Id. at 75.

101. See Fiss, supra note 63.

102. That legal scholars too frequently ignore this or downplay it is a powerful theme in M. Tushnet, *Red, White, and Blue: A Critical Analysis of Constitutional Law* (1988). In particular, see id. at 123–133. See also R. Dahl, supra note 88, at 105–112 (1956). The case for the historical sagacity and necessity of judicial review with respect to the blocking of Congressional action is painfully weak. On the other hand, my view of the courts' record vis a vis state and local legislation is much the other way. Perhaps Madison was on to something in *Federalist* 10.

103. See Brest, "Interpretation and Interest," 34 *Stan. L. Rev.* 765 (1982).

104. I do not mean to suggest that an eclectic outlook is a sufficient condition for wise policy. The partiality of everyone's outlook is inevitable, however broadminded one might try to be. Moreover, the possession of perfect knowledge is no guarantee of wise policy.

105. Cf. Minow, "Law Turning Outward," 73 *Telos* 79, 97 & 99 (1987) (emphasis added): "I assert a feminist commitment to communication. By that, I mean simply a willingness to relinquish the claim of exclusive truth, and a concomitant willingness to hear competing vantage points, *all of which are partial*. . . . By arguing that the projects of legal theory should focus on particular, concrete, social problems, I predict that eclectic approaches will become more familiar and more well-developed. This direction does risk undermining the analytic coherence of each school of theory; eclecticism also rejects the claim to exclusive truth or greater power implicit in each of the schools. These are strengths, not weaknesses, of a theoretical project if we take seriously the feminist challenge to any point of view that would claim transcendence or neutrality. Once there is more than one point of view, no point of view can be treated as not a point of view."

106. I would join those who argue that participation can be a valuable means of self-realization, and I think that the country's meager efforts to encourage participation are shortsighted. I agree with those who argue that we are social animals, but I do not believe that political participation in a large political country is constitutive of human nature. There is also a strong case for democratic participation proceeding from notions of respect for individuals, a case that does not depend on the argument that such participation produces good consequences overall. Nonetheless, the notion of respect can not of itself dictate which aspects of the system should be marked by popular participation and which should not.

107. Redish, supra note 8, at 602, 614 (1982).

108. See J. Pennock, *Democratic Political Theory* 12 (1979) ("[T]he Communist countries also lay claim to the term *democracy*. They claim that the goals of liberty and equality are theirs as well as ours. In fact, they claim that they understand, appreciate, and indeed realize these goals to a far greater extent than we do."). From the beginning Lenin fought for what he described as "social-democracy." He contended that the principles of social-democracy were expounded in the *Communist Manifesto*. See Lenin, "The Tasks of the Russian Social-Democrats," in *The Lenin Anthology* 3, 8 (R. Tucker ed. 1975). The democratic goal, according to Lenin, was embodied in "the fight against absolutism aimed at winning political liberty in Russia and democratizing the political and social system of Russia." Id. at 3–4. Moreover, he contended that democracy is what the revolution achieved: "Proletarian democracy, of which Soviet government is one of the forms, has brought a development and expansion of democracy unprecedented in the world, for the vast majority of the population, for the exploited and working people. . . . Proletarian democracy is a *million times* more democratic than any bourgeois democracy; Soviet power is a million times more democratic than the most democratic bourgeois republic." Lenin, "The Proletarian Revolution and the Renegade Kautsky," in *The Lenin Anthology,* supra at 461, 469 & 471 (emphasis in original).

109. Resolution of Congress of the Communist International (1920), quoted in J. Randall, *The Making of the Modern Mind* 660 (50th Anniversary ed. 1976).

110. Lenin, "What Is to Be Done?," supra note 108, at 29 (emphasis in original). Although the statement was made in the context of revolutionary party organization in 1902, the philosophy carried well beyond. See, e.g., 2 L. Kolakowski, *Main Currents of Marxism* 489 (1978) (describing stifling of opposition within the party). Compare also, for example, Lenin's characterization of freedom of the press in 1918: "The old bourgeois apparatus—the bureaucracy, the privileges of wealth, of bourgeois education, of social connections, etc. (these real privileges are the more varied the more highly bourgeois democracy is developed)—all this disappears under the Soviet form of organisation. Freedom of the press ceases to be hypocrisy, because the printing-plants and stocks of paper are taken away from the bourgeoisie. The same thing applies to the best buildings, the palaces, the mansions and manor houses. Soviet power took thousands upon thousands of the best buildings from the exploiters at one stroke, and in this way made the right of assembly—without which democracy is a fraud—*a million times* more democratic for the people." Lenin, "The Proletarian Revolution and the Renegade Kautsky," supra note 108, at 470 (emphasis in original).

111. S. I. Benn & R. S. Peters, *Social Principles and the Democratic State* 338–339 (1959).

112. UNESCO, *Democracy in a World of Tensions* 527 (1951), quoted in S. I. Benn & R. S. Peters, supra note 111, at 332.

113. Cf. J. Pennock, supra note 108, at 14: "[I]t is at least arguable that the same substantive conception of democracy will fit both West and East."

114. Consider W. Whitman, "Democratic Vistas," in Whitman, *Leaves of Grass and Selected Prose* 468, 469 (L. Buell ed. 1981): "I shall use the words America and democracy as convertible terms."

115. See E. Purcell, *The Crisis of Democratic Theory* 258–266 (1973) (explaining and criticizing the approach taken).

116. See id.; see also Margolis, "Democracy: American Style," in *Democratic Theory and Practice* 115 (G. Duncan ed. 1983).

117. W. Connolly, *The Terms of Political Discourse* 6 (2d ed. 1983).

118. Id. at 213.

119. Mussolini, quoted in J. Randall, supra note 109, at 663.

120. Quoted in J. Randall, supra note 109, at 663.

121. Quoted in id. at 664.

122. I refer to American ideals, not necessarily to the practice. I return to the relationship between American ideals and American practice in Chapter 5.

123. 249 U.S. 47 (1919).

124. More specifically, the charge was that the defendants had violated the 1917 Espionage Act by conspiring to cause and attempting to cause insubordination in the armed forces and obstruction of the recruiting and enlistment services of the United States. Id. at 48–49.

125. Id. at 51.

126. Id.

127. Id.

128. Id.

129. Id.

130. Id. The defendants, perhaps knowing more facts than appear in the opinion—in any event, for reasons best known to them—did not deny that the jury could reasonably find against them on that point. Id.

131. Id. at 52.

132. Id.

133. Id.

134. For a scathing description of the judge who tried one of the most important cases of the period together with a rich description of the cultural attitudes then reigning, see R. Polenberg, *Fighting Faiths: The Abrams Case, The Supreme Court, and Free Speech* (1987).

135. Brandenburg v. Ohio, 395 U.S. 444 (1969), is the most important, albeit not the most recent, of the modern cases.

136. 461 U.S. 138 (1983).

137. Id. at 140.

138. Id. at 141.

139. Id.

140. Id.

141. Id. at 146. A page before the Court used the phrase "a matter of *legitimate* public concern." Emphasis added.

142. Id. at 145, quoting Pickering v. Board of Educ., 391 U.S. 563, 571–572 (1968).

143. Id. at 146. Nonetheless, the Court suggested that "an employee's false criticism of his employer on grounds not of public concern may be cause for his discharge but would be entitled to the same protection in a libel action accorded an identical statement made by a man on the street." Id. at 147. For perceptive criticism of the Court's use of the public/private distinction in the labor speech context together with a close analysis of the *Connick* case, see Lieberwitz, "Freedom of Speech in Public Sector Employment: The Deconstitutionalization of the Public Sector Workplace," 19 *U.C.D. L. Rev.* 597 (1986).

144. 461 U.S. at 154.

145. Id.

146. Id. at 170.

147. Id. at 163.

148. Id. at 169, quoting Myers v. Connick, 507 F. Supp. 752, 759 (E.D. La. 1981).

149. See, e.g., Kateb, "Democratic Individuality and the Claims of Politics," 12 *Pol. Theory* 331, 337 (1984): The broadest point in the encouragement of democratic individuality in the writings of Emerson and Whitman (and Thoreau) is the "fear that people do not see clearly and unrelentingly enough that all social conventions are, in fact, conventions—i.e., artificial; that they are changeable; that conventions have in fact changed through time, and are different from place to place. No human life can exist without conventions. But people tend to take a given network of them as natural, as nature itself—as imperative and therefore sacred; with the result that people—even in a democracy—are too timid, too unadventurous, too conformist."

150. See, e.g., J. Porte, *Representative Man: Ralph Waldo Emerson in His Time* 106–107 (1988). Cf. id. at 105 ("[Emerson] achieved his self-definition through defiance and dissent."); J. Michael, *Emerson and Skepticism: The Cipher of the World* 40 (1988) ("[F]rom his earliest conception of his personal ambition to his last formulations of greatness and eloquence, dissent from popular belief is a crucial component of Emerson's thinking.").

151. See, e.g., B. L. Packer, *Emerson's Fall* 85–87 (1982).

152. Id. at 87–95.

153. A. de Tocqueville, *Democracy in America* 254–255 (J. P. Mayer ed. 1969).

154. B. L. Packer, supra note 151, at 95. Thus Edward Ericson writes that "Emerson was the principal prophet for several generations of men and women. . . . There is much in the American free spirit that one cannot understand unless one knows Emerson." "Introduction," in *Emerson on Transcendentalism* vii–viii (E. Ericson ed. 1986). D. Donoghue, *Reading America* 37 (1987) ("[Emerson] is the founding father of nearly everything we think of as American in the modern world. To the extent to which the sentiments of power, self-reliance, subjectivity, and independence attract to themselves a distinctly American nuance, its source is Emerson."); cf. J.

Loving, *Emerson, Whitman, and the American Muse* 177–178 (1982) (Emerson and Whitman fostered American intellectual independence and were thus "'fathers' of the American sublime"). But Emerson and Whitman did not create an entirely new tradition. They drew upon and helped to revive the spirit produced by the American Revolution: "[F]aith ran high that a better world than any that had ever been known could be built where authority was distrusted and held in constant scrutiny; . . . where the use of power over the lives of men was jealously guarded and severely restricted. It was only where there was this defiance, this refusal to truckle, this distrust of all authority, political or social, that institutions would express human aspirations, not crush them." B. Bailyn, *The Ideological Origins of the American Revolution* 319 (1967).

Moreover, without discussing Emerson or Whitman, Vincent Blasi has well summarized many of the conditions that "by and large favored the development of a tolerant attitude toward dissent," conditions which are, for the most part, thereby relevant to the favorable reception of the Emersonian perspective: "Many of the original settlers were refugees from religious persecution. The nation was conceived at a time when new ideas, scientific and political, influenced the thinking of ordinary persons; seldom have reason and experimentation seemed so closely related to social progress as in the late eighteenth century. The colonial experience left a legacy of distrust of government and a constitutional structure designed to forestall the concentration of power. The vast frontier and the patterns of social mobility that are possible in a migratory culture helped to generate an ethic of individualism. The immigration waves created a polyglot community that made pluralism the only feasible organizing principle for political life. The blessings of abundant economic resources, peaceful neighbors, oceanic protection from foreign attack, and success in military exploits made Americans a self-confident people—and self-confidence may be *the* critical variable in the calculus of toleration." Blasi, "The Pathological Perspective and the First Amendment," 85 *Colum. L. Rev.* 449, 463 (1985) (emphasis in original).

155. A. Schlesinger, *The Cycles of American History* x (1986).

156. Loving, "Walt Whitman," in *Columbia Literary History of the United States* 448, 449 (E. Elliot ed. 1988). Consider Michael Hoffman's discussion of Whitman: "It is clear from the Preface [to *Leaves of Grass*] . . . that Whitman wished to be Emerson's poet . . . . The artist must be free of any kind of institutionalized poetics or any kind of diction that follows accepted 'rules.' Poetic decorum is an institution imposed from without, and since the Transcendentalists waged war on all institutions, it is no wonder that Whitman wanted his poet to be disreputable, a 'beard,' one of the 'roughs.' By extension, only when a man can give up all the social amenities, ignore all the precepts, conundrums, and shibboleths with which society makes him so dangerously comfortable will he possibly be his own man. The poet's task is to set all men free by setting himself free." M. Hoffman, *The Subversive Vision: American Romanticism in Literature* 62 & 64 (1972).

157. Cf. Carafiol, "Reading Emerson: Writing History," 30 *Centennial Review* 431, 449 (1986): "While Emerson and his contemporaries called for a literature to match the promise of the new nation, by the First World War, scholars were increasingly willing to assume that this call had been answered and were ready to demonstrate that American literature was the adequate voice of the national character. They put Transcendentalism at the center of American literature because it was central to this project." Carafiol states that Emerson stands to Transcendentalism as Transcendentalism stands to American literature: "He is the central figure about which the rest revolves and without which there could be not even the fiction of coherence." Id. at 431. But he criticizes this focus on Emerson as the product of ideology and nationalistic assumptions.

It is hard to believe that Emerson would accept the idea of him or anyone else as a quintessential American. See R. W. Emerson, "Representative Men," in *Ralph Waldo Emerson: Essays and Lectures* 611, 630–631 (J. Porte ed. 1983). It is enough for my purposes that Emerson be recognized as an eloquent representative of an important strain in the American tradition, and even Carafiol's effort to decenter Emerson does not speak against, indeed it supports, that recognition. For my purposes it is ultimately important that Emerson be perceived as speaking from within the tradition, if not at its center. Thus I rely on Emerson and Whitman, but not Thoreau. In my view Thoreau speaks just as eloquently on themes important to my argument, and surely Thoreau is one of those dissenters the first amendment should take pains to protect. If Thoreau consciously speaks as if he is outside the community, we now see Emerson and Whitman as speaking from within. But cf. Loving, supra note 154, at 12–13 (Whitman fostered an image that left him an outsider in nineteenth-century literary history). Their posture respects the authority of the community even as they advise us to resist it. Cf. D. Robinson, *Apostle of Culture: Emerson as Preacher and Lecturer* 184–185 (1982) (because he worked within a tradition affirming human potential, Emerson could "rebel without being a rebel"). As discussed in Chapter 5, this posture has its advantages in legal argumentation.

158. Emerson's work has prompted substantially different readings in this respect. Some emphasize Emerson's focus upon the particular and look to him as an influential precursor of the pragmatists. See, e.g., H. Bloom, *Agon: Towards a Theory of Revisionism* 19–20, 39–41, 167 (1982). See generally R. Poirier, *The Renewal of Literature: Emersonian Reflections* (1987). Others place emphasis on the extent to which Emerson's material world is assimilated to a unifying subjective ideal. See, e.g., L. Chai, *The Romantic Foundations of the American Renaissance* (1987). Neither reading is unfounded. Emerson's focus upon the particular was sustained enough and eloquent enough to inspire the pragmatists, yet when the dust clears, he is a thoroughgoing idealist.

159. No general agreement exists about what Emerson's stance toward evil might be. See, e.g., S. Cavell, *In Quest of the Ordinary* 34 (1988):

"[W]hen, in 'The Genteel Tradition,' Santayana describes Emerson as 'a cheery, childlike soul, impervious to the evidence of evil' he does not show (there or anywhere else I know that he mentions Emerson) any better understanding of Emerson's so-called optimism than, say, his contemporary H. L. Mencken shows of Nietzsche's so-called pessimism—he merely retails, beautifully of course, but essentially without refinement, the most whole-sale view there is of him." Cf. Loving, supra note 154, at 179 (reading Emerson's essay on "Experience" as a "statement of willed optimism in the face of life's adversity"). See also S. Whicher, *Freedom and Fate: An Inner Life of Ralph Waldo Emerson* 46 (1953) (Emerson's inability to admit the "Reality" of evil, as opposed to its empirical existence, sustained his secure willing-ness to challenge limitations but prevented him from appreciating the tragic aspects of human experience). On the importance of appreciating the tragic aspects of human experience, see generally M. Nussbaum, *The Fragility of Goodness* (1986).

However Emerson's views on the question of evil might be characterized and however provocative of interesting commentary they might be, Irving Howe is surely right when he states on this issue that "[I]t is hard to suppose that anyone could now take Emerson as a sufficient moral or philosophical guide . . . . " I. Howe, *The American Newness: Culture and Politics in the Age of Emerson* 14 (1986).

160. "Where Emerson's ancestors ascribed infallibility to scripture, he ascribed it to the inner voice." I. Howe, supra note 159, at 9.

161. There is a powerful argument on the other side. The notion is that deep down Emerson promotes an authoritarian lack of independence. Emerson's monism, his sunny stance toward evil, and his ready assimilation of nature to mind allow persons to express things only *the* way things are, and difference in particular is said to be slighted by Emerson. As Jehlen puts it, "Tocqueville's observation that despite the remarkable diversity (ethnic, racial, religious) of American society, Americans seemed peculiarly intolerant of nonconformity, documents the process of encompassment as a broad ideo-logical phenomenon. For in the context of Emersonian pluralism, diversity connotes not difference but instead avatars of the universal. Such a concept of diversity tends in fact to deny difference precisely by expressing it, as yet another facet of the enlarged whole." Moreover, as she ultimately argues, Emerson's zeal for the acceptance of nature presses toward a conservative stance. She suggests that the conservative Carlyle "could do relatively little, or imagined he could, but everything he did changed the world. Emerson could do everything—so long as he left the world intact." M. Jehlen, *American Incarnation: The Individual, The Nation, and the Continent* 12, 120 (1986).

As I suggest in the text, I have no interest in defending Emerson's per-spectives on monism, evil, or the relationship between mind and nature. I do insist that Emerson powerfully argues as a major theme of his work that persons need to be free to criticize existing traditions, habits, and customs.

As Jehlen observes, "From the past to the future, [Emerson's] man moves not from nature to civilization but from history to nature, and himself evolves in the same direction; in history, he is encompassed all around by conventions, traditions, and other men, but his coming dominion over nature will seal his absolute independence." Id. at 93–94. This independence can give rise to the worry that promoting dissent promotes excessive individualism (but see Chapter 3 infra, and against the charge that Emerson was excessively individualistic, see J. Porte, *Emerson and Thoreau: Transcendentalists in Conflict* 21, 148–149 (1966)), and Jehlen may be right in asserting that Emerson ultimately is arguing for a deeply passive and utterly controlled "independence," but, if she *is* right, it must be said that Emerson was thoroughly self-deceived. Surely, he thought he was arguing for genuinely active independence; he thought that individuality and self-reliance could really be combined with a transcendental conception of eternal unity. And, in any event, *in terms of impact upon the culture* (and I do not understand Jehlen to deny the point), Emerson's eloquence about dissent and independence far outstripped the quietistic tendencies of his thought. Ultimately, however, I think the so-called quietism is a phantom. As Nancy Rosenblum argues: "[R]omantic sensibilities sometimes imitate stoic or otherworldly stances, but they cannot endure genuine detachment. Romantic expressivism involves a dynamic of inwardness and emergence, not inwardness alone. Despite inclinations to withdraw from prosaic society romantics are not quietist and are never resigned." N. Rosenblum, *Another Liberalism* 84 (1987). Certainly, Rosenblum's characterizations apply to Emerson and his courageous engagement with and against the powerful religious orthodoxy of his time. See, e.g., J. Porte, supra note 150, at 97–100, 101–172, 295–309, 333–334 (1988). Although Emerson for much of his life stayed out of day-to-day "political" questions (believing his emphasis on self-reliance, for example, to be of more lasting importance), he ultimately concluded that: "It is impossible to extricate oneself from the questions in which your age is involved. You can no more keep out of politics than you can keep out of the frost." *Emerson in His Journals* 497 (J. Porte ed. 1982). For brief discussion of Emerson's activities as a practicing democrat, see Gohdes, "An American Author as Democrat," in *Literary Romanticism in America* 1, 14–18 (W. L. Andrews ed. 1981). For discussion of the reform aspects of the Transcendentalist movement, see generally A. Rose, *Transcendentalism as a Social Movement, 1830–1850* (1981).

162. 438 U.S. 726 (1978).

163. Id. at 729.

164. Id. at 751.

165. Id. at 751.

166. Id. at 750 n.28 (emphasis added).

167. Thus a focus on dissent is broader than the checking value as discussed by Professor Blasi. See Blasi, supra note 8. The checking value, as he develops it, is confined not only to government action, but also to a concern about misconduct, as opposed to questions of priority or efficacy. See id. at

542. But cf. id. at 543 (courts need not apply a misconduct test under the checking value). In more recent writing, Blasi argues that first amendment doctrine should be crafted to protect dissent in pathological periods of our history. Blasi, supra note 154. Even there, his emphasis is upon particular forms of government misconduct. Id. at 494. I do not agree with the focus on government misconduct or pathological periods, but I do not claim to have directly addressed his particular argument here. Nonetheless, his work perceptively explores issues and perspectives relevant to the dissent value in ways that are fertile even for those who do not accept his starting points.

168. Laurence Tribe observes that it is unlikely that "any significant number of adults were offended by Carlin's monologue. Certainly WBAI's regular listeners were unlikely to be scandalized; in any case, the station prefaced the broadcast with warnings of the sensitive language to come. That left at risk the radio listeners who, turning the dials, stumbled briefly onto the offensive program. The number of such accidents had to be minuscule, much smaller than the number of WBAI listeners who enjoyed Mr. Carlin's satire." L. Tribe, supra note 83 §12-18, at 937–938.

169. 438 U.S. at 775 (Brennan, J., dissenting). Ralph Waldo Emerson would have agreed with Brennan. See *Emerson in His Journals,* supra note 161, at 240–241; cf. B. Erkkila, *Whitman: The Political Poet* 80 (1989) ("Recognizing the interrelation between linguistic, class, and political systems, Whitman represents language as a site of social struggle, a relationship of power in which the 'rude words' of the people struggle against the lady and gentleman words of the dominant class.").

170. More on that later. See Chapter 3 infra.

171. 391 U.S. 367 (1968).

172. See, e.g., L. Tribe, supra note 83 §12-6, at 824–825.

173. 391 U.S. at 376.

174. To be sure, a rare advertisement departs from the conventional wisdom. If cigarette companies try to tell us, for example, that cigarette smoking is not harmful to health, some dissenting values seem to be implicated in a cigarette ad. Even there, the existence of a corporate speaker seeking to maximize profits does not call up the quality of independence or rebellion that we ordinarily associate with the idea of dissent, and some might balk at admitting the existence of any dissenting values in the example. As I mention in Chapter 3, there may be a significant difference between asking whether dissent is present or whether some of the values associated with dissent are present. Moreover, as I argue at some length in Chapter 3, the presence of dissent or dissenting value is neither a necessary nor a sufficient condition for first amendment protection. I return to this example in Chapter 5.

175. Commercial advertising is an important test case. If one's focus is diversity, the case for protecting commercial advertising is strong because of the rich artistic array of images it provides. Here diversity and dissent point in different directions. See Blasi, supra note 8, at 552–553.

176. Suppose, however, that Pepsi distributes stinging attacks on Coke in

leaflets on city streets. Should that count as protest or as commercial advertisement? Clearly it is both, and because it is both it involves more first
amendment value than would a typical commercial advertisement containing no dissent. But that is my point. To make that point does not necessitate
the view that a jurisdiction should engage in ad hoc determinations about
the dissent value in particular commercial advertisements. It only demands
the recognition that the presence of dissent in commercial advertisements
inflates its first amendment value and should heighten any sense of sacrifice
involved when commercial advertisements are banned in particular times
or places. If commercial advertisements routinely implicated robust debate
about the value of particular products, the case for sustaining a ban on the
distribution of commercial leaflets in public places would be substantially
weaker.

177. Bork, supra note 6, at 20. Judge Bork has since abandoned the extreme version of this position. See, e.g., Bork, "Judge Bork Replies," 70
A.B.A. J. 132 (Feb. 1984). Nonetheless, he has continued to press for a politically based conception of the first amendment. For example, in a Worldnet
interview on June 10, 1987, he reiterated his notion that the core of the first
amendment is political, and stated that there is "a lot of moral and scientific
speech which feeds directly into the political process." He also stated that a
spectrum of protection spreads out from political speech into "moral speech
and the scientific speech, *into fiction and so forth.*" (Emphasis added.) He
added, however, that "Clearly as you get into art and literature, particularly as you get into forms of art—and if you want to call it literature and
art—which are pornography and things approaching it—you are dealing
with something now that is [not] in any way and form the way we govern
ourselves, and in fact may be quite deleterious. I would doubt that courts
ought to throw protection around that." Presumably, Judge Bork would say
that the works of Einstein and Shakespeare "feed directly into the political
process." But it is hard to believe that protection of such speech depends
upon any such finding. Even if Judge Bork gives the phrase "feeds directly
into the political process" a generous construction, literally millions of daily
conversations would fall outside Judge Bork's first amendment. Citizens in
this country say things every day that do not feed "directly into the political
process" or that are not "central to democratic government." I am certain
they would be surprised to learn that their daily freedom of speech might
hinge on a judge's assessment of what does or does not feed into the political
process or on what is or is not central to democratic government. They
rightly think that their right to speak on nonpolitical topics depends on no
such assessment.

In whatever version, Judge Bork's views are not just wrong, but, as I argue below, importantly wrong. They stem from a commonly held misperception of the nature of democracy.

178. Bork, supra note 6, at 28.

179. I do not mean to suggest that protection for free speech necessarily

depends upon constitutional arrangements. Free speech might be afforded generous protection in many societies without constitutional protection. In this country, however, appreciation for free speech values is related to its constitutional status.

180. Consider M. Hoffman, supra note 156, at 4: "[T]he mark of every major American author since the days of Poe has been an inability to find his culture adequate to his search for value, either in the universe or in his immediate society; and the new ways of looking at the world postulated by these [authors]—different as they were as individuals—were definitely subversive of what has often been called the 'official faith,' although to each writer the 'official faith' meant something different." See also Marx, "Pastoralism in America," in *Ideology and Classic American Literature* 36, 52–53 (S. Bercovitch & M. Jehlen eds. 1986). But see T. Eagleton, *Literary Theory: An Introduction* 200 & 208–209 (1983): "Departments of literature in higher education, then, are part of the ideological apparatus of the modern capitalist state. . . . Liberal humanist criticism is not wrong to use literature, but wrong to deceive itself that it does not. It uses it to further certain moral values, which as I hope to have shown are indissociable from certain ideological ones, and in the end imply a particular form of politics."

181. Judge Bork states that, "One of the freedoms, the major freedom, of our kind of society is the freedom to choose to have a public morality." R. Bork, *Tradition and Morality in Constitutional Law* 9 (1984). Or, as he has also said, "in wide areas of life, majorities are entitled to rule for no better reason than they are majorities." Bork, "Neutral Principles and Some First Amendment Problems," supra note 6, at 2. See also Bork, "The Constitution, Original Intent, and Economic Rights," 23 *San Diego L. Rev.* 823, 824 (1986). Thus, Judge Bork has decried the entry into first amendment law of what he describes as the "old, and incorrect, view that the only kinds of harm that a community is entitled to suppress are physical and economic injuries. . . . The result of discounting moral harm is the privatization of morality, which requires the law of the community to practice moral relativism. It is thought that individuals are entitled to their moral beliefs but may not gather as a community to express those moral beliefs in law." R. Bork, *Tradition and Morality in Constitutional Law,* supra at 3.

182. Consider Judge Bork's commentary on Cohen v. California, 403 U.S. 15 (1971): "A state attempted to apply its obscenity statute to a public display of an obscene word. The Supreme Court majority struck down the conviction on the grounds that regulation is a slippery slope and that moral relativism is a constitutional command. The opinion said, 'The principle contended for by the State seems inherently boundless. How is one to distinguish this from any other offensive word?' One might as well say that the negligence standard of tort law is inherently boundless, for how is one to distinguish the reckless driver from the safe one. The answer in both cases is, by the common sense of the community." Bork, *Tradition and Morality in Constitutional Law,* supra note 181, at 3.

The traditional understanding of first amendment law, however, has been that majorities have to have better reasons than that they are majorities. Majorities cannot silence speech merely because they do not like it. The whole point of the Bill of Rights is to protect minorities against the "common sense" of majorities. The Court put it well in *Cohen:* "The ability of government, consonant with the Constitution, to shut off discourse solely to protect others from hearing it is . . . dependent upon a showing that substantial privacy interests are being invaded in an essentially intolerable manner. Any broader view of this authority would effectively empower a majority to silence dissidents simply as a matter of personal predilections." 403 U.S. at 21.

183. See generally M. Yudof, *When Government Speaks* (1983).

184. To the contrary, as Professor Kateb observes, the work of Emerson, Whitman, and Thoreau "is suffused by the sense that the political arrangements of democracy conduce to a people's ability to glimpse—if only hesitantly or occasionally—the merely conventional nature of conventions, of most rules and most laws. . . . Whitman emphasizes that the skeleton of democracy, the electoral procedure, is the key to liberating democratic individuals from servility to conventions." Kateb, supra note 149, at 338.

185. Cf. L. Tribe, *Constitutional Choices* 7 (1985) (emphasis deleted): "[I]n matters of power, the end of doubt and distrust is the beginning of tyranny."

186. Michelman, supra note 63, at 75. Consider also Gordon Wood's observation: "The constitutional reformers seized on the people's growing suspicion of their own representatives and reversed the perspective: the House of Representatives, now no more trusted than other parts of the government, seemed to be also no more representative of the people than the other parts of the government. They had lost their exclusive role of embodying the people in the government. In fact the people did not actually participate in the government any more, as they did, for example, in the English House of Commons. The Americans had taken the people out of the government altogether. The 'true distinction' of the American governments, wrote Madison in *The Federalist,* 'lies *in the total exclusion of the people, in their collective capacity,* from any share' in the government." G. Wood, supra note 75, at 599 (emphasis in original), quoting *The Federalist Papers,* Number 63, supra note 79, at 382, 387.

187. See Michelman, supra note 63, at 75: "[Governmental] determinations are not our self-government." On the other hand, Michelman suggests that there *may* be a "trace" of self-government in the judicial process. He states (though it is not entirely clear whether this is Michelman's voice or Michelman's reconstruction of Ackerman, supra note 63, or both): "The Court at the last appears not as *representative* of the People's declared will but as *representation* and trace of the People's absent self-government." Id. at 65 (emphasis in original), citing Singer, "Radical Moderation," 1985 *Am. Bar Found. Research J.* 329, 339–340. Ultimately, Michelman suggests that even though the judges are not "us," they "may augment our freedom," not

mere negative freedom, but freedom understood as "socially situated self-direction—that is, self-direction by norms cognizant of fellowship with equally self-directing others." And, if freedom is understood in that sense, "then the relation between one agent's freedom and another's is additive: one realizes one's own only by confirming that of the others. This seems to hold no less for a judge than for any other agent." Supra at 75.

Warming up to Chief Justice William Rehnquist is admittedly not my cup of tea, and the norms emanating from the Court seem insufficiently cognizant of fellowship, so Michelman's suggestion is too socially situated for me in the current context. Michelman speaks here only of possibility, however. Even if the day should arrive when I would experience in the opinions of the Court—to use Michelman's elegant phrase—"self-recognition and redirection through open and empathic intersubjective encounter" (id. at 65 n.352), I could think of it as only the smallest *trace* of *self*-government. And if the gulf between self and other in this context seems great for (perhaps excessively individualist) law professors like me, how much greater for the 240 million other Americans, untold millions of whom are even more individualistic?

Michelman recognizes this difficulty both in its class-based and court-glorified aspects, see id. at 74, but it is for him a trope that has some attraction, nonetheless. What I seek to emphasize is that if Michelman's trace is the best rendition of our Constitution's commitment to *self*-government *in the governmental process*, we would be on sound footing if we recognized that for the vast majority of Americans there is next to no *self*-government in the governmental process.

188. If it exists at all.

189. John Dewey also understood this, and he appreciated Whitman's contribution. Dewey complained that there was a "social pathology which works powerfully against effective inquiry into social institutions and conditions. It manifests itself in a thousand ways; in querulousness, in impotent drifting, in uneasy snatching at distractions, in idealization of the long established, in a facile optimism assumed as a cloak, in riotous glorification of things 'as they are,' in intimidation of all dissenters—ways which depress and dissipate thought all the more effectually because they operate with subtle and unconscious pervasiveness." Dewey hoped for the day when "an organized, articulate Public comes into being" for then "[d]emocracy will come into its own, for democracy is a name for a life of free and enriching communion. It had its seer in Walt Whitman. It will have its consummation when free social inquiry is indissolubly wedded to the art of full and moving communication." J. Dewey, *The Public and Its Problems* 170–171, 184 (1927). See generally, Kateb, "Thinking about Human Extinction (II): Emerson and Whitman," 6 *Raritan* 1, 12–15 (Winter 1987); Gohdes, supra note 161, at 9 (Emerson); Scholnick, "Toward a 'Wider Democratizing of Institutions': Whitman's *Democratic Vistas*," 52 *Am. Transcendental Q.* 287, 296 (1981).

190. See Kateb, supra note 149, at 341: Emerson's "pervasive sense is that individuals are likely to be better than the laws, because 'every actual state is corrupt.' Private moral feeling, when the individual stops and takes time to think in the forum of his individual mind, is likely to be better than the moral feeling that is embodied in laws that are made by a process of publicity, exaggeration, competition, and compromise."

191. 319 U.S. 624 (1943).

192. Id. at 642.

193. Consider Whitman, supra note 114, at 486: "The eager and often inconsiderate appeals of reformers and revolutionists are indispensable, to counterbalance the inertness and fossilism making so large a part of human institutions. The latter [inertness and fossilism] will always take care of themselves—the danger being that they rapidly tend to ossify us. The former [reformers and revolutionists] is to be treated with indulgence, and even with respect. As circulation to air, so is agitation and a plentiful degree of speculative license to political and moral sanity. Indirectly, but surely, goodness, virtue, law, (of the very best,) follow freedom. These, to democracy, are what the keel is to the ship, or saltiness to the ocean."

3. The First Amendment and Dissent

1. The quotation appears in H. Steiner, *Moral Argument and Social Vision in the Courts* 206 n.1 (1987). Steiner himself in an insightful presentation argues that an understanding of tort law depends upon the recognition that social vision (which changes over time and which substantially influences outcomes) frequently appears not in the justification for the result, but, for example, in the description of the facts. As Steiner puts it in one passage: "Social vision has to do then not with reasoned elaboration but with sight and insight, with a court's grasp of a situation. It tells us salient fragments of a story about the accident's origins, parties, consequences, and context. Its graphic and sometimes expressive nature is often captured in an adjective—in, say, the contemporary empathetic images of courts of a 'hapless' consumer, 'innocent' victim, 'inescapable' risk, 'grave' danger, 'frightening' consequence, or 'devastating' loss. It is true that on its face, legal argument generally emphasizes justification. But justification necessarily absorbs and is oriented by vision. Each implies and requires the other. Legal argument, as it were, thereby joins insight to reason, the narrative to the normative, the graphic to the abstract, the expressive to the formal." Id. at 96.

Inspired by Steiner's work, I suggest that the pictorial or graphic association, negative or positive, that decisionmakers attach to the notion of a dissenter can have a substantial impact on how important free speech cases are decided. The same is true of the image associated with the media or with a defamation plaintiff. Is the media arrogant and obnoxious or is it composed of serious investigative journalists zealously on guard to preserve our right to know? Are defamation plaintiffs greedy spoilsports unable to take criticism and out seeking a pot of gold at the end of a law suit or are they the hapless victims of a powerful and greedy media conglomerate that wantonly abuses human beings in order to make a buck? Steiner focuses on accident law, but it would be interesting to explore the vision held by courts of the origins, parties, and consequences of defamation and to determine if the patterns of agreement and disagreement have changed over time. It would also be interesting to determine if the perspectives vary from state to state and from country to country. Steiner's work suggests the possibility that in defamation law too, one might learn that no sharp separation can be made between doctrine and the way the parties are described.

2. Shiffrin, "Government Speech and the Falsification of Consent" (Book Review), 96 *Harv. L. Rev.* 1745, 1745 (1983).

3. Abrams v. United States, 250 U.S. 616, 624, 628 (1919) (Holmes, J., dissenting).

4. United States v. Associated Press, 52 F. Supp. 362, 372 (S.D.N.Y. 1943) (emphasis added).

5. A. Meiklejohn, *Political Freedom* 24 (1965).

6. L. Bollinger, *The Tolerant Society: Freedom of Speech and Extremist Speech in America* 7 (1986) (emphasis in original). For perceptive commentary on the culturally constitutive aspects of law, see J. B. White, *Heracles' Bow: Essays on the Rhetoric and Poetics of the Law* 28–48 (1985). See also J. B. White, *When Words Lose Their Meaning* 231–274 (1984).

7. L. Bollinger, supra note 6, at 10.

8. I fear that a large literature may debate the meaning of a term like *cultural symbol*. I have nothing fancy in mind. See L. Marx, *The Machine in the Garden* 4 n.* (1964) ("A 'cultural symbol' is an image that conveys a special meaning (thought and feeling) to a large number of those who share the culture."). I am indifferent to the possibility that some might suggest that the first amendment is not an "image."

9. Rawls has also stressed the extent to which public values encourage a particular kind of person and that we should take that into account in determining the basic principles of justice. See, e.g., Rawls, "Kantian Constructivism in Moral Theory: The Dewey Lectures," 77 *J. Phil.* 515, 553 (1980). See also B. Barry, *Political Argument* 75–79 (1965).

10. See, e.g., R. Ladenson, *A Philosophy of Free Expression and Its Constitutional Applications* 106–107 (1983).

11. Indeed, the common law and statutory protection is quite meager. See id. at 106–143.

12. I do not mean to suggest that the "state action" requirement (the first amendment restricts governmental action, not private action) should be so narrowly construed. Far broader interpretations are possible. See, e.g., L. Tribe, *American Constitutional Law* 1688–1720 (2d ed. 1988); Van Alstyne & Karst, "State Action," 14 *Stan. L. Rev.* 3 (1961). For a somewhat narrower view, but more capacious than that currently reigning in contem-

porary Rehnquist Court doctrine, see Writers Guild of America v. FCC, 423 F. Supp. 1064 (C.D. Cal. 1976), *rev'd on different grounds*, 609 F.2d 355 (1979). The failure to find state action in the shopping center context is one of the many instances in which the present Court has denied constitutional protection by resort to an overly narrow conception of state action. See Hudgens v. NLRB, 424 U.S. 507 (1976) (attaching constitutional significance to the absence of a post office or a sewage disposal plant in the shopping center).

13. California, for example, has interpreted its own constitution to mandate access for leafleters to "private" shopping centers despite an owner's objection. See PruneYard Shopping Center v. Robins, 447 U.S. 74 (1980) (access to shopping center not required by the first amendment but California has power to mandate access and can do so without violating free speech rights or property rights).

14. A. Bloom, *The Closing of the American Mind* 26 (1987). E. D. Hirsch, Jr., *Cultural Literacy: What Every American Needs to Know* (1987), argues that American schools have followed a tradition traceable through Dewey to Rousseau, and in so doing have generally failed to promote "cultural literacy." Critical as he is of American education, he recognizes that the method employed by American schools, at least, has the virtue of encouraging "independence of mind." Hirsch would want schools to provide enough information to create a literate citizenry, but would not claim to and at least would not want to interfere with the encouragement of an independent mind. For a cogent contrast of Hirsch's project with Bloom's, see Rorty, "That Old-Time Philosophy," 198 *New Republic* 28, 31–32 (Apr. 14, 1988).

15. A common misperception about the conflict between liberalism and conservatism is that liberals think the state should be neutral about the good life and that conservatives believe the state should promote character and virtue. See, e.g., Dworkin, "Liberalism," in *Public and Private Morality* 113, 142 (S. Hampshire ed. 1978) (core of liberalism is that state should maintain "official neutrality amongst theories of what is valuable in life") (for discussion of Dworkin's evolution away from that position, see Shiffrin, "Liberalism, Radicalism, and Legal Scholarship," 30 *UCLA L. Rev.* 1103, 1131 n.105 (1983)); J. Rawls, *A Theory of Justice* §67, at 442, & §50, at 325–332 (1971) (after principles of justice are in place, government must "avoid any assessment of the relative value of one another's way of life"); W. Sullivan, *Reconstructing Public Philosophy* 181 (1986) (foundation of utilitarian liberalism is a "studied agnosticism about the nature of a good life").

No doubt, some liberals think the state should be neutral about the nature of the good life. Even there, the commitment to neutrality is largely supported by a conception of the good life that is thought to necessitate governmental neutrality. See generally V. Haksar, *Equality, Liberty, and Perfectionism* (1979); Richards, "Human Rights and Moral Ideals: An Essay on the Moral Theory of Liberalism," 5 *Soc. Theory and Prac.* 461 (1980); Shiffrin, supra, at 1119–1147.

But it is simply false as a matter of intellectual history or as a description of contemporary liberal politics to suppose that liberalism is generally characterized by a commitment to official neutrality about the character of the good life. To be sure, conservative and liberal political theories invariably conclude that the state should take a posture of neutrality about many issues. But pragmatic liberal democrats have for the most part supported museums and libraries, for example, precisely on the ground that such subsidies would support the good life. John Stuart Mill and John Dewey specifically argued that it was an important part of government's role to support a particular kind of person. See J. S. Mill, *Principles of Political Economy* §1, at 936–937, §8, at 947–950, & §15, at 968–970, in III *Collected Works of John Stuart Mill* (J. Robson ed. 1965); J. Dewey, *Liberalism and Social Action* 30–31 (Capricorn ed. 1963). Indeed, a key difference between liberals and conservatives more basically attends the question of *what type* of citizen the state should encourage rather than *whether* the state should encourage a particular type of citizen. Compare, for example, the tory emphasis of George Will with the ebullient emphasis of John Stuart Mill. In *Statecraft as Soulcraft* (1983), Will states that, "Proper conservatism holds that men and women are biological facts, but that *ladies and gentlemen* fit for self-government are social artifacts, creations of the law." Id. at 90–91 (emphasis added). By contrast, consider Isaiah Berlin's description of the ideals of John Stuart Mill: "[W]hat he came to value most was neither rationality nor contentment, but diversity, versatility, fullness of life—the unaccountable leap of individual genius, the spontaneity and uniqueness of a man, a group, a civilization. . . . [H]e set himself against the worship of order or tidiness, or even peace, if they were bought at the price of obliterating the variety and colour of untamed human beings with unextinguished passions and untrammelled imaginations." I. Berlin, *Four Essays on Liberty* 176–177 (1969). Mill's ideal, Berlin explained, is "not original. It is an attempt to fuse rationalism and romanticism . . . ." Id. at 199.

In the end, liberalism exhibits no monolithic character or deep structure. If one seeks to understand modern liberalism, and if one is forced to find *one* intellectual ancestor, I would turn to Mill (or Dewey), not Kant and not Bentham. See generally Shiffrin, supra (defending a neo-Millian eclectic liberalism).

16. See generally M. Yudof, *When Government Speaks* (1983); Shiffrin, "Government Speech," 27 *UCLA L. Rev.* 565 (1980).

17. Cf. Rawls, supra note 9, at 553: Once a publicity condition concerning the principles of justice is imposed, "a moral conception assumes a wide role as part of public culture. . . . [Citizens] are presented with a way of regarding themselves that otherwise they would most likely never have been able to entertain. Thus the realization of the full publicity condition provides the social milieu within which the notion of full autonomy can be understood and within which its ideal of the person can elicit an effective desire to be that kind of person." Nonetheless, Rawls maintains that his

approach abstracts from and does not rely upon particular conceptions of the
good (see id. at 325–332, 446–452, 542–543), but that contention rests on a
technical distinction between the right and the good which is no part of the
ordinary citizen's lexicon. His appeal to fairness is thus not as straightforward as it might initially appear. Moreover, it leads to conclusions most
liberals would resist. Rawls, for example, would too often use the concept of
fairness to bar subsidies of the arts. See Chapter 4, infra. Even on its own
terms, his use of the distinction between the right and the good is vulnerable. See, e.g., Haksar, supra note 15; Kymlicka, "Rawls on Teleology and
Deontology," 17 *Phil. & Pub. Aff.* 173 (Summer 1988). See generally Galston, "Moral Personality and Liberal Theory," 10 *Pol. Theory* 492, 506
(1982) ("If justice is desirable because it aims at our good as moral persons,
then justice as fairness rests on a specific conception of the good, from which
the 'constraints' of right and justice are ultimately derived.").

18. But "Harold Bloom" [an interview], in *Criticism in Society* 44, 58 (I.
Salusinszky ed. 1987): "Literature does not make us better, it does not make
us worse; the study of it does not make us better, it does not make us worse."

19. For a recent attempt, however, see C. Larmore, *Patterns of Moral
Complexity* xiii, 40–68 (1987). Larmore concedes that his justification is not
neutral with regard to all conceptions of the good life, though his admission
is not sweeping. Id. at 55, 60 (neutrality necessary in part for "civil peace"
and thus does not appeal to fanatics and "would-be martyrs"). It is not clear
whether those who do not believe civil peace depends upon neutrality are
also "fanatics" though it would appear Larmore would regard them as
merely misguided. In a more expansive admission, he concedes that "full
neutrality in a modern society may prove too empty to generate any substantive political principles." Id. at 67. Nonetheless, he contends that principles can be devised in a "spirit of neutrality" by adhering to the principle
that "one should institute only the least abridgment of neutrality necessary
for making a decision possible." Id. at 67–68.

Larmore maintains that his philosophy is a form of liberalism; indeed,
Kant and Mill, in his eyes, betray the liberal spirit by endorsing controversial aspects of the good life in their political theory. Id. at 129–130. His insistence on abstracting from controversial conceptions of the good life, however, leads him toward positions that most American liberals would find it
difficult to accept. In his form of liberalism, government could not encourage
lives that prize autonomy or experimentalism. See id. at 43 & 66. It would
have to be neutral, for example, between autonomous lives and lives based
on "uncritical acceptance of traditions and forms of life." Id. at 65. But few
liberals would be likely to accept that form of neutrality.

At another point, Larmore suggests that the state must be "neutral with
regard to the interests of rich and poor." Id. at 129. It is not clear what he
means by that, but he thinks that it may support, for example, transferring
wealth from Scarsdale to Harlem. Id. at 128–129. But he also thinks it may
not, and it seems clear that Larmore's neutrality principle would take prior-

ity over redistribution of wealth from rich to poor if he thought neutrality and redistribution conflicted. In this respect too he departs from the views of most liberals. If in fact they saw a conflict, it seems clear that the neutrality principle would give way before dispensing with a commitment to redistribution.

20. Stanley Fish apparently would disagree. He argues that "all contexts are equally (if differently) constraining" (Fish, "Critical Legal Studies (II)," 7 *Raritan* 1, 11 (Winter 1988)), "no context is looser—more open to revision—than any other," (id. at 12), "no context is more set—less open to revision—than any other" (id.). He states that if one moves from one vision to another, "the resulting practice will seem larger, more capacious than the practice he has left behind; but this capaciousness will be evident and palpable only from within the perspective that now becomes his horizon. For another person the new practice will seem not larger at all, but have the aspect of a restriction on the human capacity for growth and self-realization." Id. at 6. Although I agree that all contexts constrain, I think some (the American context) constrain less than others (Nazi Germany). This may be evident and palpable to me only within the perspective that is my horizon, but, as Fish would agree, I can only experience the world within the perspective that is my horizon (although that horizon may constantly change). If distinguishing between "loose" and "set" contexts requires an impossible point outside contexts to judge, it would also seem that the only way one could know that no context is looser or more set than any other would be to find a privileged point outside contexts to evaluate their looseness, but that Fish admits we cannot do. Even if one agreed with Fish in the abstract, we would return to our practice where we experience some contexts as freer than others. Similarly, we may believe there is no free will in the abstract, but in the concrete, we will experience the world, at least in part, as an aspect of our own freedom, and we will act accordingly.

So too, Richard Rorty may enjoin us to forget the notion of truth, asking us instead to adopt what is good for us to believe. But if "we divested ourselves of our commitment to truth, we would have no grounds for choosing." Maslan, "Foucault and Pragmatism," 7 *Raritan* 94, 107 (Winter 1988). That is, we determine what is good for us to believe, at least in part by what phenomenologically we believe to be true. "Even in deciding 'what it is good for *us* to believe,' for example, we must already have beliefs about who 'we' are and what is 'good' for us—beliefs we assume are correct." Id. at 106 (emphasis in original). Even if we agreed in the abstract that there was no such thing as truth, we would return to our practice in which we experience the view that we believe things because we believe them to be true rather than the other way around.

Finally, we may come to believe in the abstract that there is no right answer in hard cases, but when we make a decision in the concrete, we will make it because we believe it to be (however weakly) the right answer. See generally R. Dworkin, *Law's Empire* (1986).

21. See, e.g., R. Bellah, R. Madsen, W. Sullivan, A. Swidler & S. Tipton, *Habits of the Heart: Individualism and Commitment in American Life* (1985); W. Sullivan, supra note 15.

22. Emerson, "Freedom of Association and Freedom of Expression," 74 *Yale L.J.* 1, 2 (1964).

23. Even "intrapersonal" speech is dependent upon communally formed discourse and in that and other ways is a social practice.

24. J. S. Mill, *On Liberty* 6 (D. Spitz ed. 1975).

25. See "Geoffrey Hartman" [an interview], in *Criticism in Society,* supra note 18, at 74, 89: "I have enough trust in the conservatism of any mind, no matter how radical it is, that it will stabilize itself whether it wants to or not. Going into the classroom, I'm not afraid that students will subjectivate wildly, because I've found just the opposite: that they are out for a consensus, or something tangible."

26. Comment, "Unsafe for Little Ears? The Regulation of Broadcast Advertising to Children," 25 *UCLA L. Rev.* 1131, 1136 (1978) (referring to children aged two to eleven) (citing much of the literature).

27. Clearly, there were alternatives. See, e.g., B. Owen, *Economics and Freedom of Expression: Media Structure and the First Amendment* 88–92 (1975).

28. A former chair of the FTC calculated that the average high school graduate will have seen 350,000 televised commercial messages, more than 21,000 per year. "Unsafe for Little Ears?" supra note 26, at 1136 n.27.

29. But see C. Campbell, *The Romantic Ethic and the Spirit of Modern Consumerism* 89–90 (1987): "[T]he spirit of modern consumerism is anything but materialistic. The idea that contemporary consumers have an insatiable desire to acquire objects represents a serious misunderstanding of the mechanism which impels people to want goods. Their basic motivation is the desire to experience in reality the pleasurable dramas which they have already enjoyed in imagination, and each 'new' product is seen as offering a possibility of realizing this ambition. However, since reality can never provide the perfected pleasures encountered in day-dreams (or, if at all, only in part, and very occasionally), each purchase leads to literal disillusionment, something which explains how wanting is extinguished so quickly, and why people disacquire goods as rapidly as they acquire them. What is not extinguished, however, is the fundamental longing which day-dreaming itself generates, and hence there is as much determination as ever to find new products to serve as replacement objects of desire."

30. Tocqueville's warning is chilling when applied here: "I am trying to imagine under what novel features despotism may appear in the world. In the first place, I see an innumerable multitude of men, alike and equal, constantly circling around in pursuit of the petty and banal pleasures with which they glut their souls. Each one of them, withdrawn into himself, is almost unaware of the fate of the rest. Mankind, for him, consists in his children and his personal friends. As for the rest of his fellow citizens, they

are near enough, but he does not notice them. He touches them but feels nothing. He exists in and for himself, and though he still may have a family, one can at least say that he has not got a fatherland.

"Over this kind of men stands an immense, protective power [Tocqueville was thinking of government, but consider television] which is alone responsible for securing their enjoyment and watching over their fate. That power is absolute, thoughtful of detail, orderly, provident, and gentle. It would resemble parental authority if, fatherlike, it tried to prepare its charges for a man's life, but on the contrary, it only tries to keep them in perpetual childhood. It likes to see the citizens enjoy themselves, provided that they think of nothing but enjoyment." A. de Tocqueville, *Democracy in America* 691–692 (J. P. Mayer ed. 1969).

On the general sins of television, see J. Mander, *Four Arguments For the 'Elimination' of Television* (1978); N. Postman, *Amusing Ourselves to Death* (1985); Anastaplo, "Self-Government and the Mass Media: A Practical Man's Guide," in *The Mass Media and Modern Democracy* 161 (H. Clor ed. 1974).

31. J. S. Mill, supra note 24, at 6.

32. Promoting dissent promotes engaged association, but it might be observed that the engaged association produced by dissent itself involves separation from something or someone else. Some might worry that an emphasis on dissent thus stresses separation while a more progressive orientation would stress human connection. Against this concern it might be argued that if dissent were positively valued, dissent might be generally conceived as a form of assent, a form of good citizenship and participation, not an act of separation. I doubt it, however. My suspicion is that intolerance will be too much with us late and soon for dissent to be consistently experienced as an act of connection.

Nonetheless, by discussing the relationship between dissent and association as I have, I have not purported to exhaust the associational values in freedom of speech. Similarly, by emphasizing the extent to which dissent is underappreciated in first amendment discourse and that dissent should be promoted, I have not begun to suppose that the most important aspect of the self is its rebellious or transformative side. Nor finally do I suppose that the first amendment is the only important aspect of the Constitution. The equal protection clause may be the most important constitutional source of emphasizing connection in our public values (although, again, the associational aspects of the first amendment have never been adequately explored). For perceptive exploration of the relationship between dissent and conceptions of the self, see Cornell, "Beyond Tragedy and Complacency," 81 *Nw. U.L. Rev.* 693 (1987). See also Sunstein, "Routine and Revolution," 81 *Nw. U.L. Rev.* 869 (1987).

33. R. W. Emerson, "Self-Reliance," in *Ralph Waldo Emerson: Essays and Lectures* 257, 264 (J. Porte ed. 1983).

34. R. W. Emerson, "Intellect," in id. at 417, 425–426.

35. R. W. Emerson, "Friendship," in id. at 339, 347.

36. On intimate association generally, see Karst, "The Freedom of Intimate Association," 89 *Yale L.J.* 624 (1980).

37. See Blasi, "The Checking Value in First Amendment Theory," 1977 *Am. Bar Found. Research J.* 521, 550: "The case for freedom of expression is an uneasy one if it depends on the claim that the collective decisions that result from the existing or any reasonably foreseeable processes of opinion formation are likely to be wise, to ascertain some objectively verifiable reality, to reflect the most deeply rooted intuitions of the populace, or to be 'true' in any other significant sense."

38. See, e.g., *Emerson in His Journals* 65 (J. Porte ed. 1982). For an especially powerful critique of the marketplace model, see Baker, "Scope of the First Amendment Freedom of Speech," 25 *UCLA L. Rev.* 964, 974–981 (1978). Like Baker, I claim to retain those features of the marketplace model with the greatest appeal.

39. Cf. L. Tribe, supra note 12, at 1305 (emphasis in original), partially quoted in N. Rosenblum, *Another Liberalism* 65 (1987): "[I]t is arguable that the more human activity and human personality are shaped by the forces and pressures of homogenization spawned by mass industry and the mass media—the forces that define the culture and constitute the economy—the less sense it makes to spin out special limits and duties for *government* in its dealings with individual persons and groups."

40. Part of this encouragement stems from the notion that whatever emerges in the market is presumptively right, but there is a deeper aspect. In the economic marketplace it is frequently assumed by economists that there is no objectively correct price for a product. Instead buyers and sellers through freedom of contract agree on a mutually acceptable price, and "truth" can be said to emerge in the economic marketplace in and through the particular bargains struck. Whatever the merits of this perspective in the economic marketplace, even assuming the sagacity of subjectivity of value as to product price, there is no warrant to jump from subjectivity of product price to general notions of subjectivity of value. And yet this leap is encouraged by the marketplace metaphor. Cf. Stick, "Book Review," 88 *Colum. L. Rev.* 407, 415–417 (1988) (distinguishing between subjectivity of value in law and economics and in ethics or politics).

41. One of the most penetrating aspects of Vincent Blasi's checking value article is the discussion of the underlying appeal of the marketplace metaphor as more persuasively tied to an interest in diversity of expression than to an interest in truth. See Blasi, supra note 37, at 548–554. The dissent value, thus, embraces this major appeal of the marketplace metaphor even as it distances itself from the metaphor. Moreover, as argued in the text, the dissent value forges a closer conception to truth than the marketplace metaphor.

42. I cannot find the quotation, but I am certain Kalven said it or something close to it, and if he didn't, he should have.

43. J. S. Mill, supra note 24, at 46. Cf. Nehamas, "Truth and Consequences," 197 *New Republic* 31, 32 (Oct. 5, 1987): "Derrida has been concerned to display the undecidability of a whole host of distinctions, notably the pairs presence/absence, concept/sign, intelligible/sensible, center/margin, and others. In close and detailed readings of philosophers like Plato, Aristotle, Kant, and Husserl, he has argued that in each case the first member of each pair is considered more valuable, and a better guide to the truth, only because the features it shares with the second, which make both equally fallible, have been ignored or repressed." Finally, in this connection, consider L. Kolakowski, *Toward a Marxist Humanism* 32 (1968): "[T]hinking dominated by the growth of entropy, of conservatism, has been opposed in the course of intellectual history by a way of thinking that expresses the opposite, processes of increasing tension. All realms of culture, philosophy as much as art and custom, exemplify the paradox whereby everything that is new grows out of the endless need to question all acknowledged absolutes. And though every new current of thought that tries to break away from existing finalities establishes its own ultimates, and though every rebellion is therefore metamorphosed into a conservative state, still, it makes room for the next phase, where its own absolutes will in turn be the target of criticism." Compare R. W. Emerson, "Circles," supra note 33, at 404–414.

44. For a devastating attack on those who would advocate return to societies like the Greek polis (albeit without slavery), see Holmes, "Aristippus in and out of Athens," 73 *Am. Pol. Sci. Rev.* 113 (1979). See also C. Taylor, *Hegel* 395–396 (1975) (discussing Hegel's views on why we can not return to direct democracy). See generally I. Balbus, *Marxism and Domination* (1982) (advocating radical change and not thinking such change involves fantasy, but perceptively exploring many of the structural and attitudinal barriers to such change).

45. That hierarchies and bureaucracies are inevitable does not imply that any particular hierarchy or bureaucracy should be regarded as necessary or inevitable. For a vigorous attack on the mind set implicated in the acceptance of the inevitability of bureaucracies, see Frug, "The Ideology of Bureaucracy in American Law," 97 *Harv. L. Rev.* 1277 (1984).

46. Unger, "The Critical Legal Studies Movement," 96 *Harv. L. Rev.* 563, 589, 591–593 (1983).

47. Cf. Schauer, "The Role of the People in First Amendment Theory," 74 *Calif. L. Rev.* 761, 788 (1986) ("Perhaps it is time to face up to the paternalism of the first amendment, and maybe much of the rest of the Constitution as well.").

48. See Sunstein, supra note 32.

49. The framework might be different, but whatever the framework, the effect would be to discourage dissent of some type.

50. To take another example, the establishment clause chills the speech of anyone who would enforce public morality by establishing a local, state,

or federal church. Some would maintain that part of the motivation for the clause is the view that political debate divided along religious lines is too hot for a polity to handle. So understood, the establishment clause compromises our national commitment to robust debate. Whether or not it is understood that way, the clause unquestionably has a chilling effect on some speech. Yet the establishment clause is part of the first amendment, and no one is about to contend that the establishment clause violates the first amendment.

51. See, e.g., Blasi, supra note 37, at 641: "I think a proponent of the checking value should treat the mass demonstration as a preferred form of speech, important enough to justify the imposition on society of substantial costs in order to accommodate the activity. Just as with other forms of symbolic conduct, the mass demonstration can have an important emotional impact, on participants as well as observers. In addition, such gatherings often attract media coverage, and may in fact be the only way that new grievances can achieve a wide hearing."

52. Hudgens v. NLRB, 424 U.S. 507 (1976) (nothing in the first amendment prevents owner of modern shopping center complex from throwing dissenting picketers off the property).

53. See Columbia Broadcasting System, Inc. v. Democratic Nat'l Comm., 412 U.S. 94 (1973).

54. Indeed, despite a number of promising alternatives, the FCC has abolished the fairness doctrine and substituted nothing in its place. See Syracuse Peace Council, 2 FCC Rcd. 5043 (1987).

55. Columbia Broadcasting System, Inc. v. Democratic Nat'l Comm., 412 U.S. at 187 (dissenting).

56. See Miami Herald Pub. Co. v. Tornillo, 418 U.S. 241 (1974).

57. For probing discussion of access to the print and broadcast media from the perspective of the checking value (which overlaps the dissent value, see Chapter 2, note 167 supra), see Blasi, supra note 37, at 611–631 (favoring some forms of access regulation, but recognizing that other proponents of the checking value might well differ).

58. Conversely, it is not difficult to think of government regulations that are vulnerable to free speech objections but not to serious freedom of religion or equal protection objections. Consider, for example, the free speech and press limitations on libel law.

59. See L. Tribe, supra note 12, at 1157; Choper, "The Religion Clauses of the First Amendment: Reconciling the Conflict," 41 *U. Pitt. L. Rev.* 673 (1980); Moore, "The Supreme Court and the Relationship between the 'Establishment' and 'Free Exercise' Clauses," 42 *Tex. L. Rev.* 142 (1963).

60. See, e.g., Schauer, "Speech and 'Speech'—Obscenity and 'Obscenity': An Exercise in the Interpretation of Constitutional Language," 67 *Geo. L.J.* 899 (1979).

61. See Brandenburg v. Ohio, 395 U.S. 444 (1969).

62. Cf. Michelman, "Foreword: Traces of Self-Government," 100 *Harv.*

L. Rev. 4 (1986) (discussing importance of freedom of religion in the military).

63. See, e.g., Abood v. Detroit Bd. of Educ., 431 U.S. 209 (1977).

64. See Richards, "Free Speech and Obscenity Law: Toward a Moral Theory of the First Amendment," 123 *U. Pa. L. Rev.* 45 (1974).

65. See generally C. MacKinnon, *Feminism Unmodified* (1987). As one of my students argued in an excellent seminar paper commenting on this chapter, if dissent were to be regarded as central to free speech concerns, it would be important to take into account the silencing of a variety of people within the culture (e.g., young people, prison inmates, institutionalized people, homeless people, people of color, women, and gay people) who because of cultural forces either have not been allowed to say what they feel or are not heard when they speak. Gina Snyder, *Thoughts on Freedom of Expression* (1988). Cf. M. Foucault, *Power/Knowledge* 82 (1980) (through "unqualified," "disqualified" knowledge, "criticism performs its work").

66. That argument can be made on both sides does not imply that both sides are equal. In my view, MacKinnon's side has the better of the argument (see also Sunstein, "Pornography and the First Amendment," 1986 *Duke L.J.* 589 (1986)), although I recognize that legal academics and perhaps most feminist academics, legal and otherwise, take a contrary position.

As I suggest in the next paragraph of the text, the dissent perspective also has conflicting implications for how the law of defamation should tilt, but I find that conflict easy to resolve. Rodney Smolla put the point well in a passage with a strong Emersonian ring: "[I]f we take the libel suit too seriously, we are in danger of raising our cultural sensitivity to reputation to unhealthy levels. We are in danger of surrendering a wonderful part of our national identity—our strapping, scrambling, free-wheeling individualism, in danger of becoming less American, less robust, wild-eyed, pluralistic and free, and more decorous, image-conscious, and narcissistic. The media is itself partly to blame for this direction, and it would be dangerous to release it totally from the important check and balance that the libel laws provide. But in the United States, the balance that must be struck between reputation and expression should never be tilted too far against expression, for the right to defiantly, robustly, and irreverently speak one's mind just because it is one's mind is quintessentially what it means to be an American." R. Smolla, *Suing the Press* 257 (1986).

67. In a sense I am advocating a structure without a center. But cf. J. Derrida, *Writing and Difference* 278–279 (1978): "The function of this center was not only to orient, balance, and organize the structure—one cannot in fact conceive of an unorganized structure—but above all to make sure that the organizing principle of the structure would limit what we might call the *play* of the structure. By orienting and organizing the coherence of the system, the center of a structure permits the play of its elements inside the total form. And even today the notion of a structure lacking any center represents the unthinkable itself."

68. Nothing like mathematics is involved. For that reason, I am not moved by the clever objection that use of the dissent value is a form of double-counting, double-counting because dissent embraces other values, such as self-realization, that would be independently considered as well. Judicial decisionmaking is not a process of counting. Consideration of first amendment values from a variety of perspectives may enhance appreciation of such values, but it does not unfairly load the process.

69. Cf. Rorty, "Solidarity or Objectivity?" in *Post-Analytic Philosophy* 8 (J. Rajchman & C. West eds. 1985) (comparing and contrasting the application of criteria to cases as a mode of rationality with the "continual reweaving of a web of beliefs" as a mode of rationality).

70. 483 U.S. 378 (1987).

4. The First Amendment and Method

1. By *method,* I do not mean to imply anything scientific, technical, determinative, or rule-applying. But cf. H. Gadamer, *Truth and Method* xi, 18 (1982) (equating method with scientific method). I mean that to resolve a case one must have a way to resolve it. As will become clear, to the extent the term *method* connotes something more, I agree with Laurence Tribe, *Constitutional Choices* viii (1985): "[T]he very idea of 'method,' with its illusory suggestion of the precise and the systematic, is mostly an outgrowth of technocratic thought and practice and is thus the antithesis of humane struggle with those commitments and visions that are the stuff of genuine constitutionalism." Compare J. Ellison, *Emerson's Romantic Style* 228–229 (1984) (discussing the connection between the romantic tradition and the refusal to be bound by method).

2. Sometimes doctrine will, however. See Chapter 5, note 169 infra.

3. This claim is to some extent supported by the earlier chapters. Part of the goal of this chapter and the one that follows is to provide more pointed support for that claim.

4. For many, the term *passions* connotes more emotion and wildness than "desires," "preferences," or "wants." Nonetheless, I use the term to include both mildly and intensely held (or felt) desires, preferences, wants, or emotions.

5. One of the most original and insightful discussions of the richness of Kantian thought is H. Arendt, *Lectures on Kant's Political Philosophy* (R. Beiner ed. 1982). Other particularly original and appreciative accounts of aspects of Kantian thought include Scanlon, "Contractualism and Utilitarianism," in *Post-Analytic Philosophy* 215 (J. Rajchman & C. West eds. 1985), and C. Taylor, *Philosophy and the Human Sciences: Philosophical Papers 2* ch. 12 (1985).

6. I have taken fuller steps in that direction in Shiffrin, "Liberalism, Radicalism, and Legal Scholarship," 30 *UCLA L. Rev.* 1103 (1983).

7. As the notes to this chapter show, however, the model is not a work

of *pure* fiction. The kinds of appeals I discuss do appear in the writings of important Kantian scholars. I show this at some length in the notes because I do not want to clutter the text, but I do want to head off any denials that the appeals I describe are just straw. Ironically, those denials have come most vehemently from those who are most familiar with and attracted to the model I describe. The documentation in the notes is accordingly designed to be more than merely suggestive; at the same time, however, it is not intended to be an up-to-the-minute report on the latest twists and turns in Kantian scholarship. Thus, for example, I do not take account of Rawls, "The Priority of Right and Ideas of the Good," 17 *Phil. & Pub. Aff.* 251 (1988), an article that is Kantian in the sense I use the term, but not Kantian in the sense Rawls uses the term there and in some of his prior articles. See note 12 infra.

8. Someone anxious to provide a firm foundation for first amendment rights could be of the mind that acceptable general theory, however desirable, might not be devisable. For someone of that mind, it might be thought crucial to have at least a coherent and unified approach to doctrine, an overall strategy for the crafting of first amendment doctrine that would confine the discretion of judges. Thus Vincent Blasi has argued for clear and simple doctrine wherever possible. His belief is that lean first amendment doctrine is best suited to protect us in the worst of times. Blasi, "The Pathological Perspective and the First Amendment," 85 *Colum. L. Rev.* 449, 479 (1985). Similarly, Frederick Schauer worries that the extension of first amendment doctrine to areas such as commercial advertising risks trivializing the first amendment. See, e.g., Schauer, "Commercial Speech and the Architecture of the First Amendment," 56 *U. Cin. L. Rev.* 1181, 1201 (1988). He argues generally that the scope of the first amendment should be confined. He suggests that if first amendment doctrine becomes too complex, public officials will have neither the will nor the understanding to take the strictures of the first amendment seriously when they make decisions on the "front lines." Id. at 1200–1201. Thus, Schauer's ultimate concern is less about how judges decide cases than on the impact of doctrine outside the courts. Blasi is not unconcerned about that dimension, but his argumentation is more judge-focused than Schauer's; on the other hand, Blasi's development of the argument is more culture-focused than Schauer's. In quite different ways Blasi and Schauer argue that we need to husband first amendment resources for the truly big issues.

9. See note 103 infra.

10. Some radicals have produced free speech theory by drawing upon Kantian premises. C. Edwin Baker is the most important of the American legal scholars. Baker, "The Process of Change and the Liberty Theory of the First Amendment," 55 *S. Cal. L. Rev.* 293 (1981); Baker, "Realizing Self-Realization: Corporate Political Expenditures and Redish's *The Value of Free Speech*," 130 *U. Pa. L. Rev.* 646 (1982); Baker, "Scope of the First Amendment Freedom of Speech," 25 *UCLA L. Rev.* 964 (1978); Baker, "Com-

mercial Speech: A Problem in the Theory of Freedom," 62 *Iowa L. Rev.* 1 (1976). His general adherence to Kantian principles has become even more explicit in recent years. See, e.g., Baker, "Scope of the Freedom of Speech," supra at 991, 1000–1001, 1016 n.46, 1021, 1023–1024; Baker, "Outcome Equality or Equality of Respect: The Substantive Content of Equal Protection," 131 *U. Pa. L. Rev.* 933 (1983) (proposing an equality of respect model and arguing that his liberty theory of the first amendment would be among the principles that people in Rawls's position "could most plausibly and rationally choose," id. at 960). See also Baker, "Sandel on Rawls," 133 *U. Pa. L. Rev.* 895 (1985) (defending central themes of Rawls against criticisms of Sandel). Although Baker hopes to reach conclusions in the political realm by resort to the principle that persons in a political community must be treated with "full and equal respect and concern as autonomous persons" (Baker, "Equality of Respect," supra at 938), he recognizes that our reason is always "historically bounded." Baker, "Sandel on Rawls," supra at 924.

Outside of law the most conspicuous example is Jurgen Habermas. For criticism of Habermas's formalism, see Heller, "Habermas and Marxism," in *Habermas: Critical Debates* 21, 22 (J. Thompson & D. Held eds. 1982): "Habermasian man has . . . no body, no feelings; the 'structure of personality' is identified with cognition, language and interaction. Although Habermas accepts the Aristotelian differentiation between 'life' and 'the good life', one gets the impression that the good life consists solely of rational communication and that needs can be argued for without being felt." See also I. Balbus, *Marxism and Domination* 233 (1982) (criticizing Habermas's perspective on reason and passion). For a response to charges such as these by Habermas (also discussing the connection of his thought to Kant), see Habermas, "A Reply to My Critics," in *Critical Debates,* supra at 219. See also Habermas, "Questions and Counterquestions," in *Habermas and Modernity* 192, 211–216 (R. Bernstein ed. 1985) (responding to charges that his thought had "too much Kantianism"). For a clear statement of Habermas's embrace of Kantian thought, see Habermas, "Law and Morality," in 8 *The Tanner Lectures on Human Values* 217 (1988). In particular, see id. at 241 (emphasis in original): "Only theories of morality and justice developed in the Kantian tradition hold out the promise of an *impartial* procedure for the justification and assessment of principles."

11. If pragmatism was inaugurated with the hope of an egalitarian legal tilt in the twentieth century (see R. Summers, *Instrumentalism and American Legal Theory* 28–29 (1982); Grey, "Langdell's Orthodoxy," 45 *U. Pitt. L. Rev.* 1 (1983)), it had an antiegalitarian spin in the nineteenth century. Consider M. Horwitz, *The Transformation of American Law: 1780–1860* (1977) (in first part of nineteenth century instrumental conception of private law promoted antiegalitarian distribution; formal conception of private law later functioned to lock in the changes): "If a flexible, instrumental conception of [private] law was necessary to promote the transformation of the postrevolutionary American legal system, it was no longer needed once

the major beneficiaries of that transformation had obtained the bulk of their objectives. Indeed, once successful, those groups could only benefit if both the recent origins and the foundations in policy and group self-interest of all newly established legal doctrines could be disguised. There were, in short, major advantages in creating an intellectual system which gave common law rules the appearance of being self-contained, apolitical, and inexorable, and which, by making 'legal reasoning seem like mathematics,' conveyed 'an air . . . of . . . inevitability' about legal decisions." Id. at 254. Horwitz contends that during an important part of the nineteenth century a formal conception of public law coexisted with an instrumental conception of private law. Formalism in the public law worked to prevent legislatures from making egalitarian redistributive moves while instrumentalism in the private law "invariably tolerated and occasionally encouraged disguised forms of judicially sanctioned economic redistribution that actually increased inequality." Id. at 255.

Morton White argues in *Social Thought in America* 6 (1976) that: "Pragmatism, instrumentalism, institutionalism, economic determinism, and legal realism exhibit striking philosophical kinships. They are all suspicious of approaches which are excessively formal; they all protest their anxiety to come to grips with reality, their attachment to the moving and the vital in social life." Nonetheless, it is important to consider what they regard as vital and where they want to move. But as Summers, supra at 137, observes: Aside from a general progressive tendency, "The instrumentalists agreed more on their negations than . . . their affirmations . . . ."

12. J. Rawls, *A Theory of Justice* (1971). His approach deviated from Kant in important ways (see note 14 infra), and he has since modified his approach in ways that distance him even further from Kant. See Rawls, "The Idea of an Overlapping Consensus," 7 *Oxford J. Legal Stud.* 1 (1987); Rawls, "Justice as Fairness: Political Not Metaphysical," 14 *Phil. & Pub. Aff.* 223 (1985). *Compare A Theory of Justice,* supra at viii (theory is "highly Kantian in nature"); id. at 251–257 (emphasizing the Kantian character of his theory and expressing the view that the theory is for the most part faithful to Kant's intentions); and Rawls, "Kantian Constructivism in Moral Theory: The Dewey Lectures," 77 *J. Phil.* 515, 552 (1980) ("[I] regard justice as fairness as a Kantian view"—but pointing to ways in which it differs from Kant) *with* "Overlapping Consensus," supra at 5 ("While I believe that in fact any workable conception of political justice for a democratic regime must indeed be in an appropriate sense liberal . . . its liberalism will not be the liberalism of Kant or of J. S. Mill, to take two prominent examples." Nonetheless, I think Rawls's move away from Kant is primarily cosmetic. The influence of Kant continues to be enormous. His liberalism remains Kantian in the sense that Rawls uses the term: "[T]he adjective 'Kantian' expresses analogy and not identity; it means roughly that a doctrine sufficiently resembles Kant's in enough fundamental respects so that it is far closer to his view than to the other traditional moral conceptions that are

appropriate for use as benchmarks of comparison." Rawls, "Kantian Constructivism," supra at 517. See note 58 infra.

13. R. Dworkin, *Taking Rights Seriously* (1977). See text accompanying note 14 infra.

14. Dworkin, "Philosophy and Politics," in *Men of Ideas* 240, 259–260 (B. Magee ed. 1978). See generally Richards, "Human Rights and Moral Ideals: An Essay on the Moral Theory of Liberalism," 5 *Soc. Theory and Prac.* 461, 465 (1980) ("Kant . . . is, I believe, the most profound philosophical theorist of liberalism"). See generally D. Richards, *Toleration and the Constitution* (1986); D. Richards, *The Moral Criticism of Law* (1977); D. Richards, *A Theory of Reasons for Action* (1971).

See also B. Ackerman, *Social Justice in the Liberal State* (1980). Ackerman is certainly a general liberal theorist, but it is likely that he would resist a characterization of his work as Kantian. In a move adopted by Rawls in his more recent work, Ackerman argues that there is more than one path to liberalism, and he roots arguments for state neutrality toward the good life in a conception of undominated dialogue that some would regard as post-Kantian. See Ackerman, "What Is Neutral about Neutrality?," 93 *Ethics* 372, 375 n.1 (1983). Weale, "Book Review," 65 *Minn. L. Rev.* 685, 689–692 (1981). Nonetheless, Ackerman's rejection of utilitarianism and intuitionism and his emphasis on rationality, respect, and autonomy is distinctly Kantian. See *Social Justice,* supra at 57, 75, 111, 182, 255, 289, 302, 320, 347, 354. In particular, see id. at 367–368. Most of what I ultimately say about Kantian theory applies to Ackerman's work as well.

From the beginning, however, the modern Kantian scholars have departed from Kant in many aspects. For example, they do not subscribe to Kant's easy toleration of the massive inequality of wealth. Kant, "On the Common Saying: 'This may be True in Theory, but It does not Apply in Practice,'" in *Kant's Political Writings* 75 (Reiss ed. 1970). "This uniform equality of human beings as subjects of a state is, however, perfectly consistent with the utmost inequality of the mass in the degree of its possessions. . . . Nevertheless, they are all equal as subjects *before the law*." Id. (emphasis in original). But cf. I. Kant, *The Metaphysical Elements of Justice* 134 (J. Ladd trans. 1965) (permitting state funds for the poor, the disabled, and the sick). These scholars presumably do not share his stern views of punishment (id. at 98–108, 131–132) or his absolutist views about the moral duty to obey the law (id. at 86–87; Kant, "Theory and Practice," supra at 81). Nor do they necessarily subscribe to Kant's comprehensive views on morality. See, e.g., Rawls, "Overlapping Consensus," supra note 12. Like Kant, however, they do reject utilitarianism, exalt rights, and emphasize the concepts of respect and dignity. They are all abstractionists, believing or hoping that many of the most important political issues of our time can be solved by attention to and deduction from, or interpretation of, basic principles.

Kant is usually regarded as a horrible writer, but he has written an accessible summary of his political thought. See Kant, "Theory and Practice," supra, and Kant, "Idea for a Universal History with Cosmopolitan Intent," in *The Philosophy of Kant* 116 (C. Friedrich ed. 1949). The latter essay (or his *Critique of Judgment*) is indispensable for understanding his moral thought, and the failure to attend to the principles there embraced has caused some scholars to misinterpret Kant's most important moral writings. See note 77 infra.

15. As Gadamer, supra note 1, at 31, observes: "[Kant] developed his moral philosophy in downright opposition to the doctrine of 'moral feeling' that had been worked out in English philosophy. Thus he totally excluded the idea of [common sense] from moral philosophy." See, e.g., I. Berlin, *Vico and Herder: Two Studies in the History of Ideas* 164 (1976): "Kant drew a sharp line of division between, on the one hand, individual morality, universal, absolute, free from internal conflict, based on a transcendent rationality wholly unconnected with nature and history and empirical reality, and, on the other, the disharmonies of the processes of nature, the aim of which was the preservation of the species, and the promotion of progress by competition and strife." From Kant's perspective, the use of specific examples might serve to motivate people, but had no place in the *determination* of what might be morally right. See C. Larmore, *Patterns of Moral Complexity* 1–5 (1987). By contrast, consider Gadamer, supra at 36–37: "[O]ur knowledge of law and morality is always supplemented from the individual case, even productively determined by it. The judge does not only apply the law in concreto, but contributes through his very judgment to the development of the law . . . . Like law, morality is constantly developed through the fecundity of the individual case."

Most modern Kantians would not go nearly as far as Kant, but an emphasis on the general persists.

16. See, e.g., I. Kant, *Foundations of the Metaphysics of Morals* 46–47, 53–54 (L. Beck trans. 1959) (by contrast with humans, nonrational beings, which clearly include animals in Kant's usage, see note 17 infra, are things that can be treated as means that have a price but that have no dignity and are owed no respect). "Autonomy is . . . the basis of the dignity of both human nature and every rational nature." Id. at 54.

17. D. Richards, *Toleration and the Constitution,* supra note 14, at 72 (1986), quoting Frankfurt, "Freedom of the Will and the Concept of the Person," 68 *J. Phil.* 5, 7 (1971). Kant took this position to quite extreme lengths. He stated that: "Everything in creation which [man] wishes and over which he has power can be used merely as a means; only man, and, with him, every rational creature, is an end in itself." I. Kant, *Critique of Practical Reason* 90 (L. Beck trans. 1956). He explicitly maintained that no duty of any kind was owed to animals. See I. Kant, *The Metaphysical Principles of Virtue* 105 (J. Ellington trans. 1964). If only the animal were taken into account, nothing would prohibit animal torture. Nonetheless Kant argued that cruelty to animals was immoral because one has a duty to oneself not to engage in activities that reduce compassion because that "predisposition [is] very ser-

viceable to morality in one's relations with other men" and would be "weakened and gradually obliterated" if cruelty to animals were allowed. Id. at 106.

18. Kant frequently compared humans with animals as a part of his constructive argument. I find no similar emphasis in the writing of modern Kantians. But the emphasis on autonomy and the other concepts associated with it marks modern Kantian writing. Moreover, discussion of animals, to the extent it is raised, is strongly influenced by the initial Kantian conception of what is important about human beings. Rawls, for example, does not require that animals be included in the system of justice. He assumes that justice is not owed to those who inherently lack the capacity to have a sense of justice. J. Rawls, *A Theory of Justice,* supra note 12, at 504–512. He emphasizes the tentative character of his conclusions, opines that cruelty to animals is morally wrong, and recognizes that man's relation to animals and nature is a question of metaphysics beyond his work. Id. at 512.

19. He labels himself a "neoconservative," but, for our purposes, the "neo" adds nothing. In the specific essay I discuss, he calls himself a "liberal," a usage that gives the word just enough *new* meaning to rob it of *any* meaning. I. Kristol, "Pornography, Obscenity, and the Case for Censorship," in Kristol, *Reflections of a Neoconservative* 43, 54 (1983).

20. Id. at 47.

21. Id. at 45. Cf. Kant's treatment of the morality of animal torture, note 17 supra.

22. See generally V. Haksar, *Equality, Liberty, and Perfectionism* (1979). Shiffrin, supra note 6, at 1136–1140, 1172–1174 (1983).

23. See I. Kant, *The Metaphysical Elements of Justice,* supra note 14, at 35, 43–44. For discussion of the contrast between Kant's freedom principle and Mill's harm principle, see Shiffrin, supra note 6, at 1150–1153 (1983).

24. Cf. J. Rawls, *A Theory of Justice,* supra note 12, at 204: Assuming a particular type of society, "a basic liberty covered by the first principle can be limited only for the sake of liberty itself, that is, only to insure that the same liberty or a different basic liberty is properly protected and to adjust the one system of liberties in the best way." See also id. at 243–250; Rawls, "The Basic Liberties and Their Priorities," in 3 *The Tanner Lectures on Human Values* 3, 69 (1982) ("[A] basic liberty can be limited or denied solely for the sake of one or more other basic liberties, and never . . . for reasons of public good or of perfectionist values.") (discussing ways of accommodating conflicts between basic liberties in ways different from his earlier work).

Compare R. Dworkin, supra note 13, at 191 (interference with right justified if it interferes with another right, but allowing for the possibility of interference "to prevent a catastrophe, or even to obtain a clear and major public benefit" though stating that if the latter ground were accepted the right would not be among the most "important or fundamental"). See also Baker, "Scope of the First Amendment Freedom of Speech," supra note 10 (freely chosen speech protected unless it "coerces" another).

25. Richards, *Toleration and the Constitution,* supra note 14, at 207.

26. Again, this model is somewhat more extreme and oversimplified than the more complex versions presented in contemporary Kantian writing.

27. For a sample of the style of argument, see, e.g., D. Richards, *Toleration and the Constitution,* supra note 14, at 178–187. It is easy for a Kantian to explain why respect for persons demands protection for subversive advocacy. It is hard for a Kantian to explain why advocacy, however effective, should ever be proscribed. The state can punish those individuals who make the autonomous decision to commit illegal acts (unless the state has outlawed an act that persons have a right to engage in). Professor Richards argues, however, that advocacy of illegal action that is "imminently highly probable, very grave, and not rebuttable in the course of further dialogue" (id. at 182) can be outlawed not on utilitarian grounds (those grounds I would understand), but rather because the speech involves an "incendiary context in which our deliberative moral powers are not at play." Id. at 186.

It is unclear how the gravity requirement is derived by non-utilitarian analysis. It is unclear why the decisionmaking of the listener is not the exercise of a deliberative moral power. The notion that free speech applies only to the exercise of "deliberative moral powers" could be applied in ways that would be exceedingly dangerous to dissent. For analysis that has difficulties at the same point, but in a somewhat less focused (perhaps less consistent) way, see Rawls, supra note 24, at 51, 55–72.

If I understand Professor Baker's analysis, advocacy of illegal action is always protected, but providing information to help bank robbers would constitute unprotected participation in a coercive act. See Baker, "Scope of the First Amendment Freedom of Speech," supra note 10, at 1000–1005. On his analysis, engaging in espionage by secretly providing information of importance to a foreign nation is *protected* unless it is reasonable to conclude that the information "increases the coercive power of another country" (making it like the bank robbery example). Aside from the thinness of the line between advocacy and participation, and conceding that "espionage" should not be a label beyond first amendment scrutiny (consider the publication of information authorities do not want published—should an espionage label automatically permit censorship? for any and all private conversations?), Professor Baker's conclusions will suggest to many that his methodology does not leave enough room for consequentialist considerations.

28. For telling criticism of the Kantian position using the same example (albeit somewhat differently developed), see Hart, "Rawls on Liberty and Its Priority," in *Reading Rawls* 230 (N. Daniels ed. 1975).

29. I. Kant, *The Philosophy of Law* 138 (W. Hastie ed. 1887).

30. See id.

31. See Baker, "Scope of the First Amendment Freedom of Speech," supra note 10, at 1000–1001 (allowing one to decide whether to use speech "to

affect the world" even in ways that undermine reputation is "central to a respect for one's autonomy and integrity as a person"). Cf. Baker, "Press Rights and Government Power to Structure the Press," 34 *U. Miami L. Rev.* 819, 831 n.38 (1980) (more guarded claim that his theory provides a "plausible" ground for abolishing the tort of defamation).

Rawls does not list a right of reputation in his enumeration of basic liberties, though the right to hold property is mentioned. See J. Rawls, *A Theory of Justice,* supra note 12, at 61. Rawls's listing does not purport to be comprehensive, however. What is missing is a clear methodology for determining what should count as rights. For cogent criticism using the defamation example, see Hart, supra note 28, at 230–252.

Rawls responds to Hart in the *Tanner Lectures,* supra note 24. In discussing defamation he leans heavily on the importance of speech that relates to the basic structure of society or on the freedom of political speech. His discussion of defamation of nonpolitical figures is cryptic: "Libel and defamation of private persons (as opposed to political figures) has no significance at all for the public use of reason to judge and regulate the basic structure, and it is in addition a private wrong." Id. at 51.

Why should it matter that such speech may not be related to the basic structure? Why, for example, is talking freely about nonpolitical persons not important for "forming, revising, and rationally pursuing a conception of the good over a complete life." Id. at 50. If the pursuit of the conception of the good can ground freedom of conscience and freedom of association (and for Rawls, it can—see id.), why is not freedom of speech about nonpolitical persons part of that freedom of association? Even if one were to concede that the only speech one should care about is political speech or speech relevant to the basic structure, Rawls's statement would be quite problematic unless *political* were broadly defined (consider business leaders). Alternatively, what is a "private wrong"? Is reputation needed for self-respect? For the self-respect of political leaders?

32. R. Dworkin, supra note 13, at 193 (emphasis added).

33. This is at least a plausible and certainly the most common reading of Dun & Bradstreet, Inc. v. Greenmoss Builders, Inc., 472 U.S. 749 (1985), though, strictly speaking, the case is confined to the constitutional rules affecting damages.

34. Gertz v. Robert Welch, Inc., 418 U.S. 323 (1974) (fault showing required, at least against media defendants (and perhaps confined to certain issues), of those plaintiffs who are not public figures or public officials).

35. See id. (public official or public figure must show that defendant entertained serious doubts about the truth of the statement or knew it to be false, at least against certain defendants on certain issues).

36. See, e.g., Barr v. Matteo, 360 U.S. 564 (1959) (affording absolute immunity from libel judgments to federal officials with respect to statements made in the course of their duties).

37. See, e.g., Paul v. Davis, 424 U.S. 693 (1976) (in the absence of a state-created entitlement, reputation not part of the liberty or property protected by due process of law).

38. Indeed Professor Richards makes a heroic attempt to do just that. See D. Richards, *Toleration and the Constitution,* supra note 14, at 195–203 (assessing the extent to which equal respect demands that reputational integrity be a "general good" giving rise to a protected right). As he develops the argument, equal respect ends up demanding a public/private distinction and a change in the law of remedies affecting defamation. These conclusions turn in part on what Richards would concede to be controversial judgments about the effectiveness of replies in various contexts in securing reputation. An interest in reputation is characterized as a thing "free and rational persons would want as conditions of the self-respecting pursuit of whatever else they want." Id. at 196. But a legally protected interest in reputation is not something free and rational persons want whatever else they want. Free and rational persons just disagree about whether they want a legally protected interest in reputation and the extent to which they want it, if at all. Indeed, in an interesting way, many academics are behind the veil. They have reputations, and they want to speak. But they can come to no consensus about what the law should be. It is hard to see how the argument is advanced by phrasing it in terms of equal respect. Indeed, there is a way in which the theory could hurt because it presses one to accept the protection of reputation as a *right,* at least to the extent free speech is to be compromised on its behalf. Thus, under Kantian theory, governments would be required to protect reputation in all those instances in which they were permitted to do so. Such rigidity might be desirable, but there is no good reason as a matter of theory to be precommitted to such a conclusion.

39. For a particularly persuasive attack, see Hart, supra note 28.

40. No Kantian would posit a general right to be free of mental distress. Moreover, there may be reluctance to focus upon mental distress as the source of any right. But, as discussed below, a number of problems can be clustered around the concept of mental distress, but which do not seem to lend themselves to solution at any high level of abstraction. For a provocative critique of the tort of intentional infliction of emotional distress, see F. Haiman, *Speech and Law in a Free Society* 148–156 (1981).

41. J. S. Mill, *On Liberty* 87–88 (D. Spitz ed. 1975).

42. This device is also crucial in discussions of John Stuart Mill's harm principle. For debate about the scope of the principle, compare, e.g., Rees, "A Re-reading of Mill on Liberty," 8 *Pol. Stud.* 113 (1960), with, e.g., Wollheim, "John Stuart Mill and the Limits of State Action," 40 *Soc. Research* 1 (1973). For general criticism from a radical perspective, see R. Wolff, *The Poverty of Liberalism* (1969); from a more conservative perspective, see McCloskey, "Liberty of Expression: Its Grounds and Limits," 13 *Inquiry* 219 (1970); McCloskey, "Mill's Liberalism—A Rejoinder to Mr. Ryan," 16 *Phil.*

Q. 64 (1966); McCloskey, "A Critique of the Ideals of Liberty," 74 *Mind* 483 (1965). See also Baker, "Scope of the First Amendment Freedom of Speech," supra note 10, & sources cited in note 43 infra.

43. This denial is common to followers of both Mill and Kant and has particularly prompted criticism that it leads to evasion or to counterintuitive results in cases involving publicly offensive conduct. That theme is a recurring one in discussions of John Stuart Mill because he was willing to prohibit public sexual activity as indecent (see J. S. Mill, supra note 41, at 91) despite his otherwise fervent call for insisting that activity must cause harm to the interest of others (beyond that of causing offense) before it might be prohibited. See, e.g., Honderich, "Mill On Liberty," 10 *Inquiry* 292, 294 (1967); McCloskey, "Mill's Liberalism," 13 *Phil. Q.* 143, 151 (1963); Monro, "Liberty of Expression: Its Grounds and Limits," 13 *Inquiry* 238, 240 (1970). The same line of argument has been urged against Rawls and Dworkin. See V. Haksar, supra note 22, at 290–291. Dworkin has since adjusted his position in a way that tries to address the objection (though Haksar's work is not specifically discussed). See R. Dworkin, *A Matter of Principle* 363–365 (1985). It is not obvious how Dworkin's even more recent account about how rights should be determined would deal with this question. See Dworkin, "What Is Equality? Part 3: The Place of Liberty," 73 *Iowa L. Rev.* 1, 31–34 (1987). For a perceptive guide to many of the pitfalls in this area, see Ellis, "Offense and the Liberal Conception of the Law," 13 *Phil. & Pub. Aff.* 3 (1984).

44. One important limiting stratagem is to limit the operative definition of personal freedom to basic liberties or fundamental rights or primary goods.

45. For a crisp statement of the difficulties, see R. Dworkin, supra note 43, at 336–337.

46. Baker, "Scope of the First Amendment Freedom of Speech," supra note 10, at 1019 n.153, argues that public nudity designed to confront the public should be constitutionally protected under a liberty theory of the first amendment.

47. See D. Richards, *Toleration and the Constitution,* supra note 14, at 195: To permit abridgement on grounds of offense "would sanitize authentic exercises of the moral powers of a free people."

48. For perceptive discussion of the harms implicated by Nazi marches, see L. Bollinger, *The Tolerant Society* 58–71 (1986).

49. For discussion, see Arkes, "Civility and the Restriction of Speech: Rediscovering the Defamation of Groups," 1974 *Sup. Ct. Rev.* 281, 310–311.

50. For the case for regulating racial insults, see Delgado, "Words That Wound: A Tort Action for Racial Insults, Epithets, and Name-Calling," 17 *Harv. C.R.-C.L. L. Rev.* 133 (1982).

51. I do not mean to suggest that those who write in the Kantian tradition would oppose restrictions in every one of these cases. I do suggest that these examples present a general challenge to Kantian theory in all of its

forms. For an interesting attempt to respond to the challenge in an analysis that modifies his earlier conception of the substantive content of rights, see R. Dworkin, *A Matter of Principle,* supra note 43, at 335–372 (public displays of pornographic material determine the environment for those who object and alter the character of their sexual experience, and he would, therefore, consider a prohibition of public display to be consistent with a "right of moral independence," a compromise recommended by it rather than a compromise of it (id. at 365)). For criticism of the public/private distinction in this context, see Baker, "Counting Preferences in Collective Choice Situations," 25 *UCLA L. Rev.* 381, 387–391 (1978).

52. In response to criticism from Hart, Rawls now emphasizes that the conception of justice he endorses "is not to be regarded as a method of answering the jurist's questions, but as a guiding framework, which if jurists find it convincing, may orient their reflections, complement their knowledge, and assist their judgment. *We must not ask too much of a philosophical view.*" Rawls, supra note 24, at 84 (emphasis added). So understood, Rawls moves away from the Kantian model and toward the eclectic model described infra (although he excludes considerations an eclectic approach would not exclude). Nonetheless, Rawls's emphasis is directed at the general framework, and he purports in the *Tanner Lectures* to draw conclusions, often firm conclusions, about advocacy of illegal action, defamation, commercial speech, and campaign finance. An eclectic would insist that, Rawls's caveat aside, he asks too much of a philosophical view.

53. For a different example emphasizing the importance of context as against reasoning from abstract principles, see M. Tushnet, *Red, White, and Blue: A Critical Analysis of Constitutional Law* 112–118 (1988).

54. I do not mean to suggest that the appeals I discuss have necessarily been consciously made by Kantian writers or that they necessarily reflect anything about the psychology of particular Kantian writers. Indeed, there is often a mismatch between the political ideals of an individual and his or her personality. See I. Berlin, supra note 15, at 205 n.1 ("[Herder's] vision of the unity of the human personality . . . was the polar opposite of [his] own character and conduct. . . . His ideals seem at times a mirror image of his own frustrations.") Cf. Frug, "Argument as Character," 40 *Stan. L. Rev.* 869, 896 n.86 (1988) (analysis of the character evoked by a speech given by Derek Bok without purporting to draw inferences about Bok's character). I am focused on how Kantian theory might appeal to a recipient of it wholly apart from an author's actual intent or character. At the same time, it will be obvious that many of the appeals have been consciously made by Kantian writers; indeed, some of them are also part of the substance of Kantian theory.

55. For the suggestion that freedom of thought—and in particular free moral thought, including the freedom to think for ourselves about what the good life may be—is at the heart of Kant's notion of freedom, see H. Putnam, *The Many Faces of Realism* 50–51 (1987) (stating that the characteristic

with respect to which Kant sees us as equal is that "We all are in the same predicament, and we all have the potential of thinking for ourselves with respect to the question of How to Live").

56. This external freedom of individuals is by no means the essence of Kantian freedom, however. For Kant, the essence of freedom is moral autonomy and that moral autonomy demands submission to the dictates of reason. For Kant, moral autonomy does not mean slavery to the passions. To be moral is to act from the motivation of duty. Acting out of a sense of duty might produce happiness, but it might not. For Kant, happiness is not the point of moral personality. On the other hand, Kant's hope is that societies will emerge in which morally autonomous individuals will lead happy lives. In the final analysis, Kant thought the "creator's unique intention is neither human morality in itself nor happiness in itself, but the highest good possible on earth, the union and harmony of them both." See Kant, "Theory and Practice," supra note 14, at 65. For a brief and cogent exposition, see C. Taylor, supra note 5, ch. 12.

57. Cf. Scanlon, supra note 5, at 229 (essence of moral motivation is the desire to be able to justify actions to others on grounds they could not reasonably reject). This understanding, however, is, of course, compatible with a variety of different conceptions of autonomy and of methodological choices. It need not lead one to be optimistic about the possibilities of justification at high levels of abstraction. For different conclusions about aspects of free speech, both of which seem compatible with Scanlon's account of moral motivation, compare Scanlon, "A Theory of Freedom of Expression," 1 *Phil. & Pub. Aff.* 204 (1972), with Scanlon, "Freedom of Expression and Categories of Expression," 40 *U. Pitt. L. Rev.* 519 (1979).

58. Interestingly, when Rawls moves away from Kantian theory, he does so on the ground that it can not produce a consensus, not on the ground that such theory is itself defective. See generally, Rawls, "Overlapping Consensus," supra note 12. Thus, in this sense, he adheres to a basic Kantian appeal: he wants to find a principle that can effectively transcend the myriad passions of the society. Moreover, he continues to follow what he has described as a Kantian view: "We may suppose that [such a view] takes as fundamental certain first principles of right and justice that assign rights and liberties, liabilities and responsibilities to individuals and requires that basic institutions and social cooperation generally take a certain form, or satisfy certain constraints." Rawls, "The Independence of Moral Theory," 48 *Proc. and Addresses of the Am. Phil. A.* 5, 18 (1975). He maintains, however, that he does not rely on the comprehensive moral ideals of Kant because he does not want to rule out other conceptions of the good. In particular, he has mentioned that nothing in his theory requires endorsement of the application of Kant's treatment of the categorical imperative to everyday life. Rawls, "Kantian Constructivism," supra note 12, at 552.

Quite true. Nonetheless, in pursuit of the objective of transcending the passions, he continues to hold to the veil of ignorance ("Overlapping Consensus," supra at 7 n.13; Rawls, "Political Not Metaphysical," supra note 12, at 234–239) for which he has supplied a Kantian interpretation that remains fully applicable. See note 12 supra. Moreover, the basic premise leading to the veil is that persons are free and equal (id. at 229–234) (with the notion of freedom including rationality, see id. at 233–234), a premise he has identified as Kantian. See Rawls, "The Independence of Moral Theory," supra at 13; Rawls, "Kantian Constructivism," supra note 12, at 518. This basic premise further assumes that people wish to participate in a fair scheme of social cooperation ("Political Not Metaphysical," supra at 231–234). Finally, he continues to adhere to essentially the same substantive political principles. Id. at 227–228 (some modifications in light of criticism by Hart). Thus, if he has moved further from Kant, he has not moved far. (For the contention that he could not coherently avoid a strong conception of the good, see V. Haksar, supra note 22; Shiffrin, supra note 6. See also note 129 infra.

59. Some of Rawls's more recent writing superficially appears to avoid transcending the passions and, in that respect, can be characterized as removed from the Kantian project. First, he characterizes justification as proceeding from premises shared within the culture ("Political Not Metaphysical," supra note 12, at 229) or as "implicit or latent in the public culture" (id. at 231 n. 14; see "Overlapping Consensus," supra note 12, at 6). Thus the goal is not "a conception of justice that is true, but one that can serve as a basis of informed and willing political agreement between citizens viewed as free and equal persons." Rawls, "Political Not Metaphysical," supra, at 230. In a sense Rawls is now relying on a hermeneutic justification, one that is claimed to rise out of an interpretation of the deepest intuitions of the culture. With respect, however, I regard this as "fake hermeneutics," one that dips into the passions momentarily to seize on general abstractions of freedom and equality only to leap even further up the ladder of abstraction to the veil of ignorance.

The assumption that this turn in the project might produce a consensus over the long run is ambitious, particularly since the consensus Rawls seeks applies not only to the principles of justice but also to the question of their application. See "Overlapping Consensus," supra at 8. The analysis, however, seems to blink considerations of power, to overestimate good will, and to underestimate the diversity of American society.

Even on its own terms, the analysis is offered as an alternative to utilitarianism, which is characterized by Rawls as dominant in our tradition (see "Political Not Metaphysical," supra at 226), but utilitarianism is to be excluded from Rawls's overlapping consensus (unless it is modified along Millian lines) ("Overlapping Consensus," supra at 12). If utilitarianism truly were dominant in our tradition (does Rawls's assumption confuse pragmatism with utilitarianism?), this exclusion would have to be regarded as a serious problem, for Rawls's system strives to be built on shared values. But this difficulty reaches beyond utilitarianism. For, unless I misread him,

Rawls means to exclude from the consensus all who would embrace "perfectionism" (which among other things would use government to promote a conception of the good life) in any form and that, on Rawls's analysis, would mean, for example, in many circumstances that government could not use tax dollars to support the arts, the sciences, or the culture. (See J. Rawls, *A Theory of Justice,* supra note 12, at 329–332, discussed in Shiffrin, supra note 6, at 1132–1133.) In that posture Rawls would be advancing a particular type of liberalism that is probably unacceptable in one way or another to most Americans. If it were advanced as just and true, this would not be philosophically problematic. But Rawls now offers his system, however speculatively, as a practical basis for consensus and that gives some bite to the criticism. For criticism of Rawls's opposition to perfectionism, see generally Shiffrin, supra, and Nielsen, "The Choice between Perfectionism and Rawlsian Contractarianism," 6 *Interpretation* 132 (1977).

60. Rawls, "Overlapping Consensus," supra note 12, at 15 n.24.

61. J. Rawls, *A Theory of Justice,* supra note 12, at 121. See also note 66 infra. But cf. id. at 121 (although his argument "aims eventually to be strictly deductive" it "[u]nhappily" is conceded to be "highly intuitive throughout"); Rawls, "Political Not Metaphysical," supra note 12, at 239 n.21 ("Although the aim cannot be perfectly achieved, we want the argument to be deductive, 'a kind of moral geometry'"). The metaphor connecting law and geometry is perceptively explored in Grey, supra note 11. As he observes, "The geometric ideal pervades the literature of the whole rationalist movement to create exact sciences of ethics, politics and law that dominated European thought from Grotius to Kant, and that still remains strong in European legal scholarship today." Id. at 16.

62. See note 125 infra.

63. Cf. Okin, "Reason and Feeling in Thinking about Justice," 99 *Ethics* 229 (1989) (feminist critique of Kant and Rawls, but arguing that the original position can be rescued from criticism by emphasizing its capacity to reflect values of empathy and benevolence).

64. But cf. note 129 infra.

65. W. James, "The Sentiment of Rationality," in *The Writings of William James* 317, 318 (J. McDermott ed. 1977). Kant clearly understood this appeal. See text accompanying Chapter 1, note 3 supra. And Robert Nisbet observes generally that: "In the Enlightenment . . . simplicity was in every sense of the word a theme. It was virtually taken for granted that reality in any sphere would be known by its simplicity. . . . Simplicity was, in sum, a theme of the Enlightenment in that it underlay nearly all the concrete efforts toward either understanding or reconstruction in social thought." R. Nisbet, *Sociology as an Art Form* 35 (1977). Although James describes the appeal of simplicity in great detail, he was quite hostile to it. See James, supra at 320–321: "[T]he simple classification of things is, on the one hand, the best possible theoretic philosophy, but is, on the other, a most miserable and inadequate substitute for the fulness of the truth. It is a monstrous

abridgement of life, which, like all abridgements is got by the absolute loss and casting out of real matter. This is why so few human beings truly care for philosophy."

66. See R. Dworkin, *Law's Empire* 302 (1986): "My argument is not deductive. It does not show that once anyone accepts the root idea of equality of resources he will automatically and inevitably be driven to the conclusions I report. I argue only that he will be required to make a series of choices refining that conception for the cases we are considering and that plausible choices would then direct him to market simulation in most ordinary cases." See also Rawls, "Kantian Constructivism," supra note 12, at 572 (under a constructivist view "the original position is not an axiomatic (or deductive basis) from which principles are derived"). But cf. note 61 supra.

67. See R. Dworkin, *A Matter of Principle,* supra note 43, at 357: "The process of making an abstract right successively more concrete is not simply a process of deduction or interpretation of the abstract statement but a fresh step in political theory." Notice that the process, in Dworkin's view, remains one of making the abstract right concrete. In an important sense, then, the abstract statement *is* being interpreted. See Michelman, "Foreword: Traces of Self-Government," 100 *Harv. L. Rev.* 4, 28 (1986): "Judgment mediates between the general standard and the specific case. In order to apply the standard in the particular context before us, we must interpret the standard."

68. As Professor Joel Feinberg notes, such recognition can be grudging. J. Feinberg, *Rights, Justice, and the Bounds of Liberty* 257 (1980), referring to J. Rawls, *A Theory of Justice,* supra note 12, at 303: "At some point the priority of rules for nonideal cases will fail; and indeed, we may be able to find no satisfactory answer at all. But we must try to postpone the day of reckoning as long as possible, and try to arrange society so that it never comes."

69. Rawls contends that stability depends upon the members of the society perceiving the distribution of the fruits of their cooperation as "sufficiently" just. Rawls, "Kantian Constructivism," supra note 12, at 536. See generally Rawls, "Overlapping Consensus," supra note 12 (without agreement on the principles of justice and methods for their application, society is fragile and lacks sufficient stability). By contrast, most eclectics would deny the possibility of any such agreement and might well deny that the failure to reach such agreement means that social cohesion is fragile or society unstable. Cf. A. MacIntyre, *After Virtue* 206 (1981): "Traditions, when vital, embody continuities of conflict." See also note 75 infra.

70. Although the rhetorical appeal is present, I would not contend that Kantians necessarily regard it as an affirmative part of their argument. Kant did not, for example. See C. Larmore, *Patterns of Moral Complexity,* supra note 15, at 77: "Abstracting from our own conception of the good life is not, for [Kant], something we do for the particular purpose of arriving at

common political principles. Instead, Kant held that maintaining a certain distance toward such conceptions should shape our lives throughout, because it is an emblem of our nature as moral beings."

71. See, e.g., Dworkin, "What Is Equality?" supra note 43, at 32 (offering an alternative to any theory that hopes to make liberty contingent on the "convictions or preferences that people happen to have, or would have under specified conditions or should have").

72. Cf. R. Unger, *Social Theory: Its Situation and Its Task* 143 (1987) ("The persuasive force of the case against modest eclecticism depends to a large extent upon the availability of alternatives. . . . The sole argument with a chance to convince would be the actual formulation of an alternative theoretical practice. We would have to work out the ideas that can in fact dispense with the makeshift compromises of modest eclecticism and carry forward the antinaturalistic view of society."); see also J. Rawls, *A Theory of Justice,* supra note 12, at 39 (using the label intuitionist instead of eclectic) ("A refutation of intuitionism consists in presenting the sort of constructive criteria that are said not to exist").

73. In this regard the eclectics have received unwitting aid from general theorists. The first task of any general theorist is to show that every other general theory is misguided. Thus the general theorists lead the way in gathering support for the view that general theory is unpromising.

74. In a sophisticated discussion of the role of abstract principles in legal and political theory, Jeffrey Blum argues that the content of abstract principles not only must grow out of our historical circumstances, but must also be controversial. "Controversy," he says, "is a sign not of intellectual failure but of there being something important at stake. When thought is both rational and controversial, then it is likely that the indispensable processes of human mental adaptation are at work." Blum, "Quest for Substance" (Book Review), 35 *Buffalo L. Rev.* 735, 738 (1986). Blum is no Kantian, and his message is not particularly directed at Kantians, but it is an interesting question as to how much of Kantianism turns upon the desire for moral geometry or for proof acceptable to all free and rational persons. Presumably, a person wedded to Kantian notions of autonomy might accept Blum's perspective. Another interesting aspect of Blum's contribution is his explicit recognition that the content of theory should be selected not with the hope of dictating results, but with an eye to molding preferences and passions. Indeed, on the latter point, Rawls also recognizes the extent to which preferences will and ought to be affected by society's adoption of the principles of justice. See, e.g., J. Rawls, *A Theory of Justice,* supra note 12, at 259–263, 515–516.

75. Consider Mouffe, "Rawls: Political Philosophy without Politics," 13 *Phil. & Soc. Criticism* 105, 115–116 (1987): "In a modern democratic society there can no longer be a substantial unity, and division must be regarded as constitutive. . . . If Rawls had possessed such an understanding of the political and been able to see the democratic tradition not as a simple collection

of shared meanings, institutions and intuitive ideas but as a specific mode of institution of the social, he would have realized that there never could be, in a modern democracy, a final agreement on a single set of principles of justice."

76. See, e.g., J. Rawls, *A Theory of Justice,* supra note 12, at 263: "[T]he two principles of justice are not contingent upon existing desires or present social conditions." But cf. Rawls, "Political Not Metaphysical," supra note 12, at 250 ("[W]e are forced to consider at some point the effects of the social conditions required by a conception of political justice on the acceptance of that conception itself.").

77. Some suppose that Kant hoped to generate a moral theory from the bare idea of rationality itself. As Rawls states, however, "The categorical imperative often gives reasonable results, but it does so only because additional features, which are not part of the concept of a purely rational being, have been introduced." Rawls, supra note 58, at 10; see also Rawls, *A Theory of Justice,* supra note 12, at 251 (would be a mistake to emphasize the place of universality and generality in Kant's moral theory—its force lies elsewhere). Kant, however, apparently thought that his normative conception of human nature came from reason. That is, he thought we could not know that the world we appear to see is the world as it is. But it is reasonable for us to act *as if* it is and to act *as if* an intellect designed nature with a purpose and human nature with a purpose. The failure to recognize Kant's belief that man is the end of nature and that practical reason should be guided by an account of nature's purpose has led many to attack Kant's moral theory as being merely empty and merely formal. See, e.g., A. MacIntyre, supra note 69, at 52; R. Wolff, *The Autonomy of Reason* 176 (1973); R. Unger, *Knowledge and Politics* 85–86 (1975). Kant did not maintain that we could *know* the purpose of nature, but he did think that our practical reason could be guided by *assumptions* about that purpose. Only in a limited sense then does Kant deny a teleological view of human nature. See generally Kant, *Critique of Judgment,* supra note 14. For pointed and cogent discussion of this question, see Riley, "On Ladd's Review of *Kant's Political Philosophy,*" 12 *Pol. Theory* 597 (1984). See also Riley, "The 'Elements' of Kant's Practical Philosophy," 14 *Pol. Theory* 552, 564 (1986) (contending that Kant's teleology clamps Kantianism together and contending that moral ends are *knowable* in Kantian theory while the ends of nature and art are interpreted teleologically, id. at 567).

If one accepts that this teleological reading of Kant is correct (obviously it is controversial), the weakness of Kant's theory lies in the character of his assumptions about human beings and the weight he gives them; he can not properly be faulted for failure to have a moral theory about the nature of human beings. On any reading, however, rationality plays too strong a role in Kantian theory.

78. See J. Rawls, *A Theory of Justice,* supra note 12, at 516–517: "The veil of ignorance prevents us from shaping our moral view to accord with

our own particular attachments and interests. We do not look at the social order from our situation but take up a point of view that everyone can adopt on an equal footing. In this sense we look at our society and our place in it objectively: we share a common standpoint along with others and do not make our judgments from a personal slant." Of course, this passage, in addition to appealing to a desire for objectivity, also makes claims on a sense of community, cooperation, fairness, and equality, and an antipathy against bias.

79. Cf. Rawls, "Kantian Constructivism," supra note 12, at 533: "[T]he desire to act from the principles of justice, is not a desire on the same footing with natural inclinations; it is an executive and regulative highest-order desire to act from certain principles of justice in view of their connection with a conception of the person as free and equal."

80. Rawls would have the principles of justice be chosen without reference to one's particular conception of the good or by "affections for this or that group of persons, association, or community." He wants to screen out "lower-order impulses" and rely only on the "highest-order interests of moral personality." To do otherwise would be to rely on desires that "we might think of . . . as heteronomous and not as autonomous." See "Kantian Constructivism," supra note 12, at 527.

81. See J. Rawls, *A Theory of Justice,* supra note 12, at 263, 584 (claiming to have established an Archimedean point for judging the basic structure of society not contingent upon existing social desires or social conditions). But cf. note 76 supra.

82. One can appeal to a desire for objectivity without using the word or even disclaiming that the notion of objectivity adds anything. Thus Ronald Dworkin appeals to a desire for objectivity when he insists on the existence of a single right answer in most hard cases (see *Taking Rights Seriously,* supra note 13, at 279–290; *Law's Empire,* supra note 66, at viii) even though he argues that there is no point in insisting that political or moral arguments are "objective." See R. Dworkin, *A Matter of Principle,* supra note 43, at 171; *Law's Empire,* supra at 80–86.

83. The notion of integrity has emerged as an important working concept in Dworkin's most recent book. R. Dworkin, supra note 66, at chs. 6–7. See, e.g., id. at 167: "[I]ntegrity . . . is the life of the law as we know it." I mean something less complex (and less extreme) than that which is developed in *Law's Empire.* That is, before Dworkin gave integrity a central role in his legal theory, one of the rhetorical appeals of his work and that of other neo-Kantians was that readers might think better of themselves for opting into a system that explicitly or implicitly prized integrity. That appeal is conveyed, for example, by the title of Dworkin's immediately prior book, *A Matter of Principle,* supra note 43. For a telling attack on Dworkin's use of integrity, see Cornell, "Institutionalization of Meaning, Recollective Imagination and the Potential for Transformative Legal Interpretation," 136 *U. Pa. L. Rev.* 1135, 1172–1178, 1220–1224 (1988). Consider id. at 1175:

"Indeed, Dworkin is very serious when he says that we should understand the community as a single author. He introduces a very strong associative notion of community only to have it disappear before our eyes. We are left with an account of a judge with integrity, a hero, a super-individual, Hercules. We can be pleased that Dworkin offers us a hero with such principles. Even so, we are left with a new version of the proclamation, 'the state is I.' Dworkin may find notions of the objective spirit both foreign and 'scary,' but surely this version of community personified is much 'scarier.'"

84. The association of the passions with selfishness and the contrast between reason and the passions is explicitly denied by another general, but anti-Kantian, theory, namely utilitarianism. In most of its forms utilitarianism can not be characterized as selfish because it seeks to maximize social utility, not individual utility. It does not set reason against the passions. Rather reason's job is to serve the passions and to serve the passions one has to be deeply immersed in finding out what they are. Finally, the utilitarian has the integrity to stand by principle, namely the principle of utility.

85. See, e.g., R. Dworkin, supra note 66, at 166: "Integrity becomes a political ideal when we make the same demand of the state or community taken to be moral agent, when we insist that the state act on a single, coherent set of principles even when its citizens are divided about what the right principles of justice and fairness really are. We assume, in both the individual and the political cases, that we can recognize other people's acts as expressing a conception of fairness or justice or decency even when we do not endorse that conception ourselves. This ability is an important part of our more general ability to treat others with respect, and it is therefore a prerequisite of civilization." A major challenge to Dworkin's view is the possibility that compromise might play a larger role in a civilized system than is suggested by his insistence upon a "single, coherent set of principles." For his response to that challenge, see id. at 176–190, 216–224, 266–275.

86. Allied to this is an appeal to a sense of fairness and tolerance. This appeal, for example, is implicit in the Kantian suggestion that we should be neutral toward others' conceptions of the good life. The appeal is sometimes explicit: "The virtues of political cooperation that make a constitutional regime possible are, then, *very great* virtues. I mean, for example, the virtues of tolerance and being ready to meet others halfway, and the virtue of reasonableness and the sense of fairness." Rawls, "Overlapping Consensus," supra note 12, at 17 (emphasis in original). See also id. at 21: contention that Rawls's proposal will "encourage the cooperative virtues of political life: the virtue of reasonableness and a sense of fairness, a spirit of compromise and a readiness to meet others halfway . . . . "

87. See Baker, "Sandel on Rawls," supra note 10, at 924: "In criticizing the established order, the attempts to devise and think through the implications of principles that are treated as universals may provide effective leverage against the inherent conservatism of intuitions that are informed primarily by the status quo."

88. See note 81 supra.

89. For an excellent review of an important debate on this issue, see Mendelson, "The Habermas-Gadamer Debate," 18 *New German Critique* 44 (1979).

90. I do not mean to suggest that a Kantian would describe it that way. A Kantian might say the core is respect for persons, autonomy, dignity, or the like. I am looking at Kantian thought here from an eclectic perspective.

91. The word *emphasize* is important. No Kantian would suggest as a matter of theory that first amendment decisionmaking could be reduced to a mere analytic puzzle. But the Kantian would emphasize the importance of conceptual clarity and the need to focus on particular concepts while the emphasis of the eclectic is upon attention to the diversity and particularity of social reality.

92. This requires empathy, but not necessarily sympathy. Minow, "Foreword: Justice Engendered," 101 *Harv. L. Rev.* 10, 77 (1987), on one reading appears to take the view that empathy is not required: "The plea for judges to engage with perspectives that challenge their own is not a call for sympathy or empathy, nor a hope that judges will be 'good' people. Sympathy, the human emotion, must be distinguished from equal respect, the legal command."

Even allowing for the difficulty of truly understanding the perspective of another, I would insist that empathy must precede any genuine respect for a particular perspective. Perhaps Minow only intended to get across the idea that she was not engaged in a goody-two-shoes sermon. On this reading Minow would agree that empathy is required: she would not have put a call out for it, however.

On the other hand, there are emotional costs and limits accompanying empathy in decisionmaking. Consider M. Nussbaum, *The Fragility of Goodness* 81 (1986) (emphasis in original): "If, for example, we could ever see clearly and be moved by the value of each unique person in the world, we could never without intolerable pain and guilt be able to act so as to benefit any one of them rather than any other—as love, or justice, might in some cases require. (If I saw and valued other people's children as I do my own, my own could never receive from me the love, time, and care that she *ought* to have, that it is just and right for her to have.) But we must stop somewhere in these necessary and even just blindnesses, balancing open responsiveness against order in some appropriate way."

93. For an articulate defense of the notion that dialogue should occupy center stage as a "regulative ideal," see Cornell, "Toward A Modern/Postmodern Reconstruction of Ethics," 133 *U. Pa. L. Rev.* 291 (1985).

94. See Michelman, supra note 67, at 33: The dialogic themes in modern social theory "express the vision of social normative choice as participatory, exploratory, and persuasive, rather than specialized, deductive, or demonstrative." By contrast, the Kantian would stress that emphasis on the passions encourages the view that belief systems are incommensurable and their conflicts not rationally resolvable. Thus, from the Kantian perspec-

tive, it is possible to claim that Kantian arguments spur more dialogue, debate, and criticism because they impart a duty to respond to criticism.

95. Drawing attention to the concrete is not, however, an escape from the abstract. The particular is always an instance of many general categories, and the conception of a particular could not exist without a more general idea. As Peter Thorslev writes, "A world of 'unique particulars' would be a world in which there could be no generalizations: it could not in any sense 'enlarge' our lives, since it would make any mental life impossible." P. Thorslev, *Romantic Contraries* 4 (1984). Moreover, as Gadamer, supra note 1, at 258–259, observes: "[W]e must understand the whole in terms of the detail and the detail in terms of the whole. This principle stems from ancient rhetoric, and modern hermeneutics has taken it and applied it to the art of understanding. It is a circular relationship in both cases. The anticipation of meaning in which the whole is envisaged becomes explicit understanding in that the parts, that are determined by the whole, themselves also determine this whole." In an earlier passage, he remarks: "Fundamentally, understanding is always a movement in [a] kind of circle, which is why the repeated return from the whole to the parts, and vice versa, is essential. Moreover, this cycle is constantly expanding, in that the concept of the whole is relative, and when it is placed in ever larger contexts the understanding of the individual element is always affected." Id. at 167.

96. In contrast, consider R. Dworkin, supra note 67, at 219–220 (emphasis added): "In the end, however, *political theory can make no contribution to how we govern ourselves except by struggling*, against all the impulses that drag us back into our own culture, *toward generality* and some reflective basis for deciding which of our traditional distinctions and discriminations are genuine and which spurious, which contribute to the flourishing of the ideals we want, after reflection, to embrace, and which serve only to protect us from the personal costs of that demanding process."

97. See Karst, "The First Amendment and Harry Kalven: An Appreciative Comment on the Advantages of Thinking Small," 13 *UCLA L. Rev.* 1 (1965).

98. P. Feyerabend, *Against Method* 45 n.12 (1975).

99. Cf. R. Unger, supra note 72, at 45 ("The effort to escape from this predicament by finding decision procedures neutral with respect to clashing interests or ideals will never be more than partly successful. . . . [I]t will be indeterminate to the extent that it remains neutral, and it will lose its neutrality as it gains determinacy."). See also Grey, supra note 11, at 32: Classical legal thought "could not in the end make too much of a virtue of its flexibility without undermining its promise of determinate geometric order."

100. F. Nietzsche, "Twilight of the Idols," in *The Portable Nietzsche* 463, 470 (W. Kaufmann trans. 1968). Compare Schlegel: "It is equally fatal for the mind to have a system and to have none. It will simply have to decide to combine the two." Quoted in P. Thorslev, supra note 95, at 161.

101. This is not to say that eclectic reasoning is unprincipled in the sense

that honesty and integrity are lacking. Quite the contrary, see Chapter 5 infra.

102. A truly "fundamentalist" Kantian might wholly deny any concern about consequences, but those who press for first amendment general theory would be quick to deny that the consequences called for by their theory are unacceptable, and Kant himself took consequences into account in determining applications of the categorical imperative.

103. In 1907 William James wrote that, "The history of philosophy is to a great extent that of a certain clash of human temperaments." W. James, *Pragmatism* 19 (1955). James understood that the clashes he described were not confined to philosophy. He referred to the conflict in manners between the formalists and the free-and-easy persons, in government to the authoritarians and the anarchists, in art to the classics and the romantics. Id. at 20. What James said of professional philosophers is for the most part also true of legal commentators, "Of whatever temperament a professional philosopher is, he tries, when philosophizing, to sink the fact of his temperament. Temperament is no conventionally recognized reason, so he urges impersonal reasons only for his conclusions. Yet his temperament really gives him a stronger bias than any of his more strictly objective premises." Id. at 19. Nietzsche made the point with less delicacy in 1855: "Every [philosopher] pretends that he has discovered and reached his opinions through the self-development of cold, pure, divinely untroubled dialectic (in distinction to the mystics of every rank who, more honest and fatuous, talk about 'inspiration'), whereas, at bottom, a pre-conceived dogma, a notion, an ['inspiration'], or mostly a heart's desire, made abstract and refined, is defended by them with arguments sought after the fact. They are all of them lawyers (though wanting to be called anything but that), and for the most part quite sly defenders of their prejudices which they christen 'truths'—*very* far removed they are from the courageous conscience which admits precisely this . . . . The spectacle of old Kant's Tartuffery, as stiff as it is respectable, luring us onto the dialectical crooked paths which lead (or better, mislead) to his 'categorical imperative'—this spectacle makes us, used to diversions as we are, smile." F. Nietzsche, *Beyond Good and Evil* 5 (M. Cowan trans. 1955; in this edition the translation of "Eingebung," which should be "inspiration" (as amended here), is misprinted as "institution"). Nietzsche continues: "Gradually I have come to realize what every great philosophy up to now has been: the personal confession of its originator, a type of involuntary and unaware memoirs . . . ." Id. at 6. On the latter point, see R. Solomon, *History and Human Nature* (1979).

104. Consider Fish, "Consequences," 11 *Critical Inquiry* 433, 438–439 (1985): "This then is why theory will never succeed: it cannot help but borrow its terms and its content from that which it claims to transcend, the mutable world of practice, belief, assumptions, point of view, and so forth. . . . [T]heory cannot reform practice because, rather than neutralizing interest, it begins and ends in interest and raises the imperatives of interest—of some local, particular, partisan project—to the status of universals."

105. Modern writers in the Kantian tradition ordinarily do not even purport to do so. See, e.g., Rawls, "Political Not Metaphysical," supra note 12. See also note 59 supra. But then the key argument is why some particular value is elevated above others in such important ways.

106. See generally M. Walzer, *Interpretation and Social Criticism* (1987). For a strong statement of the possibility of immanent criticism, see Gadamer, supra note 1, at 495–496: "Fundamentally in our world the issue is always the same: the verbalisation of conventions and of social norms behind which there are always economic and dominating interests. But our human experience of the world, for which we rely on our faculty of judgment, consists precisely in the possibility of our taking a critical stance with regard to every convention. In reality, we owe this to the linguistic virtuality of our reason and language does not, therefore, present an obstacle to reason."

107. They are not the only materials. Moreover, effective criticism can also challenge the ideals of the system. Even then the argument is likely to rely on other ideals held within the community.

108. Cf. R. Unger, *Law in Modern Society* 153–154 (1976): "The deepest root of all historical change is manifest or latent conflict between the view of the ideal and the experience of actuality. In liberal society, there is a constant and overt struggle between what men are led to expect of society and what they in fact receive from it."

109. See Minow, supra note 92, at 95: "Through deliberate attention to our own partiality, we can begin to acknowledge the dangers of pretended impartiality."

110. Notice the double modifier. An eclectic need not value dissent or change at all, let alone to the degree suggested in this book. Those eclectics who do value dissent and change need not possess the psychological disposition I describe in the text. Finally, I in no sense claim that one need be an eclectic to value dissent.

111. Cf. R. Rorty, *Philosophy and the Mirror of Nature* 388–389 (1979) (referring to the "fear that there will be objectively true or false answers to every question we ask, so that human worth will consist in knowing truths, and human virtue will be merely justified true belief. This is frightening because it cuts off the possibility of something new under the sun, of human life as poetic rather than merely contemplative.").

112. Cf. E. Said, *The World, the Text, and the Critic* 241 (1983): "Theory we certainly need . . . . What we also need over and above theory, however, is the critical recognition that there is no theory capable of covering, closing off, predicting all the situations in which it might be useful. . . . [U]nless theory is unanswerable, either through its successes or its failures, to the essential untidiness, the essential unmasterable presence that constitutes a large part of historical and social situations . . . , then theory becomes an ideological trap."

113. Cf. Richard Poirier's commentary on William James: "James's fear of stagnation and of inaction extended into his fear of speculation itself,

especially when this led, as he felt it often had done in philosophy, to the system building of 'intellectualists,' to entrapment within concepts, to the danger of fixation even within one's own formulations." R. Poirier, *The Renewal of Literature: Emersonian Reflections* 64–65 (1987).

114. There certainly is no logical contradiction. The categories "locked in" are arguably of a different order, and the locking in is arguably of a different kind.

115. Compare Dean Bollinger's description of what he calls the fortress model, as a method of defending free speech (a model he does not endorse): "Given this view of the world, it seems both sensible and imperative to take a position in defense of free speech in which essentially no thought is permitted: free speech is simply a 'right' that each individual possesses against the larger society and that need not be defended on any other basis. It is elemental, beyond argument, a priori." L. Bollinger, *The Tolerant Society* 90 (1986). Kantian theory, at least, tries to justify its position so it can not fairly be equated with that aspect of the fortress model, but it arguably tries to cut off the conversation and in that sense it shares another feature of the model. As Bollinger describes it: "The primary ingredient in this strategy is the idea that the people should be made to feel the suppression of speech is both unthinkable and unlikely to be successful and that the judges should be led to think they have no choice but to protect the speech if the public should decide to suppress it." Id. at 100. Cf. Cornell, supra note 93, at 349–350 (comparing Hegel's fortress model–like attack on positivity in religion with an interpretation of attacks on "liberal rights theory" by some writers associated with the Conference on Critical Legal Studies).

For an eloquent example of an appeal that seems to fit the fortress model, see Kateb, "Democratic Individuality and the Claims of Politics," 12 *Political Theory* 331, 336 (1984): "Obviously if respect for rights characteristically resulted in havoc or in utterly trivial uses, the question of why rights (or a particular right) should be respected would legitimately arise. But the question is forced into existence usually because a particular matter or some specific condition seems to beg for a remedy that respect for rights is thought to obstruct. This forcing of the question is a sign that there is no underlying respect for rights on the part of those doing the forcing. They want some other kind of society than one in which rights are respected. To keep on demanding an answer to this question—even to ask it as if it were just another question that could be reasonably argued about—is already to be on the way to abandoning respect for rights. It is exemplary that the Bill of Rights contains no rationale."

116. This tension is not confined to Kantians. It applies to many of those who press for simplicity in first amendment law. Thus Vincent Blasi, a vigorous (non-Kantian) defender of tolerance and dissent, plots strategies in support of dissent, such as simplicity in first amendment law, in the hope that the first amendment will have sufficient *authority* to cause citizens to forgo their preference for intolerance in pathological periods. Blasi, supra note 8, at 453 & 458–459.

117. I reiterate: noneclectics can prize the dissent value, and eclectics could prize the dissent value without the psychological disposition I describe. See note 110 supra.

118. This particular facet of Kantian theory places a substantial roadblock in John Rawls's hope for an overlapping consensus to be joined by followers of Mill. Rawls places significant emphasis on the values of cooperation and agreement. He states that: "Faced with the fact of pluralism, a liberal view removes from the political agenda the most divisive issues, pervasive uncertainty and serious contention about which must undermine the bases of social cooperation." Rawls, "Overlapping Consensus," supra note 12, at 17. Within limits, followers of Mill are more likely to regard division and uncertainty as promoting individuality and are less likely than Rawls to think that division about questions of the good life, for example, really threatens social stability in a worrisome way. Moreover, for the reasons stated in the text, many followers of Mill would be reluctant to join in the notions of public reason and methodology for which Rawls would seek consensus. In a footnote, Rawls suggests that followers of Isaiah Berlin might reach Rawlsian principles through a methodology different than his (id. at 15 n.24), but that analysis assumes that those followers are hoping to find an overall pattern (as opposed to diversity) and it seems to discard the Rawlsian notion that the principles to be settled upon call for simple principles applied in a way that everyone can accept. That notion would be resisted by the Millian tradition prizing diversity and individuality. Rawls could argue that it would be a mistake to see it that way and that he speaks about a small corner of human existence. Nonetheless, followers in the Millian tradition could be expected to resist joining the overlapping consensus.

119. Cf. R. Poirier, supra note 113, at 65 ("With Nietzsche and Emerson, and in anticipation of Foucault and Deleuze, James was essentially trying to release himself and the rest of us from any settled, coherent idea of the human, from the conceptual systems and arrangements of knowledge by which man has so far defined himself. In his work and in his life, he was drawn to the marginal, the transgressive, the misfits.").

120. It is also a central concern of many eclectics.

121. See Rawls, "Overlapping Consensus," supra note 12, at 8.

122. Thus, Nietzsche sniped that Kant was "'in the end an underhanded Christian,'" by which he meant that Kant had attempted to salvage the notion of free will in an underhanded way—by assuming it hypothetically. See P. Riley, *Will and Political Legitimacy* 139 (1982), citing F. Nietzsche, supra note 100, at 484.

123. R. Nozick, *Anarchy, State, and Utopia* 45–47 (1974). See also id. at 35–42.

124. There are other paths as well. For an intriguing debate, compare Regan, "Utilitarianism, Vegetarianism, and Animal Rights," 9 *Phil & Pub. Aff.* 305 (1980), with Singer, "Utilitarianism and Vegetarianism," 9 *Phil. & Pub. Aff.* 325 (1980).

125. In Rawls's *A Theory of Justice,* supra note 12, this priority is evinced

in many ways. The veil of ignorance presupposes a conception of the self. As Rawls says, the original position "already includes moral features and must do so, for example, the formal conditions on principles and the veil of ignorance. I have simply divided up the description of the original position so that these elements do not occur in the characterization of the parties, although even here there might be a question as to what counts as a moral element and what does not." Id. at 585. Indeed, Rawls states that he is not trying to show that a committed egoist should be persuaded by his theory (id. at 568); the most he says to the question "why be moral?" is to say about those who disagree: "[T]heir nature is their misfortune." Id. at 576. By building into the original position the requirement that each person's plan of life be respected so far as possible, Rawls also quite deliberately sets up the veil in a way that precludes a utilitarian conception of the self: "The parties regard moral personality and not the capacity for pleasure and pain as the fundamental aspect of the self. They do not know what final aims persons have, and all dominant-end conceptions are rejected. Thus it would not occur to them to acknowledge the principle of utility in its hedonistic form." Id. at 563.

In more recent writing, Rawls argues that he has not taken a metaphysical position about the self, but only a political position designed to generate an overlapping consensus. See sources cited in note 12 supra. But if Rawls is to answer the question of why results arising from the veil are just, he would be forced into a metaphysical conception of the self just as he was in the theory of justice. Alternatively, Rawls might not claim justice, but he would argue that people should accept the principles in order to reach consensus. This would prompt the response as to why consensus was important enough to give up on justice or other values an individual would regard as important. It would not take much further conversation to lead back again to a metaphysical conception of the self.

Rawls maintains that Ronald Dworkin's conception of justice is political, but not metaphysical. But there are passages in Dworkin's work that speak against that view. He, for example, denies that his conception of justice and equality is grounded in skepticism and also denies that "the liberal says there is no answer to the question how human beings should live . . . ." Dworkin, supra note 14, at 251. Indeed he approvingly interprets Rawls to say that the right of persons to equal respect is "'owed to human beings as moral persons,' and follows from the moral personality that distinguishes humans from animals." R. Dworkin, supra note 13, at 181. For general discussion, see "What Liberalism Isn't," N.Y. Rev. Bks. 47 (Jan. 20, 1983).

Moreover, it is clear that the Rawlsian conception of moral personality is built on an opposition between reason and passion. The original position is an attempt to duplicate the Kantian ideal where "men exhibit their freedom, their independence from the contingencies of nature and society . . . ." J. Rawls, A Theory of Justice, supra note 12, at 256. Rawls contends that "'to be governed by appetite alone is slavery, while obedience to a law one prescribes to oneself is freedom.'" Id. at 264 n.4. For Rawls, this is the point of both the original position and what it means to be a moral person. See id. at 251–257. As Rawls puts it, when a person acts autonomously, principles are adopted as the "most adequate possible expression of his nature as a free and equal rational being. The principles he acts upon are not adopted because of . . . specific things that he happens to want." Id. at 252. To act on the latter would be to act "heteronomously" not autonomously. Id. For a particularly clear and perceptive discussion of the assumptions of Kantian liberalism, see Richards, "Human Rights and Moral Ideals," supra note 14.

126. See note 125 supra.

127. See note 125 supra.

128. See note 125 supra. By contrast, consider C. Campbell, *The Romantic Ethic and the Spirit of Modern Consumerism* 190 (1987) (quoting Wordsworth and describing his views): "Pleasure is no less than the poet's medium of truth, his means of acknowledging the beauty of the universe, and his manner of giving expression to the essential dignity of man; pleasure is, in effect, 'the grand elementary principle' through which man 'knows, and feels, and lives, and moves.'"

129. Thus Rawls's decisionmakers in the original position have no particular conception of the good but do believe it is important for them to be able to implant a rational plan of life. See generally *A Theory of Justice,* supra note 12, at 395–452. Second, after the principles of justice have been established government must "avoid any assessment of the relative value of another's way of life." Id. at 442. See generally id. at 325–332.

So too Ronald Dworkin has argued that justice requires abstraction from people's various conceptions of the good life. At one point, he argued that liberalism centered on the principle that "government must be neutral on what might be called the question of the good life." Dworkin, "Liberalism," in *Public and Private Morality* 127 (S. Hampshire ed. 1978). Later he championed a somewhat narrower version of that principle (see note 58 supra), namely that government could not engage in actions that characterized people's lives as "ignoble" or "wrong." In place of neutrality about the good life, he emphasized a right of moral independence. More recently, he has advanced an approach that would determine rights by reference to an imaginary auction which by abstracting from people's plans and projects is said to best show equal concern for the lives of all. In particular, see Dworkin, supra note 43, at 25–29.

What the veil of ignorance and the imaginary auction have in common is an artificial separation of reason from desire in which it is thought crucial to be fair to virtually all conceptions of the good. For criticism of that view, see Nielsen, supra note 59. For writing criticizing the purported connection between neutrality toward conceptions of the good life and liberalism, see V. Haksar, supra note 22; Galston, "Defending Liberalism," 76 *Am. Pol. Sci. Rev.* 621 (1982); Raz, "Liberalism, Autonomy, and the Politics of Neutral Concern," 7 *Midwest Stud. Phil.* 89 (1982); Shiffrin, supra note 6.

Of course, the veil of ignorance has been arrived at through a process of reflective equilibrium and thus in an important sense is grounded in a methodology that recognizes the interaction between reason and desire. But when it is asked why the veil is just (as opposed to why it can assist in promoting a stable society), the answer that has emerged from reflective equilibrium is one that characterizes the fundamental aspect of the self in a way that separates reason from desire. See note 125 supra.

130. R. Solomon, *The Passions* 120 (1983). For a short recent statement of Solomon's conception of the relationship between reason and desire, see Solomon, "On Emotions as Judgments," 25 *Am. Phil. Q.* 183 (1988).

131. S. Wolin, *Politics and Vision* 318 (1960).

132. Indeed another major rhetorical appeal of Kantian theory despite its individualism is the appeal to a sense of community, that is, surely we all ought to be able to agree on the *basic* principles of the society. See note 78 supra.

133. J. Rawls, *A Theory of Justice,* supra note 12, at 563.

134. For general discussion of eclectic methodology in the first amendment context, see Shiffrin, "The First Amendment and Economic Regulation: Away from a General Theory of the First Amendment," 78 *Nw. U.L. Rev.* 1212 (1983); Shiffrin, "Government Speech," 27 *UCLA L. Rev.* 565 (1980). See generally Shiffrin, supra note 6 (defending eclectic liberalism). There is a vast anti-Kantian and antiutilitarian literature, most of which I consider eclectic though different labels and different concepts are their principal focus (consider intuitionistic, pragmatic, practical reason, hermeneutic, deconstructionist, feminist), and major differences exist within that literature. Some of that literature is cited within this section. Some authors specifically use the "eclectic" label though here again important differences are put in the background. See, e.g., Farber & Frickey, "Practical Reason and the First Amendment," 34 *UCLA L. Rev.* 1615 (1987); Alexander & Schwarzschild, "Liberalism, Neutrality, and Equality of Welfare vs. Equality of Resources," 16 *Phil. & Pub. Aff.* 85, 109–110 (1987); Minow, "Law Turning Outward," 73 *Telos* 79, 99–100 (1987). There is a general family resemblance, a set of shared values among the authors cited in this section, but many would resist an eclectic label; many would resist characterizations made in the text; many violently disagree among themselves on a range of issues.

135. It might be thought that complication is not the right concept. For example, even in a very simple society (is that possible?) speech values might have to yield to competing values because a competing claim is more important. By calling a society "complicated," however, I mean to suggest not only the pluralism of society but also that society is not so simple that speech values should invariably trump others.

136. Cf. Farber & Frickey, supra note 134, at 1645 (1987) ("An impressive array of recent legal commentary has suggested a movement away from grand theory toward something new . . . .") (citing much of the literature in and outside of law).

137. Cf. R. Rorty, *Consequences of Pragmatism* (1982); R. Rorty, supra note 111. The Court's method has been compatible with much of Rorty's attack on foundations but has by no means exhibited agreement with his notion of truth.

138. See, e.g., I. Berlin, *Against the Current: Essays in the History of Ideas* (1980); I. Berlin, *Four Essays on Liberty* (1969); Alexander & Schwarzschild, supra note 134, at 109–110.

139. See generally C. Gilligan, *In a Different Voice* (1982); Sherry, "Civic Virtue and the Feminine Voice in Constitutional Adjudication," 72 *Va. L. Rev.* 543 (1986). In my view law generally pretends to be Gilligan's male but is better understood as Gilligan's female, at least with respect to the contextualized aspects of decisionmaking—which, in my view, is not to say the law is feminist. See C. MacKinnon, *Feminism Unmodified* 8–10, 38–39 (1987). If, for example, feminism is defined as "the theory of, and the practice of resistance to, the oppression and subordination of women" (Littleton, "Feminist Jurisprudence: The Difference Method Makes" (Book Review), 41 *Stan. L. Rev.* 751, 763 n.55 (1989)), the common law is not feminist. Similarly, if feminist method grows out of and is grounded in the experience of women (see id. at 763–766), the common law does not use feminist method.

If Littleton's uses of the term *feminist theory* were accepted, the arguments of this book as presented would not be a part of feminist theory or of feminist method. But, I would hope that the perspectives of the first amendment offered here are compatible with the best feminist theory. Certainly, present law is not.

140. Alexander, "Interpreting Legal Constructivism," 71 *Cornell L. Rev.* 249, 257–259 (1985); Shiffrin, supra note 6; Shiffrin, supra note 134. Two cheers for intuition can also be found in Tribe, "Technology Assessment and the Fourth Discontinuity: The Limits of Instrumental Rationality," 46 *S. Cal. L. Rev.* 617, 659 (1973), though he ultimately hopes for an approach to reason that reciprocally links subject with object (id. at 652) and calls for "an idea of rationality that is more personal and more deeply rooted in the life history of the individual than is true of abstract, universal reason" (id. at 654). See also Tribe, "Policy Science: Analysis or Ideology?," 2 *Phil. & Pub. Aff.* 66 (1972).

141. See, e.g., Michelman, supra note 67, at 24–36 (stressing practical reason but with a more generous interpretation of Kant than that presented here). For general discussions of practical reason from quite different perspectives, compare R. Bernstein, *Beyond Objectivism and Relativism: Science, Hermeneutics, and Praxis* (1983), with A. MacIntyre, supra note 69. On the relationship of practical reason to culture, judgment, common sense, and taste (together with a reading of Kant stressing his attempt to root moral theory outside individual feelings, even if widely shared), see H. Gadamer, supra note 1, at 5–39. See also id. at 278–289 (discussing the relationship of Aristotle's notions of reason with hermeneutics). For an appreciative reading of Kant, focusing on the concept of judgment, see H. Arendt, supra note 5.

142. For the intriguing suggestion that synchronization may be a better metaphor, see Cornell, supra note 83, at 1189, 1210–1212.

143. In fairness, it is not clear who is prepared to ignore consequences entirely. Judge Posner, for example, defines Kantian theory as one that rejects "any form of consequentialism." But, Dworkin replies that on that definition, even Kant is not a Kantian. R. Dworkin, supra note 67, at 411 n.10. Certainly Posner is right if consequentialism is taken to mean that everything depends on the consequences. On that definition, there are different forms of consequentialism (depending on what consequences are thought to matter, e.g., beauty, happiness, discovery of truth). To take consequences into account (which Kant surely did) is not the same as consequentialism (unless everything is said to depend on them). Similarly, Kantians could say that something is right no matter what the consequences, *save total disasters* (some Kantians would reject—as would Kant—or consider rejecting the savings clause, see C. Fried, *Right and Wrong* 31 (1978)), and acceptance of the savings clause would not turn them into consequentialists. See Williams, "A Critique of Utilitarianism," in J. Smart & B. Williams, *Utilitarianism: For and Against* 93 (1973).

144. Particularly important in this movement is Gadamer's *Truth and Method*, supra note 1, but H. Gadamer, *Reason in the Age of Science* (1981) is an accessible entrée to the larger work. Gadamer has exerted substantial influence, but not hegemony on such important philosophers as Bernstein, supra note 141, Rorty, supra note 111, and, of course, Habermas. See Rabinow and Sullivan, "The Interpretive Turn: Emergence of an Approach," in *Interpretive Social Science* 16 (P. Rabinow & W. Sullivan eds. 1979) (Habermas able to move beyond the pessimism of the Frankfurt School as "a result of his encounter with the interpretive tradition, particularly with the work of Hans-Georg Gadamer"). Gadamer's footprints are even evident in R. Dworkin, *Law's Empire,* supra note 66, at 62. For discussion of the relationship between Dworkin's conception of interpretation and Gadamer's, see Note, "Dworkin and Subjectivity in Legal Interpretation," 40 *Stan. L. Rev.* 1517, 1535–1541 (1988). For general discussion of the "interpretive turn," see, e.g., C. Geertz, *Local Knowledge* 19–35 (1983); see generally the essays in *Interpretive Social Science,* supra.

145. C. Geertz, supra note 144, at 21.

146. Cf. "Harold Bloom" [an interview], in *Criticism in Society* 44, 73 (I. Salusinszky 1987) (emphasis in original): "What Emerson is always telling us: which is that every received text—even Shakespeare, even the Bible—is secondary. [The readers] are primary. *They* are the text. The Bible or Shakespeare is a commentary upon them. There are no texts. There are only ourselves."

Some—I do not read Bloom this way—would mean to say literally that there are no texts, that in interpretation there are all subjects and no objects. For example, some insist that history is a statement about the historian rather than a statement about the past. In my view, it is plainly both.

In response to the historical skeptic, Gregory Alexander writes that: "External analysis of historical thought-structures becomes possible as such structures recede in time. Historians are thus defined as Hegel's Owl of Minerva, 'one who imposes pattern on thrusts of creativity after they are over, critic to the historical actor's artists.'" Alexander, "The Dead Hand and the Law of Trusts in the Nineteenth Century," 37 *Stan. L. Rev.* 1189, 1194 n.10 (1985), quoting J. Pocock, *Politics, Language and Time* 273, 279 (1971). Even there—and I doubt that Alexander would disagree—I would contend that analysis of many historical thought-structures is possible long before dusk, and that even if genuine analysis of historical thought-structures must wait until dusk, analysis of contemporary thought need not. The dragon to be slain here is not nihilism (though that dragon deserves to be slain), but solipsism. In the end, if there are no texts, it is easy to slide to the conclusion that there are no objects, and if there are no objects, there are no subjects.

147. Thus Irving Howe comments that America is a country "which makes the refusal of history into a first principle . . . . " I. Howe, *The American Newness: Culture and Politics in the Age of Emerson* 4 (1986). But see M. Jehlen, *American Incarnation: The Individual, the Nation, and the Continent* 7 (1986): "[The consensus that Americans lack a sense of history] fails to account for the fact that Americans are in another way highly conscious of their national heritage and, as much as any people, celebrate a gallery of monumental heroes and events; it might be argued, on the contrary, that they are *too* faithful to founding principles that, after two centuries, remain axiomatic."

148. I refer to the traditional reading of Emerson. See, e.g., Howe, supra note 147, at 4: "Calling himself 'a seeker with no Past at his back'—a piece of impudence possible only to an American—Emerson wrote: 'it is a mischievous notion that we are come late into nature, that the world was finished long ago.'" There are, of course, more complicated readings. See, e.g., S. Cavell, *In Quest of the Ordinary: Lines of Skepticism and Romanticism* 36–37 (1988): "Whether you find Emerson entitled to such a gloss will depend on who you think Emerson is, something I am trying to leave, or to get, open. It would be, to my mind, key enough if Emerson's thought here opens to us the thought, or opens us to the thought, that our past solutions to these mysteries, however philosophical in aspect, are themselves mythology, or as we might more readily say today, products of our intuitions, and hence can progress no further until we have assessed which of our intuitions are satisfied, and which thwarted, by the various dramas of concepts or figures like fate, and freedom, and foreknowledge, and will." Emerson himself was fully aware, at least some of the time, of the historically situated character of the self: "[T]he new art is always formed out of the old. . . . No man can quite emancipate himself from his age or country, or produce a model in which the education, the religion, the politics, usages, and arts of his times shall have no share. Though he were never so original, never so wilful and fantastic,

he cannot wipe out of his work every trace of the thoughts amidst it grew."
R. W. Emerson, "Art," in *Emerson: Essays and Lectures* 429, 431–432 (J.
Porte ed. 1983), quoted in part in A. Schlesinger, *The Cycles of American
History* 373 (1986). But cf. J. H. Hexter, *Reappraisals in History* ch. 1 (2d ed.
1979) (historian can live in present while escaping many of its assumptions
and, instead, allow a view of the past to dominate the present).

149. R. W. B. Lewis, *The American Adam: Innocence, Tragedy, and Tradition in the Nineteenth Century* (1955).

150. This does not mean, however, that a transcendental point outside
the passions is needed for criticism. The passions cannot be escaped, but a
metaphor that would conceive of politics exclusively in terms of reading
texts would limit our vision. See C. Geertz, supra note 144, at 30–33 (discussing the limits of the text analogy and comparing it with other analo-
gies). Of course, Gadamer's project was aimed at elucidating the idea of
understanding, and was not presented as a total framework for political decisionmaking.

151. For the argument that the subject-object framework itself (together
with the attitude of uncovering meaning, deep or otherwise) obscures the
power relationships that need to be explored, see generally H. Dreyfus & P.
Rabinow, *Foucault: Beyond Structuralism and Hermeneutics* (2d ed. 1983).

152. "Justices . . . *are* molders of policy, rather than the impersonal vehicles of revealed truth." Frankfurter, quoted in J. Harris, *The Advice and
Consent of the Senate* 313 (1953) (emphasis in original).

153. For thoughtful commentary on the sources and interpreters of constitutional interpretation relating the dispute over those sources and interpreters to similar debates in theological circles, see S. Levinson, *Constitutional Faith* 9–53, 185 (1988).

154. Cf. Redish, "The Value of Free Speech," 130 *U. Pa. L. Rev.* 591, 595
(1982) (making a stylistically similar set of comparisons with his own different theory, one that reduces all first amendment values to "one true value,"
individual self-realization).

155. Thus I agree with Professors Farber and Frickey: "First amendment
law needs . . . more coherence and even grandeur than pure eclecticism can
provide." Farber & Frickey, supra note 134, at 1628. On the other hand, in
application, there is no pure eclecticism. Moreover, no court can balance
without an overall vision, however partial or conflicted, of the society. But
cf. id. at 1637.

5. The First Amendment and Romance

1. G. Wood, *The Creation of the American Republic, 1776–1787,* at 606
(1969).

2. Id.

3. Id.

4. A. Lovejoy, *Essays in the History of Ideas* 228–253 (1948).

5. Id. at 235.

6. For a perceptive discussion of the problems associated with labels like *Hegelian* or *Marxist,* see Riley, "Introduction to the Reading of Alexander Kojeve," 9 *Pol. Theory* 5 (1981); L. Kolakowski, *Toward a Marxist Humanism* 173–187 (1968).

7. Lovejoy stated that "The one really radical remedy—namely, that we should all cease talking about Romanticism—is, I fear, certain not to be adopted." A. Lovejoy, supra note 4, at 234. Lovejoy, we are told, ultimately found more unity in romanticism than he previously had seen. According to Stromberg, he found "the fundamental Romantic trait to be diversity, as over against Enlightenment standardization and simplification—the search for unique particulars, rather than universals and generals." R. Stromberg, *An Intellectual History of Modern Europe* 219 (1976).

8. F. Baumer, *Modern European Thought* 269 (1977). See also C. Campbell, *The Romantic Ethic and the Spirit of Modern Consumerism* 180 (1987).

9. Much of the phrasing of this description is influenced by Berlin, "Preface," in G. Schenck, *The Mind of the European Romantics* xiii (1966) (excellent brief description of the romantics). See generally sources cited in note 8 supra & notes 10 & 17 infra.

10. Berlin, supra note 9, at xvi. See also Broyard, "About Books: Can Art Make the World Safe for Romanticism," *New York Times Book Review* 13 (Feb. 7, 1988) ("[A] romantic is in constant rebellion—perhaps without a cause, for causes so often fail."); P. Thorslev, *Romantic Contraries* 170 (1984) (referring to the romantics' "passionate resistance to closure"); M. Gilmore, *American Romanticism and the Marketplace* 6 (1985) ("Ample evidence exists to support this conception of American romanticism as a movement of dissent"; referring also to conformity as Emerson's "special bugbear").

11. Quoted in F. Baumer, supra note 8, at 270. Baumer continues: "The romantics thought [the] world too narrow, because of its addiction, as they believed, to geometric thinking and the allied doctrine of neo-classicism, or else to Lockean empiricism. The geometric spirit, though metaphysically bold, tried to subject all life to reason, and thus to mechanize and demean it." Id. at 270–271. See also R. Stromberg, supra note 7, at 210 (romanticism a reaction against eighteenth-century rationalism, mechanistic materialism, and classicism).

12. See Chapter 4, note 14 supra.

13. Consider C. Campbell, supra note 8, at 179, quoting K. Klaus, *The Romantic Period in Music* 13–14 (1970): "Romanticism can justifiably be presented as more of an impulse than a unified system of ideas, and what is more, an impulse toward chaos. Logically, therefore, not only is 'a closed definition of romanticism . . . not very romantic', but, 'if one important aspect of romanticism is the spirit of rebellion, then rebelling against romanticism could also be romantic.'"

14. See, e.g., H. Gadamer, *Truth and Method* 242, 249–250 (1982) (in opposing the enlightenment, romantics—Gadamer's focus is probably on

German romantics—exalted the old and the traditional as against abstract reason, regarding the traditional as natural); M. Peckham, *Romanticism and Behaviorism* 68–69 (1976) ("[A]mong those individuals who are generally agreed to have been Romantics, there was a full spectrum of political attitudes, from the extreme right to the extreme left, and . . . a number who were politically indifferent.") Cf. "Frank Kermode" [an interview], in *Criticism in Society* 97, 106 (I. Salusinszky 1987) ("There's no necessary correlation between romanticism and left wing politics."); Sullivan, "Hearts and Rights," *New Republic* 35, 36 (March 7, 1988): "[Nancy Rosenblum in *Another Liberalism* argues] long and hard for the compatibility of the English Romantics with liberalism, but the fact remains that Southey, Wordsworth, and Coleridge ended up creative Tories. It is indeed [odd] . . . that Rosenblum shows little interest in the Tory political tradition, whose very identity was formed by the struggle to reconcile the Romantic impulses she admires with the liberalism she respects." Nonetheless, Rosenblum's work, infra note 17, shares the view of this book and perceptively explores the view that the anticonventional form of romanticism has much in common with and much to contribute to liberal thought. Moreover, Sullivan's particular emphasis to the contrary, there is strong support for the proposition that English romanticism is best understood as being firmly rooted in the liberal tradition of supporting dissent. See generally H. Bloom, *The Visionary Company: A Reading of English Romantic Poetry* (rev. ed. 1971). See, e.g., id. at xvii: "Like that of all the English Romantic poets, Hazlitt's religious background was in the tradition of Protestant dissent, the kind of nonconformist vision that descended from the Left Wing of England's Puritan movement. There is no more important point to be made about English Romantic poetry than this one, or indeed about English poetry in general, particularly since it has been deliberately obscured by most modern criticism."

15. J. Randall, *The Making of the Modern Mind* 404 (50th Anniversary ed. 1976): "When to this distrust of reason is added the positive feelings for familiar institutions endeared by long association, it is easy to see how romanticism became the bulwark of beliefs that had seemed to crumble before the onslaughts of rational criticism." But compare id. at 409: "[W]hile the new appeal to faith as against reason found expression in these great popular revivals of doctrines drawn from the older religious tradition, it was just as strongly a radical force as well. The feelings, the passions, and the intuitions of the natural man, when made the ultimate source of all knowledge and aspiration, led as easily to principles and attitudes that were genuinely subversive of the whole established order."

16. Compare C. Campbell, supra note 8, at 194: "'[A]dverse imagination' of the culture could drive the Romantic into that form of inner exile from society which day-dreaming and fantasizing represented, finding in his 'inner eye' both the bliss which soothed despair and the inspiration necessary for renewed attempts to convert others. But disgust with a world in which people 'lay waste [their] powers' by 'Getting and spending', also

caused the Romantic to distance himself physically from society, finding comfort and consolation in the natural landscape of remote places."

17. See, e.g., P. Thorslev, supra note 10, at 175: "As Schlegel maintains, and as Kierkegaard agrees, what the romantic ironist aims at above all is freedom, an ultimate and unconditioned freedom. He can gain such freedom, however, as Kierkegaard insists, only by forgoing any sense of destiny, by ironizing ('negating,' in Hegel's term) all the claims of 'actuality,' by cutting himself free from the claims of society and history. The progress of Romantic irony in literary history: estheticism, narcissism, camp. The only imperative which finally remains is to burn with a hard, gem-like flame." See also N. Rosenblum, *Another Liberalism: Romanticism and the Reconstruction of Liberal Thought* 48–53 (1987).

18. J. Shklar, *After Utopia: The Decline of Political Faith* 85 (1957): "The rejection of manners and convention in Bohemia is infinitely less a desire for freedom than a demonstration of contempt for lesser men. The worship of individuality is inseparable from egoism, and from genius-consciousness."

19. C. Campbell, supra note 8, at 201 & 207, for example, argues that by legitimizing pleasure the romantics played a role in bringing about the very hedonism and consumerism that they opposed. Cf. Graff, "American Criticism Left and Right," in *Ideology and Classic American Literature* 91, 95–96 (emphasis on breaking of restraints encourages ideology of consumption) (S. Bercovitch & M. Jehlen eds. 1987).

20. See generally N. Rosenblum, supra note 17, at 9–33 (1987) (describing and criticizing this aspect of romanticism).

21. A part of romantic thought that particularly lends itself to totalitarian leanings is the notion of society as organic "in which common goals animate and harmonize all the different elements of the totality" (C. Larmore, *Patterns of Moral Complexity* 96 (1987)) or in which the society is "fused by a single conception of the good life" (id. at 25). The notion of organic society or an organic universe is a strong theme in English and German romanticism, but there are more open and pluralistic visions in romantic writing. See, e.g., P. Thorslev, supra note 10, at 142–186 (discussing the conception of the "open universe" in romantic writing). Moreover, the concept of an organism need not connote a harmonization of the different elements of the totality, nor need it connote totalitarianism as, for example, Emerson and Whitman's writings clearly show. See, e.g., Graff, supra note 19, at 106. See generally F. O. Matthiessen, *American Renaissance* (1941).

Larmore, supra, argues, however, that a principal weakness of romanticism is the emphasis on organic society and the related (but to my mind quite different) idea, "namely the expressivism that supposes that the highest ideals of the political order must mirror what are our highest personal ideals." Larmore, supra, at 121. Larmore argues that the political order should not be conceived as expressing personal ideals (id. at 118) and should be independent of any conception of the good life not shared by all (id. at 67

& 118), and that expressivism confuses the political realm with the aesthetic realm (id. at 99). By engaging in this confusion, he writes, liberalism has been exposed to "just the sort of controversiality from which it has sought to escape." Id. at 118.

Larmore's perspective takes insufficient account of the possibility that the principles of the political order will shape and mold personal ideals even if it is characterized as neutral and that if this effect will occur, it might be important to debate and consider what the impact will be and what it ought to be. I presume he would concede that it is possible to conceive of society expressing Millian notions of a free, diverse, and exciting people. See id. at 118. And that conception, he would have to concede, is a form of expressivism far removed from the monistic totalitarianism so often associated with notions of organic society. It has the *advantage* of aesthetic appeal (an advantage Larmore would forgo), an appeal that taps into revered traditions in this country. See text accompanying notes 115 to 119 infra.

Of course, that perspective does not escape controversy; *neither does Larmore's.* It may not escape the kind of controversy that Larmore would like to avoid, but Larmore can fairly equate his conception of liberalism (which is close to the later writings of Rawls, see Chapter 4, note 12 supra) with only one strand of liberalism. This becomes particularly clear when he claims that "Liberals such as Kant and Mill, who have coupled their political theory with a corresponding notion of what in general ought to be our personal ideal, have betrayed in fact the liberal spirit." Id. at 129. He continues: "The fundamental liberal insight is the inescapable controversiality of ideals of the good life and thus the need to find political principles that abstract from them." Id. at 129–130. That is an insight shared by many liberal academics, including Larmore. As a matter of intellectual history, however, it misdescribes American liberalism, which is far more pragmatic and more suspicious of abstraction than is Larmore's liberalism. See Chapter 3, note 15 supra.

22. Much feminist writing has emphasized how females have been associated with the passions and males with reason. For example, Frances Olsen writes of a "series of complex dualisms—reason/passion, rational/irrational, culture/nature, power/sensitivity, thought/feeling, soul/body, objective/subjective. Men, who have created our dominant consciousness, have organized these dualisms into a system in which each dualism has a strong or positive side and a weak or negative side. Men associate themselves with the strong side of these dualisms and project the weak sides upon women." Olsen, "The Family and the Market: A Study of Ideology and Legal Reform," 96 *Harv. L. Rev.* 1497, 1575 (1983). As she observes, the choices for women can be described in terms of these dualisms. Women can accept the hierarchy and argue that conceptions of them have been mistaken, that they too are as closely associated with the "strong" side of the hierarchy as men. Alternatively, women can accept the stereotypical views but insist that the hierarchy is upside down, that women are better than men. Olsen instead takes

the route of androgyny and on the way states: "It is the acceptance and the sexualization of the dualisms that is the chief problem. . . . We cannot choose between the two sides of the dualism, because we need both." Id. at 1577. .

From one perspective, I am arguing that the idea of passion integrates reason because it is not possible to have desires, preferences, emotions, or passions (I use the latter term to include all) without cognition and because the passions are ordinarily part and parcel of a developed personality that has integrated values through conscious choice. See generally R. Solomon, *The Passions* (1983). Moreover, without passion *abstract* reason is a dead end. Indeed, *it* is irrational.

Nonetheless, however much passion and reason might be integrated, the ability to abstract can be analytically separated from the fact of human desire even if they be symbiotically interconnected. I emphasize the passions in the context of legal discourse precisely because it has been downplayed. Thus I adhere to the view of Mill quoted in Chapter 3, text accompanying note 43 supra, that the suppressed side of an important duality is likely to be underappreciated. As I suggested in the previous paragraph in the text, if I were placed in a den of hippies, I would begin to stress the other side of the dualism. I do not think the dualism can ever be entirely transcended.

23. Those connections in many instances might be both complicated and contestable. For brief discussion of the some of the issues concerning the connections between feminism and the themes of this book, see note 22 supra; Chapter 3, note 32 supra; and Chapter 4, note 139 supra.

24. As I mentioned in Chapter 2, however, I have left parts of Emerson behind.

25. C. Campbell, supra note 8, at 218.

26. See D. Donoghue, *Reading America* 39 (1987) ("[Emerson] can be quoted to nearly any purpose"). But any picture of Emerson as muddle-headed or contradictory is simplistic and false. Rather, Joel Porte is on the mark when he points to "the characteristic ebb and flow of Emerson's nature, as he attempts to attain an approximation to personal truth through a dialectic of opposites." *Emerson in His Journals* 89 (J. Porte ed. 1982). Moreover, Emerson was acutely aware of this. See, e.g., id. at 185, 221, 350.

27. Perhaps the most influential exposition of this view is S. Whicher, *Freedom and Fate: An Inner Life of Ralph Waldo Emerson* (1953) (stressing the changes in Emerson's thought over time). But Whicher's understanding has been challenged from a variety of perspectives. See, e.g., J. Michael, *Emerson and Skepticism: The Cipher of the World* (1988); J. Ellison, *Emerson's Romantic Style* (1984); D. Robinson, *Apostle of Culture: Emerson as Preacher and Lecturer* (1982). See also J. Bishop, *Emerson on the Soul* 216–221 (1964) (suggesting that the earlier and bolder Emerson is the Emerson worthy of our attention, pointing in particular to Emerson's "lively critique of habitual passivities and excuses" and suggesting that his writings are an antidote to "moral anaesthesia"; id. at 218–219).

28. See, e.g., J. Ellison, supra note 27, at 228–229: "[L]ike the major German and English Romantics, Emerson rejects generic conventions . . . . Emerson's animus against 'stiff conventions' arises from the fact that he associates method with prescriptions and limits imposed upon him and with the 'exact respect' tradition requires from him."

29. Quoted in L. Chai, *The Romantic Foundations of the American Renaissance* 66 (1987). See also *Emerson in His Journals,* supra note 26, at 209 ("[M]en are not made like boxes, a hundred, a thousand to order, & all exactly alike, of known dimension, & all their properties known; but no they come into nature through a nine months' astonishment & of a character each one incalculable & of extravagant possibilities . . . . "); id. at 294 ("All life is an experiment. The more experiments you make, the better.").

30. S. Paul, *Emerson's Angle of Vision: Man and Nature in American Experience* 25 (1952).

31. Id. See, e.g., *Emerson in His Journals,* supra note 26, at 217.

32. J. McAleer, *Ralph Waldo Emerson: Days of Encounter* 151 (1984). See also Buell, "The Transcendentalists," in *Columbia Literary History of the United States* 364, 370 (1988) (Coleridge's reworking of Kantian categories reversed Kant himself); J. Porte, *Emerson and Thoreau: Transcendentalists in Conflict* 84–90 (1966) (comparing and contrasting Emerson's views with Kant). For the definitive treatment of the many relationships between Emerson's epistemology and Kant's epistemology, see Van Leer, *Emerson's Epistemology* (1986).

33. Quoted in J. McAleer, supra note 32, at 151, & in J. Porte, supra note 32, at 85 (emphasis in original).

34. M. Gilmore, supra note 10, at 28.

35. See, e.g., G. Allen, *Waldo Emerson* 392 (1981). In truth, Emerson's views drew on a wide variety of sources and experiences. He was self-consciously eclectic. See, e.g., *Emerson in His Journals,* supra note 26, at 148; S. Whicher, supra note 27, at 17, 56, 120.

36. Supra note 10, at 158.

37. F. O. Matthiessen, *American Renaissance* 7 (1941).

38. See L. Buell, *Literary Transcendentalism* 269–271 (1973).

39. R. W. Emerson, "An Address," in *Ralph Waldo Emerson: Essays and Lectures* 73, 75–78, 84–85 (J. Porte ed. 1983). For brief discussions of the centrality of the moral intuition to Emerson's thought, see Gohdes, "An American Author as Democrat," in *Literary Romanticism in America* 1, 10–14 (W. L. Andrews 1981); S. Whicher, supra note 27, at 21, 49.

40. L. Chai, *The Romantic Foundations of the American Renaissance* 186 n.12 (1987) (emphasis in original).

41. R. W. Emerson, supra note 39, at 84–85.

42. Id. at 75–76.

43. Id. at 76.

44. Id. at 78. Professor David Leverenz puts forward a powerful critique of Emerson in "The Politics of Emerson's Man-Making Words," 101 *PMLA*

38 (1986). A major theme of his critique is that Emerson was a misogynist at many levels, including his "language of man making" and his emphasis on power. He states: "As one crucial consequence, the women's world of relations and feelings becomes irrelevant. Though Emerson challenges the social definitions of manhood and power, he does not question the more fundamental code that binds manhood and power together at the expense of intimacy. . . . In taking his female support system for granted and in reducing intimacy to faceless nurturing, Emerson cut himself off from experiencing feelings except through rivalry and detachment." Id. at 39.

No doubt, Emerson repressed many important feelings (from mourning to intimacy—though his journals are filled with regret about the latter—and in many of the respects for which he is faulted, including misogyny, he was hardly alone in nineteenth-century New England). And no doubt, Emerson took female support for granted (and otherwise participated in gender stereotyping of an indefensible character). Even if one tempered some of Leverenz's critique of Emerson's statements about power with more recognition of the dialectical quality of Emerson's views on that subject, most of his critique on that score might still be sustained.

But that critique should not obscure the point made in the text: Emerson is quite far from any view that feelings are an unimportant part of the human condition, and he did not consign feelings to one half of the human race. Throughout the major texts of Emerson, passion is a central part of the human experience. As he says in an important passage in "Nature," supra note 39, at 47: "The reason why the world lacks unity, and lies broken and in heaps, is, because man is disunited with himself. He cannot be a naturalist, until he satisfies all the demands of the spirit. Love is as much its demand as perception. Indeed, neither can be perfect without the other."

I do not understand Leverenz to deny the point made in the text. But it is important to stress that even if Emerson was repressed in important ways for many complicated reasons, there are central aspects of his philosophy that privilege the passions in ways that are deeply hostile to much writing in the rationalist tradition.

45. See note 38 supra. See also *Emerson in His Journals,* supra note 26, at 65, 344–345.

46. See, e.g., *Emerson in His Journals,* supra note 26, at 288: "Intellect always puts an interval between the subject & the object. Affection would blend the two." Cf. S. Whicher, supra note 27, at 21: "[Emerson's] problem of authority was solved when he learned from Coleridge to call the reason of the Unitarians the understanding, and to reserve the term reason for the religious sentiments. He thus could repudiate reason in the name of reason . . . . " See also note 44 supra.

47. See Chapter 1, note 1 supra.

48. See, e.g., R. W. Emerson, "The Over-Soul," supra note 39, at 386.

49. Gitlin, "Postmodernism: Roots and Politics," *Dissent* 100, 104 (Winter 1989).

50. Id. at 100.

51. R. W. Emerson, supra note 39, at 941.

52. Quoted in Berman, "Why Modernism Still Matters," 4 *Tikkun* 11 (Jan./Feb. 1989). Compare quotation from Loving in Chapter 2, note 159 supra.

53. R. W. Emerson, "The Protest," III *The Early Lectures of Ralph Waldo Emerson: 1838–42,* at 85, 89–90 (R. Spiller & W. Williams eds. 1972). Cf. B. Erkkila, *Whitman the Political Poet* 16 (1989) ("Long before [Whitman] had any contact with the self-reliant and transcendental philosophy of Ralph Waldo Emerson, Whitman was trained in the Hicksite doctrine that the 'ideals of character, of justice, of religious action . . . are to be conform'd to no outside doctrine of creeds, Bibles, legislative enactments, conventionalities, or even decorums, but are to follow the inward Deity-planted law of the emotional soul.'").

54. Berman, supra note 52, at 11. Cf. R. W. Emerson, "Circles," supra note 39, at 403–414.

55. See, e.g., Cotkin, "Ralph Waldo Emerson and William James as Public Philosophers," 49 *Historian* 49, 59 (1986). See also Chapter 2, note 158 supra.

56. For rumination on the many meanings of formalism with two cheers for its desirability, see Schauer, "Formalism," 97 *Yale L.J.* 509 (1988).

57. In particular, see Lentricchia, "On the Ideologies of Poetic Modernism, 1890–1913: The Example of William James," in *Reconstructing American Literary History* 220–249 (S. Bercovitch ed. 1986) (arguing that the "moral and political authority behind James' pragmatism is Emerson," id. at 230).

58. For an eloquent discussion of the romantic American tradition with appreciation for the connection between Emerson and Dewey, see West, "Between Dewey and Gramsci: Unger's Emancipatory Experimentalism," 81 *Nw. U.L. Rev.* 941 (1987).

59. See, e.g., H. Bloom, *Agon: Towards a Theory of Revisionism* 173–174 (1982). In particular, consider Bloom's quotation from Whitman: "'The best part of Emersonianism is, it breeds the giant that destroys itself. Who wants to be any man's mere follower? lurks behind every page.'" Id. at 173. Emerson put it best: "This is my boast that I have no school & no follower. I should account it a measure of the impurity of insight, if it did not create independence." *Emerson in His Journals,* supra note 26, at 484.

60. Supra note 39, at 57–58.

61. See Chapter 4, note 152 supra.

62. Compare R. W. B. Lewis, *The American Adam: Innocence, Tragedy, and Tradition in the Nineteenth Century* 51 (1955) (emphasis in original): "What is implicit in every line of Whitman is the belief that the poet *projects* a world of order and meaning and identity into either a chaos or a sheer vacuum; he does not *discover* it. The poet may salute the chaos; but he creates the world."

63. The emphasis on conflict is an important theme in romantic writing. See, e.g., J. Porte, *Representative Man: Ralph Waldo Emerson in His Time* 207 (1988): "Emerson . . . is a compulsively dialectical thinker . . . . " As P. Thorslev, supra note 10, at 67–68, describes it, the "Romantic dialectic [is a] method of 'reasoning' from polar opposites toward a new and higher synthesis, the theory of truth not as permanent, immutable, and necessarily self-consistent, but as provisional, indeed as growth and progress, and proceeding from conflicts or even contradictions inherent in the very nature of reality." The conflict between, for example, "self and not-self, [or] between synthetic imagination and analytic reason," was not regarded as "superimposed from without by a supreme geometer, working itself out with the cool and unimpassioned logic of an Aristotelian syllogism or mathematical equation; on the contrary, conflict was real and at the heart of things, and not to be explained away. . . . It is perhaps true that each opposition can be transcended in a higher synthesis, but this process is open-ended, the newer synthesis always unstable—it carries within itself, in Hegel's terms, the seeds of its own destruction, indeed, it depends upon this internal opposition for its very existence." Id. at 68–69.

I would not contend that balancing can be equated with the romantic dialectic, particularly to the extent that dialectic insists on seeing everything in terms of polar contraries (see id. at 77), but the emphasis on conflict in important values is a striking parallel. At least part of the reason romantics were attracted to this conception of reason was that it invited candor— particularly in those versions that did not have to pretend that the synthesis was really "higher" or that the conflict had disappeared. In this respect, as I suggested in Chapter 2, supra note 159, I do not sponsor Emerson's version of romanticism to the extent that it can fairly be read to fail to appreciate that tragic choices accompany the resolution of dialectical conflict. See, e.g., S. Whicher, supra note 27, at 46. But cf. Chapter 2, note 159 supra.

64. Kantianism appeals to the desire to avoid or resolve the conflict implicated by the complexity of social reality. Larmore puts it well: "[O]ne's moral philosophy inevitably expresses the kind of person that one, if not is, then wants to be. The simplifications that I have attacked do not stem merely from a liking for theoretical simplicity. They also embody ideals of the moral person, and draw their force from these ideals. They manifest a drive to make virtue easily masterable (by reducing it to the conscientious adherence to principle), a wish to live life as a whole animated by a single dominant purpose, and a hope for an existence uncompromised by moral loss and unriven by unsettlable conflict." C. Larmore, supra note 21, at 152. But cf. note 21 supra and Chapter 3 note 19 supra (discussing Larmore's belief that it is possible to develop political philosophy in a way that expresses virtually nothing about the kind of person one wants to be and that political life should be controlled by a principle of neutrality about conceptions of the good life).

65. For perceptive discussion of tragic choices in human decisionmak-

ing, see generally M. Nussbaum, *The Fragility of Goodness* (1986). See also B. Williams, *Moral Luck* chs. 2, 5 (1981).

66. For discussion of the connection between the experience of finitude and empathy, see Cornell, "Toward a Modern/Postmodern Reconstruction of Ethics," 133 *U. Pa. L. Rev.* 291, 343–344 (1985).

67. The lack of stability is threatening to many, but the romantic perspective is quite different: "The prime virtue of the romantic hero in an open universe is to adjust to changing circumstances which he cannot predict, and to work out his purely human and relative destiny as best he can, given his own limited endowments; and above all to retain that resiliency of character and that joy in the endless variety of life which keeps him from blaming his errors or his temporary reverses on a malevolent fate." P. Thorslev, supra note 10, at 145.

68. Any such romantic would also find Gordon Wood's characterization of the Founders' activities to be quite bizarre.

69. M. Peckham, *The Triumph of Romanticism* 35 (1970). It bears repeating that I am working within a particular part of the romantic tradition and that there are many forms of romanticism. It is possible to sketch aspects of romanticism and pragmatism or realism that are deeply at odds and in ways that go much beyond that which would be involved in merely negating Peckham's perspective. See, e.g., Fraser, "Solidarity or Singularity? Richard Rorty between Romanticism and Technocracy," 8 *Praxis Int'l* 257 (1988). Contrary to the picture of romanticism set forth by Fraser, as I set forth at length in Chapter 3: I deny that an emphasis on dissent is excessively individualistic overall, let alone that it imagines social change proceeding primarily from genius poets (if all of us suffer from and gain from a necessarily partial perspective, the sources of profitable dissent will be widespread, and promoting dissent promotes association); I recognize that an emphasis on dissent must operate within certain background assumptions about the nature and character of the basic institutions of the country, in particular that the polity is committed to free speech and dissent (that commitment promotes social constraints against those who loathe dissent and thus discourages some dissent); I do not suppose that romanticism can or should be confined to the private sphere, but I deny that romanticism in the public sphere is necessarily dangerous, and I insist that some aspects of it are unavoidable (the latter points are also developed in the final section of this chapter).

70. Cf. M. Kelman, *A Guide to Critical Legal Studies* 61 (1987): "Rules appeal to the aesthetics of precision, to the psychology of denial or skeptical pragmatism (or, alternatively, of blinding ourselves to imprecision and mistakes or believing it is . . . utopian to hope for perfection); standards appeal to the aesthetics of romantic absolutism, to the psychology of painful involvement in each situation, to the pragmatism that rejects the need for highfalutin generalities."

71. Cf. Harold Bloom's comment: "[A]ll formalisms are one." "Harold Bloom" [an interview], in *Criticism in Society,* supra note 14, at 44, 54.

72. N. Rosenblum, supra note 17, at 34–35.

73. For philosophical reflection on the value of rules and the connection of a regime of rules with formalism (without insisting that rules should always be required), see Schauer, supra note 56, at 509. For an illuminating historical demonstration of the dangers associated with discretionary power in the regulation of speech, see L. Powe, *American Broadcasting and the First Amendment* (1987).

74. R. Williams, *Culture and Society: 1780–1950,* at 36 (1983).

75. Id. at 42. For discussion of the American context with special emphasis on Emerson (relying in part on the work of Raymond Williams), see C. Porter, *Seeing and Being* 57–90 (1981).

76. L. Marx, *The Machine in the Garden: Technology and the Pastoral Ideal in America* 230–234 (1964). But cf. M. Gilmore, supra note 10, at 18–34 (1985) (stressing Emerson's move from an early distrust of the marketplace to a later embrace of it). See id. at 5: "To the early Emerson, the spread of the market meant instability and the loss of independence; the later Emerson found order and reassurance in the same circumstances from which his younger self recoiled." Even the later Emerson, however, could properly be characterized as standing (in Leo Marx's phrasing) for the "proper subordination of material concerns to other, less tangible aspects of life—whether aesthetic, moral, political, or spiritual" even though he had no desire "to renounce the amenities of modern life." Marx, "Pastoralism in America," in *Ideology and Classic American Literature,* supra note 19, at 36, 59 (commenting generally on writers drawn to pastoral imagery). The same analysis applies to Whitman, see B. Erkkila, supra note 53, at 11, 36–41, 253. For further insight into Emerson's commercial thought in a discussion of the centrality of the idea of debt in Emerson's "spiritual economy," see Grusin, "'Put God in Your Debt': Emerson's Economy of Expenditure," 103 *PMLA* 35 (1988).

77. L. Marx, *The Machine in the Garden,* supra note 76, at 231.

78. Id. at 238. See also C. Campbell, supra note 8, at 218: "[It] was Franklin, not Calvin, who was seen as epitomizing all that the Romantics hated most. In North America, where the Romantic Movement took the form of Transcendentalism, it was such inheritors of the pietistic and intensely moral Puritan tradition as Emerson, Thoreau, Melville and Poe, who repeatedly criticized what they saw as the shallow and immoral nature of Franklin's utilitarianism. Emerson, in particular, repeatedly attacked the selfish doctrine of the market-place, advocating in its place an ideal of the self as being and becoming . . . . "

79. L. Marx, *The Machine in the Garden,* supra note 76, at 238. For discussion of this theme in Emerson, Whitman, and Thoreau, see Kateb, "Democratic Individuality and the Claims of Politics," 12 *Political Theory* 331, 335, 337, 349–350 (1984).

80. W. Whitman, "Democratic Vistas," in Whitman, *Leaves of Grass and Selected Prose* 468, 487 n.* (L. Buell ed. 1981).

81. Id. at 513 n.*.

82. Id. at 522.

83. See C. Campbell, supra note 8, at 207 (but arguing that romantics unwittingly helped to bring about the consumerism they opposed). For the argument that the tradition stretches back to pastoral imagery in general, see Marx, "Pastoralism in America," supra note 76, at 59.

84. FEC v. Massachusetts Citizens For Life, Inc., 479 U.S. 238, 257 (1986).

85. J. Barzun, *Classic, Romantic, and Modern* xxi (1961).

86. Emerson understood this. At least he was prepared to defend the free speech rights of those with whom he vigorously disagreed. He, for example, opposed the jailing of Adam Kneeland (fortunately, the last person imprisoned for blasphemy in Massachusetts) despite the fact that he regarded Kneeland's views as "miserable babble" that "God himself contradicts through me & all his creatures . . . . " See *Emerson in His Journals,* supra note 26, at 142. On the Kneeland affair generally, see L. Levy, *The Law of the Commonwealth and Chief Justice Shaw* ch. 4 (1957).

87. Nonetheless, it bears repeating that the Kantians themselves prized dissent. As H. S. Thayer observed in *Meaning and Action: A Critical History of Pragmatism* 45 (2d ed. 1981): "Rationalism and romanticism in the eighteenth-century Enlightenment had this in common: both were assertions of individuality against older systems of governmental repression. . . . The common enemy is social, intellectual, and moral tyranny. To the coldly reasoned new scientific criticism and rejection of past dogmas, the romanticists added fire and imagination, zealously if not consistently announcing the new faith in the sacred right of the individual personality to free and creative self-expression and self-realization. Such were the varied and impassioned suggestions to come from Rousseau in France, Goethe and Schiller in Germany, the younger Coleridge and Wordsworth in England—and Shelley and Byron—and the New England transcendentalists, Emerson and Thoreau."

88. See N. Rosenblum, supra note 17, at 45: From the romantic perspective, "[s]incerity is opposed to artifice and, more important, connected with genuine self-expression." Cf. C. Campbell, supra note 8, at 177: "[J]ust as the dandies represented the triumph of propriety over sincerity, so the Romantics (and, especially, the romantic Bohemians) come to represent the reverse."

89. Cf. J. Randall, supra note 15, at 400 ("The virtues of the romantic attitude are its open-mindedness, its receptivity to whatever of truth and whatever of value any experience may reveal; as William James put it, although the past has uniformly taught us that all crows are black, still we should continue to look for the white crow.").

90. Cf. P. Thorslev, supra note 10, at 170 (equating the romantic "passion for inclusion," namely, the view that "nothing should be excluded for the sake of form and order, each experience should be viewed from every possible angle and in every possible context, and no view should be considered ultimate," with the romantic "passionate resistance to closure").

91. For a powerful argument to that effect also emphasizing the possibility of richer and more meaningful justifications than are likely to be produced by formalistic approaches, see Schlag, "An Attack on Categorical Approaches to Freedom of Speech," 30 *UCLA L. Rev.* 671 (1983).

92. See note 39 supra.

93. One, of course, need not affiliate with the classical republican tradition to oppose the metaphor of social engineering.

94. "Speaking generally, engineering means designing and constructing objects or processes to fit human purposes . . . . " Grobstein, "On Genetic Engineering," 7 *Raritan* 108 (Spring 1988). So understood, engineering is not inherently "scientific," and proponents of social engineering like Roscoe Pound did not pretend it was. See, e.g., R. Pound, *An Introduction to the Philosophy of Law* 45–46 (rev. ed. 1954). Nonetheless, the association of the term *science* with engineering is close. See S. Florman, *The Existential Pleasures of Engineering* x (1976). And, deliberately or not, the original proponents of the metaphor necessarily traded on associations that conveyed false notions of expertise and objectivity. See R. Summers, *Instrumentalism and American Legal Theory* 207–208 (1982); Rhees, "Social Engineering," 56 *Mind* 317 (1947) (criticizing Popper's association of social engineering with science). Nonetheless, today any notion that judges possess scientific expertise regarding the social consequences of law would be transparently preposterous. Thus, the social engineering metaphor, if anything, calls to mind the bankruptcy of any association of legal decisionmaking with science and thus tends to reinforce the notion that the decisionmakers are human.

95. W. Sullivan, *Reconstructing Public Philosophy* xiii & 19 (1986).

96. Id. at xi–xii, 55.

97. Clearly, parts of republicanism emphasize ideals that are shared with romantic eclecticism. This point applies to versions of republicanism that are quite different from each other. Compare Michelman, "Foreword: Traces of Self-Government," 100 *Harv. L. Rev.* 4, 33 (1986), with Sunstein, "Interest Groups in American Public Law," 38 *Stan. L. Rev.* 29 (1985). Both perspectives are on the left in American politics. Republicanism, in that respect, has the difficulty of sharing its label with Jerry Falwell and Ronald Reagan. On the other hand, academic "republicanism" has not been advanced as a campaign slogan, and its pressing of concepts like community and the common good (as opposed to interest group politics) has already played a role in national politics.

98. Certainly, in many situations there is no common good that transcends the accommodation of individual and group interests. One of the worst aspects of the metaphor is that it fosters an attitude that individual and group interests are themselves illegitimate. The best aspect is that it encourages an attitude of looking at the interests of the polity as a whole.

99. Of course, republicans can emphasize that this is a regulative ideal, something to be searched for and struggled over, but not necessarily achieved. The metaphor of the common good places an emphasis on com-

monality. The metaphor of social engineering stresses difference and, at the same time, emphasizes a need for the society to arrive at a solution.

100. Nor does the metaphor of social engineering imagine an interest group politics of exclusively self-interested actors. Its focus is on the judge making a decision. Is it a disadvantage that it is not focused on the citizen? See note 101 infra. Notice also that this project is designed to conjoin romance with social engineering, and I have already argued that promoting dissent promotes association and participation in politics. The differences that lie behind these metaphors, though not trivial, may be less than meet the eye.

101. Does this let the common good in through the back door? Yes and no. No, if the common good is set against accommodating individual and group interests. Yes, in that the decisionmaker is not merely involved in aggregating preferences. In any event, the common good is an object without a person. The social engineering metaphor emphasizes that someone has made a decision and thus emphasizes the presence of power. It has a lack of appeal in that the power of the social engineer is not populist power, and some would, therefore, say it is undemocratic power. This is an advantage of the metaphor, not a disadvantage, because it opens decisions to criticism. The republican vision is that the metaphor of the common good will open the paths for popular participation. That has a general appeal, but at least for first amendment decisions it is hard to reconcile with a Bill of Rights enforced by judges. Thus, the best Professor Michelman can hope to search for in his republican vision are "traces of self-government" (see note 97 supra). The contest between these metaphors was addressed at length in Chapter 2, albeit in different terms.

102. Sophisticated republicans need not contend that either. See note 99 supra.

103. The emphasis on the common good tends to minimize the role of power and conflict in the political process just as it tends toward the repression of difference in the interest of unity. On the other hand, republicanism hopes to open space for politics by encouraging citizens to participate in advancing their conception of the common good.

104. That has its advantages. See note 101 supra.

105. I am thinking of social engineers in the best sense. For some, the term *social engineer* exudes an antidemocratic odor. It calls up the image of professional expertise, the kind of expert who thinks he or she can make decisions without dialogue. In any event, there will never be enough dialogue. The knowledge of the decisionmaker will always be biased and partial. And the antidemocratic image called up by the social engineering metaphor has its advantages. See note 101 supra.

106. Bloom, "The Internalization of Quest-Romance," in *Romanticism and Consciousness: Essays in Criticism* 3, 12 (H. Bloom ed. 1970).

107. Id.

108. "Geoffrey Hartman" [an interview], in *Criticism in Society,* supra note 14, at 74, 85.

109. But cf. Alexander, "The Transformation of Trusts as a Legal Category, 1800–1914," 5 *Law and History Review* 303, 350 (1987): "Categorizing may be an inevitable activity, but no particular category is inevitable."

110. See Chapter 4, note 95 supra.

111. R. Solomon, supra note 22, at xix.

112. See Appleby, "Ideology and the History of Political Thought," *Intellectual History Group Newsletter* 10, 16 (Fall 1980), quoting C. Geertz, *The Interpretation of Cultures* 5 (1973): "[L]inguists, philosophers, anthropologists and students of religion . . . . explain the existence of structured consciousness as part of the general human 'craving for meaning.' Man, as Geertz has written, 'is an animal suspended in webs of significance he himself has spun.'" There is a danger in overemphasizing this perspective. As Appleby suggests, if one is not careful, the "reality of power relations" can be overshadowed and "[fade] away much like Alice's Cheshire cat, leaving nothing behind but the smile of culture." Moreover: "Power relations within [pluralistic societies] are frequently troubled, and men and women enjoy an access to information that can supply materials for alternative interpretations of reality. Ideologies in such societies rarely enjoy an uncontested supremacy—which is why we so often refer to them as persuasions." Appleby, "Republicanism in Old and New Contexts," 43 *Wm. & Mary Q.* 20, 28 (1986).

113. For the suggestion that much of the appeal of Kant lies in the "picture of how our virtues and ideals hang together with one another" in his "moral image of the world," see H. Putnam, *The Many Faces of Realism* 51 (1987).

114. K. Karst, *Belonging to America: Equal Citizenship and the Constitution* 194 (1989).

115. See generally P. Thorslev, supra note 10. Consider Cornell, "Beyond Tragedy and Complacency," 81 *Nw. U.L. Rev.* 693, 694 (1987): "The romantic longing to find a home in the world is countered by the romantic vision's other side: No world is or can be home for the infinite striving self."

116. Cf. J. Porte, supra note 63, at 5: "The Emersonian ego is a lonely one and longs to embrace and be embraced; but it is also proud and experimental and needs to free itself from that embrace when it feels itself trapped." But cf. P. Thorslev, supra note 10, at 19: "This sense of the burden of destiny . . . is more of a twentieth-century than a Romantic phenomenon. The English Romantic poets, at least—with the important exception of Byron— were in general too concerned with the loss of destiny to feel it as a burden." I am using the term *romantic* in a broader, less historically specific sense than Thorslev's. I certainly do not question his analysis of the English Romantic poets. As my citations to his work only begin to suggest, his analysis of the English Romantics sheds conceptual light on a variety of important modern, but recurrent, legal, political, and philosophical issues. Indeed, Thorslev, at many points, stresses the contemporary implications of Romantic thought. In particular see id. at 70, 91.

117. Consider id. at 16: "[F]reedom . . . is a prerequisite for moral responsibility, and therefore for a sense of self, but it is also essentially separative:

it confers individuality rather than a sense of community. Destiny, on the other hand, is social and collective: it gives man a sense of shared purpose and mission, of security and fellowship—with other men, with the organic world around him, and sometimes even with the stars."

118. See Rosenblum's perceptive discussion of "Liberalism as a Spectacle of Diversity," supra note 17, at 118–121 (connecting the spectacle to Whitman as well). See also id. at 121–124.

119. *Emerson in His Journals,* supra note 26, at 428: "America is the idea of emancipation. Abolish kingcraft, Slavery, feudalism, blackletter monopoly, pull down gallows, explode priestcraft, tariff, open the doors of the sea to all emigrants . . . . All proceeds on the belief that as the people have made a govt. they can make another, that their Union & law is not in their memory but in their blood. If they unmake the law they can easily make it again."

120. 319 U.S. 624 (1943).

121. Id. at 641.

122. 310 U.S. 586, 596 (1940) (emphasis in original).

123. 319 U.S. at 637.

124. Id. at 640–641 (emphasis added).

125. Id. at 637, 641.

126. Id. at 641.

127. Id. at 641.

128. Id.

129. Id. at 642.

130. See id. at 641. Of course, the question of whether one can be forced to salute a flag is different from the question of whether flag desecration should be protected under the first amendment, though I do not think that distinction should make a difference. Indeed, just as I was sending this book off to the publisher to meet a publication deadline, a copy of Texas v. Johnson, 109 S.Ct. 2533 (1989), arrived in Ithaca. The case holds that flagburning as a part of a political demonstration is protected under the first amendment. Justice Brennan, speaking for the Court, stated: "Our decision is a reaffirmation of the principles of freedom and inclusiveness that the flag best reflects, and of the conviction that our toleration of criticism . . . is a sign and source of our strength. . . . It is the Nation's resilience, not its rigidity . . . that we reassert today. The way to preserve the flag's special role is not to punish those people who feel differently about these matters. It is to persuade them that they are wrong." Id. at 2547. Emerson was not cited by Brennan, but the decision is Emersonian.

Even the opponents of the *Johnson* decision have phrased their opposition in Emersonian terms. Thus President Bush insisted that "[a]s President, I will uphold our precious right to dissent, but burning the flag goes too far and I want to see that matter remedied." *N.Y. Times,* June 28, 1989, at B7. So understood, the question posed by *Johnson* is not whether to be Emersonian, but how Emersonian to be.

131. 319 U.S. at 641.

132. The question of what aliens should reasonably be required to affirm as a condition of becoming a citizen is much more interesting and difficult, as Sanford Levinson convincingly shows in *Constitutional Faith* 122–154 (1988).

133. For extended discussion of the question of how closely citizens should bond with the American Constitution, see generally S. Levinson, supra note 132.

134. Indeed, there were moments when Emerson himself was prepared to denounce the flag. See *Emerson in His Journals,* supra note 26, at 421.

135. 319 U.S. at 642.

136. Id.

137. For a fascinating and depressing exploration of the treatment of dissenters during World War I, see R. Polenberg, *Fighting Faiths: The Abrams Case, the Supreme Court, and Free Speech* (1987). See also Kairys, "Freedom of Speech," in D. Kairys, *The Politics of Law: A Progressive Critique* 140 (1982) (exploring the divide between the reality and the ideology of free speech in American history). Much of the literature that might be cited in support of the realist's case is cited in Blasi, "The Pathological Perspective and the First Amendment," 85 *Colum. L. Rev.* 449 (1985).

138. They may, nonetheless, have considerable value. See Williams, "The Uses of Myth: A Response to Professor Bassett," 4 *J. L. & Religion* 153 (1986).

139. That question can not be avoided. As Professor James Boyd White states: "The legal case is always a narrative; and a narrative . . . can always be a way of testing the presuppositions of the culture, forcing to the bright center of the mind difficulties we wish to push back into the twilight." J. B. White, *When Words Lose Their Meaning* 265 (1984).

140. On the different perspectives from which stories are told, see Cover, "Foreword: *Nomos* and Narrative," 97 *Harv. L. Rev.* 4 (1983).

141. See Blasi, supra note 137, at 456: "The most serious lapses in toleration of dissent, such as the Alien and Sedition Acts, the Red Scare, and the McCarthy Era, have acquired an aura of ignominy that says much about the importance of free speech in the pantheon of national ideals."

142. As Irving Howe observes, "[M]yth is itself a reality, and American myth an American reality, the most powerful and enduring that we have." I. Howe, *The American Newness* 16 (1986). Cf. Northrop Frye's observation: "[A]n ideology is always a secondary and derivative thing, and . . . the primary thing is a mythology. That is, people don't think up a set of assumptions or beliefs; they think up a set of stories, and derive the assumptions and beliefs from the stories. Things like democratic, progressive, revolutionary, Marxist political philosophies: these are comic plots, superimposed on history." "Northrop Frye," in *Criticism in Society,* supra note 14, at 26, 31. One need not go as far as either Howe or Frye—I for one do not—to recognize that national myths and stories are influential.

143. See Kairys, supra note 137, at 167. For questions from a radical perspective about the desirability of channeling dissent into a conflict between theory and practice (suggesting in particular that issues so framed tend to "circumscribe the bounds of perception, thought, and desire" and exercise an "enormous conservative, restraining power"), see Bercovitch, "Afterword," in *Ideology and Classic American Literature,* supra note 19, at 418, 433–434. See also S. Bercovitch, *The American Jeremiad* ch. 6 (1978) (similar argument with substantial attention to the symbol of America in Emersonian rhetoric); C. Porter, supra note 75, at 61, 91–118.

144. "[R]omanticism could be specified as a 'tradition against tradition.'" C. Campbell, supra note 8, at 219. Cf. Gadamer, supra note 14, at 239–240: "[T]he fundamental prejudice of the enlightenment is the prejudice against prejudice itself, which deprives tradition of its power."

145. Compare the discussion of the self in Cornell, "Institutionalization of Meaning, Recollective Imagination and the Potential for Transformative Legal Interpretation," 136 *U. Pa. L. Rev.* 1135, 1224–1228 (1988).

146. Even Roberto Unger, whose commitment to change is resolute, writes that: "At any given time we *are* largely the sum of our fundamental practices. But we are also the permanent possibility of revising them. . . . When invited to change or revise a practice . . . all we can do is to consult the preponderance of our insights and ambitions, to study the available options, and to reflect upon the lessons of past efforts. . . . *Inevitably, we must accept a conservative presumption. To question the legitimacy of our fundamental practices is somewhat like asking why we should continue to be ourselves. The reasonable answer often falls somewhere between—Why shouldn't we?—and—We can't help it."* R. Unger, *Passion: An Essay on Personality* 41–42 (1984) (first emphasis in original; second emphasis added). The fact of our embodiment is both liberating and restricting at the same time. Consider B. Williams, *Ethics and the Limits of Philosophy* 57 (1985) (emphasis in original): "The fact that there are restrictions on what [a rational agent] can do is what requires him to be a rational agent, and it also makes it possible for him to be one; more than that, it is also the condition of his being some particular person, of living *a* life at all. We may think sometimes that we are dismally constrained to be rational agents, and that in a happier world it would not be necessary. But that is a fantasy (indeed it is *the* fantasy)."

147. Gadamer, supra note 14, at 250. See also id. at 100.

148. See, e.g., D. Robinson, supra note 27, at 184–185 (Emerson relied on tradition as the foundation for rejecting barriers and limits: "Because he was nurtured in a tradition which affirmed human potential, he could reject confining and damaging barriers, but could stand on firm ground to do so. He could rebel without being a rebel, for his revolutionary gestures were affirmative ones, and were not without precedent.").

149. M. Jehlen, *American Incarnation: The Individual, the Nation, and the Continent* 202 (1986) (emphasis in original). For her own part, Jehlen

ultimately argues that this form of argument does not leave enough space for radicalism. See also S. Bercovitch, supra note 143, at ch. 6; S. Bercovitch, *The Puritan Origins of the American Self* ch. 5 (1975).

150. One of the disadvantages of a term like tradition is that it denotes "a continuum of discourse" and thus tends to obscure the extent to which traditions contain "debate, perplexity, and contradiction inherent within th[e] discourse." Pocock, "Between Gog and Magog: The Republican Thesis and the *Ideologia Americana*," 48 *Journal of the History of Ideas* 325, 336 (1987). See also id. at 344–345 (discussing difficulties with the term *paradigm*).

151. Some stories do not fit at all. A Mussolini-style fascism or Hitler-style Nazism could not now be considered a plausible account of an American ideal even if either could be considered normatively desirable—which I, of course, do not suggest.

152. For general discussion, see H. Putnam, *Reason, Truth and History* xi, 134, 148–149, 214–216 (1981).

153. Cf. "Edward Said" [an interview], in *Criticism in Society,* supra note 14, at 122, 138 (emphasis in original): "If you read a lot of the critics you've talked with, the body doesn't matter at all. But in fact it *does* matter: we aren't disembodied brains or poetry-machines. We're involved in the circumstances of physical existence. . . . We're in the world, no matter how many times we scream that we're really in the tower."

154. This word may be too strong, but I doubt it. At least, it errs in the right direction.

155. Leaving aside memory loss, is it tautological that perspectives are enlarged by more experience? For the suggestion that enlargement is nonexistent, see Fish, "Critical Legal Studies (II)," 7 *Raritan* 1, 6 (Winter 1988): "Of course, for the person who has performed the act of revision, the resulting practice will seem larger, more capacious than the practice he has left behind; but this capaciousness will be evident and palpable only from within the perspective that now becomes his horizon." But cf. Chapter 3, note 20 supra.

156. On the importance of expression to the romantic conception, see C. Taylor, *Hegel* 13–50. (1975).

157. See id.

158. See generally Taylor, "Logics of Disintegration," 170 *New Left Rev.* 110 (1988).

159. Cf. R. W. Emerson, "Fate," in supra note 39, at 941, 960 (emphasis added): "[I]n man, every generosity, every new perception, the love and praise he extorts from his fellows, are certificates of advance out of fate into freedom. *Liberation of the will from the sheaths and clogs of organization which he has outgrown, is the end and aim of this world.*"

160. See Taylor, supra note 158, at 112.

161. For perceptive exploration of some of the issues involved with different tentative outcomes, see Lyons, "Utility and Rights," in 24 *Nomos: Eth-*

ics, Economics and the Law 107 (J. Pennock & J. Chapman eds. 1982), and Lyons, "Human Rights and the General Welfare," 6 *Phil. & Pub. Aff.* 113 (1977).

162. Blasi, supra note 137.

163. See L. Hand, "The Spirit of Liberty," in *The Spirit of Liberty: Papers and Addresses of Learned Hand* 143, 144 (I. Dilliard ed. 1959), criticized in Blasi, supra note 137, at 507–508. But Blasi is fully prepared to recognize the limits of doctrine: "It is unlikely that first amendment doctrine, no matter how carefully constructed, could ever actually prevent a pathology. The most we can hope for is that well-prepared methodologies and doctrines might help to blunt or delay the impact of some pathological pressures, keep a pathology in certain bounds, or stimulate the regenerative forces that permit a political community to work its way out of a pathological period. Contributions of that sort should not be undervalued." Id. at 459.

164. No absolutes are possible. Judges can lead, and courageous judges can keep a finger in the dike. Even if judges are hostage to the culture, there may be conflicting values within the culture. Moreover, there is evidence that elites (including judges) have different and more favorable views about civil liberties than the general population (see, e.g., H. McCloskey & A. Brill, *Dimensions of Tolerance: What Americans Believe about Civil Liberties* (1983)), though sometimes elites have *led* in a repressive direction. See Gibson, "Political Intolerance and Political Repression during the McCarthy Red Scare," 82 *Am. Pol. Sci. Rev.* 511 (1988). Total pessimism is not justified, but the history of what judges have done does not encourage a sunny view. See sources cited in note 137 supra. In the end, however, Professor Tribe is surely right: Judicial reaction to social forces is a "part of the normal functioning of constitutional adjudication." The Constitution is not "an empty vessel to be filled with the values of a particular historical period. . . . [But] the Constitution exists in intimate relationship with society as a whole and . . . the constitutional doctrines and choices of any particular period are outcomes of a complex interplay among text, history, and social forces. Whether one's purpose is critical or supportive, arguments grounded in social and historical context may in the long run prove more effective, and would surely be more honest, than outraged assertions of 'ancient liberties.'" L. Tribe, *Constitutional Choices* 192 (1985).

165. One of the best demonstrations of the general point of this paragraph is in *Press Law in Modern Democracies: A Comparative Study* (P. Lahav ed. 1985). One conclusion evident from the essays collected there is that the substance of press law ("on the books") is far less important than the existence and strength of liberal values within the particular culture. The example of Israel is an especially powerful instance of this point. See id. at 265–313.

166. I have in mind law schools and political science departments in the pre-Reagan era. People thought of as lunatics then are now thought of as respectable; people then in the center of the Republican party were often

characterized as dull and uninteresting. There are difficult questions here. Academic evaluations will inevitably decide what is lunacy and what is dull and uninteresting. The sense of what amounts to discrimination will inevitably be culturally specific and would demand detailed argumentation. I will have to leave my claim of discrimination at the level of assertion. But it would be difficult to underestimate the provincial character of academic evaluations.

167. See, e.g., R. Jacoby, *The Last Intellectuals: American Culture in the Age of Academe* ch. 6 (1987); Frug, "McCarthyism and Critical Legal Studies," 22 *Harv. C.R.-C.L. L. Rev.* 665 (1987).

168. Compare Michelman, "Justification (and Justifiability) of Law in a Contradictory World," 28 *Nomos: Justification* 71, 94 (J. Pennock & J. Chapman eds. 1986): "Perhaps rights like life depend for their meaning on the occasional intimation of their immortality. What we need is a theory of rights immortal, but for not too long."

169. I do think the substance of doctrine can make a difference, enough of a difference to make it worth arguing about and fighting about, but, in the end, its capacity to hold often disappoints. I do not think the general complexity or simplicity of first amendment doctrine overall is likely to affect the outcome of, for example, cases involving advocacy of illegal action (though the specific doctrine may). Still less do I think that the outcome of the latter category of such cases will likely be affected by the posture of the Court toward commercial speech, for example. This is not to say that the arguments about particular censorial attitudes being fostered by complex doctrine are altogether wrong, although I have tried to suggest that attitudes about simplicity in doctrine can cut in the same direction. It is to say that such judgments seem too speculative to "[require] courts to do injustice today in order to prepare to do justice tomorrow." See Blasi, supra note 137, at 514.

170. For a more confident expression of this point, see Redish, "The Role of Pathology in First Amendment Theory: A Skeptical Examination," 38 *Case W. Res. L. Rev.* 618, 622–625 (1987–88).

Index